The
Celestine Sibley
Sampler

The Celestine Sibley Sampler

Writings & Photographs

with tributes to the beloved
author and journalist

Written by Celestine Sibley

Edited by Sibley Fleming

PEACHTREE
ATLANTA

Published by
PEACHTREE PUBLISHERS, LTD.
494 Armour Circle N.E.
Atlanta GA 30324-4088

Jacket design by Dana Laurent and Loraine M. Balcsik
Book design and composition by Terri Fox

Manufactured in the United States of America

10 9 8 7 6 5 4 3 2 1
First edition

Library of Congress Cataloging-in-Publication Data

Sibley, Celestine
        The Celestine Sibley sampler: writings
    and photographs with tributes to the beloved
author and journalist / by Celestine Sibley:
edited by Sibley Fleming.
            p.   cm.
            ISBN 1-56145-154-1
            I. Fleming, Sibley. II. Title
        PS3569.I256A6   1997   97–16911
        813'.54—dc21   CIP

Contents

Contributors

Frederick Allen is the author of *Atlanta Rising* and *Secret Formula*.

Lawrence P. Ashmead is the executive editor and vice president of HarperCollins Publishers and Celestine Sibley's lifetime book editor.

Mark Childress is the author of two children's books and four novels, including *Crazy in Alabama* and *A World Made of Fire*.

John Egerton won the Robert Kennedy Award for his recent book *Speak Now Against the Day*. He is the author of several other books, including *Southern Food* and *Side Orders: Small Helpings of Southern Cookery and Culture*.

William A. Emerson, Jr. is the former editor of the *Saturday Evening Post* and former Atlanta bureau chief for *Newsweek* magazine.

Terry Kay is the author of seven novels, including *To Dance With the White Dog*, *Shadowsong*, and *The Runaway*.

Lee May writes food and gardening columns for the *Atlanta Journal–Constitution* and *Southern Accents* magazine and is the author of *In My Father's Garden*.

Zell Miller is the governor of Georgia and a former businessman, teacher, Marine sergeant, and author of four books, the most recent of which is *Corps Values*.

Dr. Ferrol Sams is a physician and the author of seven books, including *Run With the Horsemen*, *Whisper of the River*, and *Epiphany*.

Kathy Hogan Trocheck has been nominated for the Agatha, Anthony, and Macavity awards both for her Callahan Garrity and her Truman Kicklighter mystery series.

Introduction

A young writer needing advice would do well to seek out Celestine Sibley, a veteran who has survived. Always willing to take the time to talk, Ms. Sibley will most likely teach the novice a quick lesson by recounting one of her favorite anecdotes, one that sprung from the John Wallace murder trial in Coweta County some years ago:

"Al Henson, a lawyer who later became a judge, brought in a classy lawyer from the military to question Dr. Herman Jones, the crime lab man—to shake him," Ms. Sibley says. "He questioned the doctor about an hour. Everyone was hot and exhausted and the jury was tired. I stopped Al on the way out for recess and asked what he thought about his lawyer. He said it was a mistake. 'You find a man who says "supine" when he means "lyin' down"—you can be sure he's a damn fool.'"

Celestine Sibley does not write supine. Nor does she write lyin' down. Her words—whether about gardening, murder, family, food, or politics—flow with a simplicity that might be called *Southern haiku* if there were such a term.

Celestine Sibley prizes simplicity, in spite of the fact that she is a very complex person. Dubbed Georgia's "treasure" by some and an "institution" by others, Ms. Sibley is a woman of complicated and sometimes contradictory beliefs.

The hundreds of awards Ms. Sibley has received do not appear in her memoirs, in her twenty-odd books, or in the thousands of personal columns she has written. She's one of the longest-running columnists in U.S. history and her name appears in *Who's Who in America*. She's twice been a juror for the Pulitzer Prize Award and has served on the advisory board of the Neighborhood Justice Center.

She does not hold a bachelor's degree yet she sports two honorary doctorates. The first is from Spring Hill College in Mobile, Alabama, where she nearly flunked English during her early newspaper career. The second is from Atlanta's own Emory University.

Most recently, the Georgia Department of Transportation named a stretch of GA Highway 140 after her. She was the third woman in the state to receive such an honor (in the company of Martha Berry and Juliette Lowe) and the only living woman.

When Ms. Sibley was battling cancer in 1996, every other week brought another award. I remember visiting her in her office at the *Atlanta Journal-Constitution* where she insisted, in spite of her condition, on reporting for work. She'd already put in a full day, written two columns, and answered stacks of mail with her good friend and assistant, Debra Childers. As Ms. Sibley was packing her book bag for the long MARTA train ride home, she confided to me in hushed tones, "I'm going to be honored again." She then cocked her brow knowingly, straightened her chemotherapy wig, and announced: "They think I'm dying—*that's why*."

I do not, however, believe that it was really that life-threatening disease that produced the flurry of awards. Years ago when Georgia's political columnist Bill Shipp was the city editor for the *Atlanta Constitution*, he attempted to push Ms. Sibley out of the office to attend a luncheon at a ladies' club.

"They'll just blind you and make you dizzy and give you a brain tumor," complained his reporter, who also happened to be a struggling single mother.

"Damn it," barked the city editor, "you have to go—they're gonna give you a goddamn *reward*."

The "reward" was the Mother of the Year Award in recognition of Ms. Sibley's valiant efforts at raising three children single-handedly and maintaining her career as a journalist in an era when most women did not attempt the role of both mother and breadwinner.

To feed and clothe those children, Ms. Sibley moonlighted as a *True Confession* and *True Detective* reporter, selling stories with shocking headlines. One story bore the headline "I Sold My Baby for $300" and was published under the byline of the culprit. Another article called "I Wanted to Die," told the story of a waitress who had jumped off the Spring Street bridge. It, too, was published under the subject's name (the woman had insisted on the editorial right to delete the word "shabby" from the description of her living quarters). The latter story, written in the 1950s, earned Ms. Sibley a whopping two hundred dollars.

On another such endeavor when she was at the jail preparing an article to be titled "I Was A Junkie" (and remember, this was at a time when such an animal was rarely referred to in polite society), a photographer was sent over to get some "emotional" pictures of the accused woman. Ms. Sibley asked the warden to show them to a room where the woman might "emote" for the camera. As she was an ex-stripper, she did. She started taking off her clothes.

Unfortunately, these colorful pieces by Ms. Sibley did not survive. They did not survive because her mother, "Muv," wrapped them in brown newspaper so that not even the sanitation department could see the depths her daughter would stoop to for money. Muv preferred to save more respectable work—like the column about her granddaughter Mary praying in a public diner, which brought a respectable Christopher Award and two thousand dollars.

Eventually, the newspaper gave Ms. Sibley a raise on the condition that she would stop writing confession stories.

Rearing children was never easy, but the writer never felt comfortable about taking credit for being an outstanding mother. Speaking of the award, she shrugged, "They didn't even investigate how many times I've had children drunk and in jail."

Perhaps it is just such honest statements that are what endear the writer to her readers. Celestine Sibley sees the weaknesses and faults of humanity through a lens of compassion.

When she writes about and supports various groups and associations such as the Goodwill and Brandeis book sales, Grady Memorial Hospital, the Association for the Blind, or Alcoholics Anonymous, she doesn't make readers feel like they are being preached to by a sob sister, but rather that they are listening to a person who shares their concerns, hopes, and fears.

"I used to go to jail with the Salvation Army when they would visit prisoners," Ms. Sibley once said. "I asked this red-headed captain, 'Why don't you people have churches like other denominations?'"

To this the captain replied, "If we ever forgot the poor and downtrodden people who needed us, the Lord God Almighty would spew us up out of his mouth!"

Celestine Sibley is a self-proclaimed Presbyterian and Democrat, a mother, grandmother, great-grandmother, columnist, reporter, author, and, yes, a strong advocate for the poor and downtrodden.

Claude Sitton, retired newspaper editor and Pulitzer Prize winner, remembers sharing an office with Celestine and the late Harold Martin at the *Atlanta Constitution*. "Harold was bad about having people come in, but Celestine was worse," said Sitton. "One day this disturbing odor came wafting through the city room. A strange-looking man covered with political campaign buttons and wearing WWI leggings came in headed towards Celestine. I think he was dragging a dead cat... Anyway, flecks of lemon peel and vegetable skins were flicking off of him. As I recollect, he was bringing Celestine books he had scavenged out of the public library's garbage cans. Celestine thanked him warmly and he was gone."

The gentleman Sitton recalled so warmly was Francis Brunton, just one of the many eccentric characters Sibley befriended and subsequently wrote about.

Although Celestine Sibley made a rather inauspicious start as a cub reporter for the *Mobile Press Register*, predicting that Shirley Temple had no future as a film star and that Bing Crosby was merely another foppish dilettante, her career in journalism eventually brought her in contact with a host of famous people, among them

Marilyn Monroe, Walt Disney, and Clark Gable. Before television took over she interviewed just about every silver screen legend, including Fred Astaire, Ethel Merman, Charlton Heston, Mickey Rooney, Frank Sinatra, James Cagney, Bing Crosby, songwriter Johnny Mercer, Henry Fonda, and Susan Hayward.

She covered President Jimmy Carter and "Mrs. Roosevelt but never Mr. Roosevelt." Celestine Sibley's political writings spanned the terms of every Georgia governor from the infamous Eugene Talmadge to mountain-bred Zell Miller. Senators Russell, George, and Talmadge (Herman) have all felt the effect of her fingers on the keyboard.

Her insight and ability to get detail made her what some old time journalists call a "Big Gun." She reported the Refoule Murder, the James Earle Ray and Anjette Lyles murder trials, not to mention the shooting of Governor Wallace and countless lesser-known courtroom dramas.

T his book is a sampling of Celestine Sibley's work and is taken primarily from her books. It also includes some news stories and columns as well as other memorabilia that will be permanently housed with her papers in the archives of Emory University. Many thanks to Kathy Landwehr, Peachtree Publisher's editorial director, for her patient direction and organization and for taking more frantic phone calls than a priest. Special thanks to Stephen Goldfarb, Ph.D., of the Atlanta-Fulton Public Library for his flawless research. And special thanks to the youngest archivist in our family, Betsy Vance, for swimming in paper instead of a pool. My deep appreciation to all the esteemed writers and friends of Celestine Sibley who took time to contribute their words and wisdom to this volume, because it is they who best can describe Ms. Sibley's strength and spirit. They probably understand, as I believe I do, that it will take something far more powerful than cancer to take her away from us. It will take something really important—like the temptation of hearing Big Bethel's Heaven Bound choir, of which she is a lifetime fan. You see, a few years ago when the choir promised the writer they'd sing at her funeral, she brightened noticeably. "Oh, I'll rush right home and die tonight!" she said.

Luckily she didn't.

—Sibley Fleming

Miss Celestine Sibley

in deference to Operation Sail, Larry Ashmead has magnani... celebration of the Annual 27th Birthday Party on July 10th 7-10 pm Potts'...

Chapter 1

MEMOIR

I have known Celestine Sibley for thirty years. The first book we published together was *A Place Called Sweet Apple*. There was a lot of her life in that book, as there is in everything she writes. It wasn't until 1988 that she put it all together in a remarkable memoir, *Turned Funny*.

When she was about five years old Celestine hung around the Pensacola Seaport with a Miss Derby who loved to wave at passing ships large and small. When Celestine asked her mother if the "waving girl" was crazy, Muv replied, "No, honey, she's not crazy, she's just turned funny." The book concludes with the following anecdote which is the quintessential "Celestine Story":

> Years ago my friend Jack Spalding pegged my good fortune for me. He was a reporter on the *Atlanta Journal*; I was a reporter on the *Atlanta Constitution*. By sheer coincidence we both turned up at the [Milledgeville] state hospital for the insane at the same time to do stories. We were invited to a patients' dance that afternoon and we went. When we walked in, a gray-bearded old gentleman wearing an old-fashioned Boy Scout uniform with leggings and a Sergeant York-type hat asked me to dance.
>
> Not knowing what else to do I accepted and we stomped and whirled around that blazing-hot concrete auditorium to the recorded "Tennessee Waltz"—the only tune the patients wanted to hear—for two solid hours.
>
> When the dance finally lumbered torturously to its end, my pal Spalding came to walk me back to the hospital administration building. I lit into him.
>
> "You saw I was stuck!" I cried. "Why didn't you rescue me?"
>
> He grinned. "What are you complaining about, old girl?" he asked genially. "You never got such a rush from *sane* people."

He was, now that I think of it, absolutely right. It is one of the compensations—and they are, believe me, many—for being turned funny.

Once there was a panel of authors discussing their editors in unanimously glowing terms. As the moderator invited each author to speak, their editors puffed with pride. One author said, "my editor instinctively knows how to fix the soft underbelly of my storyline," while another claimed her editor was a "genius at writing jacket copy that captured the pure essence of the novel." One fortunate editor was even praised as a "wizard at fine-tuning the allegorical passages." When it came Celestine's turn she said, "I'm not sure Larry even knows the difference between *that* and *which,* but he always reads my manuscripts overnight and he taught me that it's all right to mix red and pink geraniums."

Celestine does know a lot about not very important details such as the difference between *that* and *which,* and she's one of the wisest people I know—certainly my favorite author. She is also a fiercely courageous woman who has lived a life of hard-won happiness with many pains and griefs, hardships, and downright tragedies. Throughout it all, the good times and the bad, she is steadfast in her love of family and friends, city and country. As for writing about her life, she's right up there with the best of them.

Lawrence P. Ashmead

—Lawrence P. Ashmead

Beginnings

Through the years I listened to stories of my forebears, alternately embarrassed and uncomfortable. They sounded so poor, so dirt poor, so heartbreakingly hangdog and hopeless. Even Muv's grandmother, who was said to be a "real lady," looks stringy and hard-bitten in the murky tintype that was left to us. Muv liked to talk about her beloved Grandma, who grew up in south Georgia and "had advantages," which included a melodeon in the parlor and some education at a nearby female academy.

Her undoing, as Muv used to tell it, was that she fell in love with "a sorry renter." Anybody who didn't have the git-up-and-git to own a piece of land was patently poor husband material. And Susan Nix's parents didn't want her to marry King Hinson. He must have had charms that were never perceived by his children and grandchildren because Susan was determined to marry him, and she started assembling pots and pans and dishes and quilts with marriage in mind. For years we had a little glass cream pitcher, all that was left of Susan's house fixings, which Muv said she bought at Henry Paulk's store in Willacoochee back in 1845.

Her mother, who was obviously no more gentle or diplomatic than women in our family have ever been, is said to have remarked: "You might as well buy dishes. *He'll* never get you any."

He must have bought dishes because they had twelve children who had to eat out of something. But apparently he was not given to indulging his Susan or their children in many of life's amenities. He stopped being a "sorry renter" and acquired land, a lot of land, which he tilled with the passionate devotion of the formerly landless. I know so little about him except that his children and grandchildren hated him as a harsh taskmaster, who made them work in the fields from can-till-can't. The older boys went off to fight with the Confederate Army and the girls took over the farm work. All I know about them is fragments, passed on by Muv from time to time through the years.

They weren't sent to school, she said, because "old King," as they called their father, did not consider education important, especially to females. Aunt Rose Ann, according to the stories, married a well-to-do widower, who lived in a painted house with glass windows, and since she couldn't read or write, she had to dictate the exuberant accounts of her new affluence to the folks at home.

"Just put down there," she directed to a niece or nephew, "that I'm a-settin' up here a-lookin' out my glass winders."

Aunt Dilly, the eldest of the girls, had been "promised" to a boy named John, who went off to fight in the Civil War and never returned, leaving her, at the age of fifteen years, a confirmed spinster, who would live the rest of her life in the role of servant and poor kin to the rest of the family.

Elizabeth, called Babe, was a sharp-tongued old lady when I knew her and I suppose she had good reason to be.

As a young girl she was working in the cotton field one day when some young people from a neighboring plantation passed by on their horses. She knew the young man in the crowd and, I suppose, thought that he had noticed her and been attracted to her. To have him catch her in the cotton field in a dirty, draggle-tailed skirt and sunbonnet, laboring like the slaves on his father's land, was more than she could bear.

She hid, face down, on the ground between the rows and refused to budge until the laughing and carefree young riders had gone their way. On her knees on her cotton sack, according to the story, she took a solemn vow that she would never, never work in the fields again. She would do anything that needed doing around the house but she would not pick cotton or hoe corn or harvest tobacco or ever again be caught in the role of field hand.

"Pa can beat me," she said, "but he can't make a field hand out of me."

I don't know if her pa did beat her. He may have had hands enough among his other children. But he didn't help them to the schooling they longed for or see that they learned to read and write. I know now that he wasn't alone in this. There were no public schools and only those who could afford private schooling were taught. But Aunt Babe was never reconciled. She taught herself, as well as she could, and when she was an old lady I remember her letters to my mother sometimes broke off and became drawings. We laughed when she wrote about getting some rabbits to raise and, unable to spell "rabbit," drew pictures of one. Now I know that it wasn't funny. Nor was it funny that Aunt Dilly, in her eighties, insisted on going to a circus with me and some of my teenage friends.

Why would an old lady like that want to horn in on the outing of a group of young folks? I asked my mother.

"Because," Muv said, "she wanted to go to the circus all her life. Once when she was a girl a circus came to Berrien County, Georgia, and she wanted to go bad. She found somebody who would pay a few cents apiece for guana sacks if she washed them. It wasn't easy work. Guana is smelly fertilizer. But she made enough money to buy tickets for herself and Aunt Babe and Aunt Molly. The day of the circus was Saturday, and they knocked off work and filled washtubs and bathed themselves and got dressed and ready to walk the five miles to Nashville to see it. Their father drove up in the yard as they were getting ready to leave and made them get back to the field."

What was the matter with that "real lady," Grandma, that she didn't intercede for her children? I don't know. But my impression is that she was relieved when the old tyrant died and she was free to travel around and visit with her married children.

Aunt Molly married a fun-loving Irishman named John Welch, who drank a little whiskey and played the fiddle and left her with three children when he died young and penniless. Aunt Babe married a railroadman named David Alonzo Kennedy, who was solid citizen

9

enough to establish a home for his family, which became a refuge for all his wife's poor kin. Aunt Dilly and Aunt Molly and my mother were among this number, as were Aunt Babe and Uncle Lon's daughter, Theda, called Sister, when she divorced Uncle George Chapman and came home with their son, Roy. My mother's mother, my grandmother, named Susan for her mother, was the most puzzling of the lot to me.

Sue, as her sisters called her, was said to be the prettiest of the girls, fair-skinned and red-headed, and full of mischief and fire. At the age of sixteen she married an older man of forty named John Barber and went to live in the little south Georgia town of Pearson. I know nothing of John except that my mother always regarded him as a gentleman from a good family, who was able to provide his wife with a nice two-story white house on the town's main street. He might not have been a good husband, but, on the other hand, Sue was not the most biddable wife. When her first and only child, my mother, was born in that tall white house, she took her and went home to the farm, where she dumped her baby and took off.

Muv, named Evelyn but called Dixie, found out later that John came looking for them, but her grandparents hid her and told him they didn't know where Sue had gone. He never found either of them and, according to family lore, was so grief-stricken his reason slipped and he was eventually committed to Milledgeville State Hospital for the Insane, where he died. My mother told me she wasn't sure of that and always meant to visit the hospital and ask them to check their records for her father's name. Years later, when I was a reporter covering stories at the hospital, I saw a cemetery with many unmarked graves and I wondered but did not ask if my grandfather John Barber lay there.

Meanwhile, Sue became what my mother called "a traveling woman." Restless, never content to stay in one place more than a few days, she prowled the countryside, stopping to visit relatives, occasionally taking a job of some kind, usually as a housekeeper. When her daughter was old enough to go with her she took her along.

"Going, going, walking, walking, always traveling," Muv said.

Once they had a berth with a widower, who fell in love with Sue and asked her to marry him. She agreed and little Dixie was ecstatic.

"A good home and plenty at it," she told me.

The wedding was set and the bridegroom's married daughters came home to take a hand with the arrangements, helping to outfit Sue and Dixie with new finery and launching a cooking marathon to have a suitable feast for the wedding guests.

"I was so happy," Muv told me. "I loved that house and that old man, and I thought I was going to get to stay put and maybe go to school and church like other children."

The night before the wedding Sue slipped out of the house, taking Dixie with her. They walked to the nearest railroad line and flagged the first passing train.

"I never got over it," Muv said. "My, that would have been a nice home!"

I don't know how many years Sue's traveling went on before Dixie parted company with her. One night when they were visiting some aunt or cousin little Dixie saw the signs she had come to recognize in her mother—a restless tramping around and singing, too-ready laughter.

"I knew she was fixing to go again," she told me. "I knew I couldn't do it anymore. I was done with it. I went to the woods and hid out, and when she looked for me in my bed and I wasn't there, she left without me."

On the map East Bay looked—and still does—like the tail on the big blue rooster of Pensacola Bay, a south-curving prong of indigo water. Century-old live oaks, twisted and lichened by the turbulent winds, shaded the white-sand shoreline.

11

The main street was a dirt road running along the bayside, but it was a lively thoroughfare, lined with the bright-painted houses of Swedish settlers named Anderson, Nelson, and Bengston. From them came the laughter and play sounds of many children because families in that community frequently numbered ten or twelve children each. (One of my father's uncles had a record eighteen by two wives and a neighbor known only as Florence. He claimed them all.) There was also the smell of good cooking, exotic foreign-named cakes and strudels, brought from Scandinavia, and rich fish chowders, which my mother could never quite emulate and never quite forgot.

The Broxsons, my father's maternal ancestors, may have come from Sweden originally but they had been in the United States for generations. Robert Broxson, the first one to settle in the Florida panhandle, was born in South Carolina in 1812 and was apparently a planter there, because he had thirteen slaves.

He moved to Florida several years before it attained statehood in 1845 and, according to William J. Wells, who wrote a delightful book about the area (*Pioneering in the Panhandle*), farmed until the Emancipation Proclamation freed his slaves in 1863. Then he switched to lumbering. According to a family story, some of the slaves followed the Broxsons to Miller Point on East Bay, where they moved into a mill house next door and continued to work for and were fed by the Broxsons.

Robert and his wife, the former Mary Ellen Lovett, of Holmes County, Florida, had ten children, the second of whom was my grandmother, Susan, born in 1850. According to the stories told to my mother, who, of course, didn't arrive until a few years after Susan's death in 1911, she was a beautiful woman and well loved by countless East Bay children, who called her Aunt Sook.

William Henry Colley was in the logging business on Yellow River with her younger brother, Joseph, and must have begun to pay court to Susan when he came home from the Civil War. For, although he was a native of Barbour County, Alabama, he fought with a Florida company, Company F, First Florida Regiment, which went on to Shiloh. He may have been married twice, although I never heard that, but there is a headstone in the Holley Cemetery that reads "W. H. Colley, Jr. Born April 22, 1862. Died October 31, 1889." There is no marked grave of a first wife. Anyhow, Henry and Susan were married July 20, 1871, and were elderly for that time, forty-eight and forty respectively, when my father, called Little Henry, was born in 1890. (I don't know when his older brother, Clark, was born.)

According to legend still current on East Bay, there were "salt-water Broxsons and fresh-water Broxsons." Many of them were both, moving from river to bay and bay to river and back again. Henry Colley, Sr., made a salt-water Broxson of his bride, Susan, taking her from Yellow River to a beautiful wooded spot on the bay. There they built a neat white house back of the Harper post office and store and the substantial wharf, from which barrels of turpentine, from L. D. Bryan's still a couple of miles inland, were shipped out to Pensacola three days a week.

The bridegroom had bought from the government a full lot of land, less four and a half acres designated for a Baptist church and grave-yard. There they reared their two sons, Clark and Henry, establishing them on neighboring homesteads—the great land bonanza responsible for settling much of the area. In order to persuade settlers to go west, the Homestead Act of 1862 had offered 160 acres to anybody who would settle on the land and care for it for five years. The offer also applied to Florida, a newcomer among states and still largely unsettled. Clark and Henry claimed 160 acres each, which gave that branch of the Colley family a fair chunk of the beautiful Santa Rosa peninsula.

Years later, when my mother grew restless and dissatisfied with life as she was living it, she would say, "I'm going to get me a homestead." I

13

don't think she knew that the offer was withdrawn in 1934 when President Franklin D. Roosevelt abolished the homestead system.

But her arrival at East Bay in 1915 was an occasion for celebration among Little Henry's friends and relatives. His brother, Clark, had married Ellen Anderson, daughter of Swedish neighbors, and moved down near the mouth of the bay on a tract from the Andersons' homestead. Little Henry and Henry, Sr., batched together and definitely felt the need of a woman's hand in the house. When Henry had reached the age of twenty-three with no indication that he was interested in the local girls, his friends and neighbors were concerned. According to William James Wells, a friend told Little Henry about the Lonely Hearts Club, which published a matrimonial bulletin. It was the place to write to get himself a bride, they said. Little Henry gave it a try and had response enough, according to Bill Wells, who thought my mother had been one of the applicants. (She emphatically denied it.)

Anyhow, he met and married Dixie, and when he brought her home to the bay, the population, numbering chiefly his kinfolks, turned out to welcome them. Their first night, to my mother's chagrin, they were "shivareed" by the exuberant young blades of the bay. French settlers of Florida had called it a *charivari*, a noisy serenade to newlyweds. The American pioneers pronounced it "shivaree" and it meant the same—a tumultuous night-long commotion around the honeymoon house, engendered by moonshine and good feelings and punctuated by pistol shots. My mother hated it and the series of "frolics" that followed.

She never forgot one such party in the little white clapboard Methodist-Congregational church at Holley, where there were bountiful food and drink and fiddle music and singing, interrupted by the arrival of a bunch of roistering young fellows, who rode their horses around the church, cracking the long whips used on oxen logging teams, and shooting off their pistols. She had already backed timidly into a corner when the young bucks dismounted and came rolling merrily into the church with the avowed intention of kissing the bride.

Little Henry, to her surprise, did not attempt to rescue her.

"I had to look after myself and I was ready for them," she recalled. "I had a hatpin and I used it!"

That night may have been the tip-off that Little Henry wasn't going to look after her. She didn't notice it as long as his father lived, for they truly had a good home and plenty at it. And, when she became pregnant with me, Henry, Sr., was delighted and spoiled her, ordering off to Pensacola for special foods not available in the store, and yard goods from which to make baby clothes. He encouraged her efforts to fix up the house and was apparently far more interested than his son when she bought cheesecloth to paste over the plank walls and flower-sprigged wallpaper to paste on the cheesecloth. She made scrim curtains and cut fancy paper valances for the mantels and planted flowers everywhere, drawing freely on seeds and cuttings from her neighbors, as well as ordering from the catalogues.

Henry, Sr., bought her a saddle horse, and she rode around the bay visiting families she was to remember with affection all her life. Aunt Sister and her little boy Roy arrived to spend the winter with Dixie, and the two cousins put in many happy hours making baby clothes for the expected one. Grandpa ordered a pair of Keen Kutter scissors for the enterprise and Dixie cherished them as long as she lived, keeping them sharp and frequently angrily rescuing them from various playhouses when I reached doll-clothes and paperdoll age. The day after her funeral when my children and I were preparing to go back to Atlanta, my daughter Susan said, "Maybe you should take some of Muv's things that you want to keep. Her silver?"

Muv had bought a service for eight with money she saved from teaching school during World War II years and I knew she valued it. But I had no inclination to pick through her things and take them out of her house. Not so soon. Then I remembered her scissors, the ones the grandfather I never knew bought, the ones she used to cut out my baby dresses and those of my children and grandchildren. I opened her work basket and picked them up and took them home with me.

Grandpa died in 1917 shortly after I was born and by that time my little brother was on the way. Things at the Colley homestead seem to have changed drastically. The store closed. My father lost the post office. Storms buffeted the little house, and Little Henry's legs broke out with sores, which were to bedevil him all his life.

"He wouldn't get out of bed to put the mail bag on the boat," Muv told me later. "I did it until I was so pregnant I was ashamed to be seen. I'd call and call him, trying to get him out of bed, and one morning I saw him flying down the wharf with the mail bag, wearing nothing but his shirt, the tail flapping in the breeze!"

Dixie was delighted with my little brother, naming him Vernon Castle for the famous dancer. But there was no indulgent grandfather to buy him Horlick's Malted Milk and a silver cup, as he had bought me, and life was getting increasingly precarious for the whole family. Dixie, proud and energetic and determined never to be anybody's "poor kin" again, did not want help from even the kindest of Little Henry's relatives, although most of them were considered well-off by local standards, and all of them treated her husband with the affection and indulgence they had accorded the gangling, good-humored giant all his life.

"Old High Pockets," they would say fondly. "Nary a bit of harm in him."

Dixie agreed. He was amiable and gentle and kind to her and his children, but he wouldn't or couldn't earn a living. When the house and store and post office were gone, they moved to Bagdad, a little mill town to the north, and Little Henry went out looking for work.

I don't know how long he was gone, but we ran out of food and my little brother, never robust, seemed to sicken on biscuits and flour gravy, which was all that was left in the larder. Taking him in her arms and me by the hand, my mother walked across the railroad trestle to a store where she had bought food in the past.

She asked to get a few things on credit. Her husband was away looking for work and would pay when he returned.

"I'm sorry, Miss Dixie," the grocer said. "I can't give you any more credit. Little Henry ain't good for it."

Dixie lifted her chin proudly and turned away quickly. The baby in her arms saw a pile of bright red apples on the counter and reached out his hand.

"Ap, Ma," he implored. "Ap?"

Humiliated and angry at him for reaching for what she was powerless to give him, Dixie slapped her baby's hand—a blow that left a bruised place in her own heart as long as she lived.

"He got sicker during the night," she told me. "I knew he needed nourishment and my colored neighbors—Lord, they was good!—they must have known it too. They came and brought a frying-size chicken cooked tender and juicy with gruel. We tried to feed him, a spoonful at the time, but it was too late. He died that day."

They took his body back to East Bay on the *Monroe W.*, the passenger launch that ran between the bay and Pensacola. It was a windy, rainy day, but Dixie sat in the stem of the boat and held on to the little coffin, which swayed and rocked with the boat's rough passage.

Vernon Castle was buried in an unmarked grave in the Harper cemetery beside his Colley grandparents. Muv never meant to leave his grave without a headstone, and months later in Pensacola she bought a small angel of some insubstantial material. She had it on a table by her bed, ready to take back to East Bay, when she could go, but I was bouncing on the bed one day, pretending to drive a horse, and I knocked the angel to the floor. It shattered.

When anyone speaks of ineradicable childhood guilts I remember that. Muv slapped me and I cried and then she held me in her arms and we cried together.

Although the marriage was not legally severed (it never was, as a matter of fact), it was over. Whatever affection she had once had for the awkward, boyish fellow she married turned to hatred. She despised the slow, plodding way he moved. The country occupation of whittling, universally pursued by a man with a sharp knife, a good piece of wood, and time on his hands, filled her with rage. She hated the way he smelled, the sores he wouldn't get treated, and the way he dressed. And, when he took up Bible reading and quoting scriptures to answer any question she had about some workaday matter, she took a perverse pleasure in attacking God, the church, and all religions—this despite her own previously strong religious convictions.

There must have been some effort at reconciliation on Little Henry's part, and I think his relatives probably considered Dixie unreasonable and peremptory to leave him. I have a foggy recollection of being on the bay with him when she wasn't there and being taken to a little house beside a bridge where it crossed a beautiful stream that flowed like amber over white sand. He must have told me that mama was coming and that we might live there, because I found a left-behind broom and swept the vacant rooms. There was a crapemyrtle bush by the back door and I broke off a flowering branch and set it in a jar of creek water. Like my mother, I wanted a home and I clung to the fantasy, fostered by my father, that we would all be together again.

18

Letting the People Know

Every newspaper reporter who has seen people in trouble or in need and been able to help them by writing about them or seen social and political evils corrected or improved because the public was informed has a mighty respect for the so-called power of the press. My experience with the magic in "letting the people know" came in a small way but it was an awesome thing to me—and it still is.

That first summer on the Mobile *Press*, when news seemed dull or nonexistent and little seemed to be stirring in the sleepy old seaport town except an occasional breeze, which died when it hit the sun-baked pavements, our city editor got a call about a minor crisis at the Family Welfare Bureau. You have to understand that welfare was a small business then. Miss Florence Van Sickler, the director, a secretary, and one caseworker constituted the staff, and they operated from two rooms over a downtown store. Their budget had to have been infinitesimal or they wouldn't have called for help for three newborn babies.

But they did call and the city editor sent me down to talk to Miss Van Sickler. There were three infants just born who had not a diaper to their names and were literally crying for milk, which their scrawny, undernourished mothers could not provide. If by some miracle we could get milk contributed to them, there was then the problem of ice to keep it. Perhaps a small notice in the paper, Miss Van suggested.

Distressed and alarmed that the babies might die (infant mortality rate was still high then), I wrote a little story, which the paper carried on page one.

The response was overwhelming. Layettes enough to outfit hundreds of babies to come poured in. Milk enough for the newborns and all the children in many families was provided. Ice companies rallied, not only with every-other-day delivery of the standard fifty pounds of ice but with old wooden iceboxes in which to keep it. I was both astonished and perhaps a little impressed that words of mine had wrought such a miracle.

Miss Van saved me from smugness. She praised me for caring and for the words that evoked the response, but she showed me that the problem of hunger and need was still big and heartbreaking and certainly beyond the skill, if not the comprehension, of a kid who could use a typewriter. For the Depression was on the land and just beginning to reach out octopus tentacles to our town.

I spent a lot of time around the Family Welfare Bureau that summer. Miss Dorothy Bennett, the sole caseworker, was finding that her load was growing, and she took on her first assistant, a college girl named Mary McMullen, who came to intern with them.

Between them they introduced me to many things I had not dreamed of. Hookworm was rampant. (I had thought it was inevitable.) Pellagra, which many old people I knew took for granted, was a deficiency disease that could be cured. We distributed many cans of salmon to old people in cottonmill villages, convincing them—and me—that nutrition could save them. I, who only dimly suspected where babies came from, heard about birth control, a procedure my social-worker friends favored for cutting down on the number of feeble-minded and demented couples.

As the Depression deepened, my visits to the Family Welfare Bureau and my stories about need increased. People called me about cases that were unknown even to the caseworkers. There was a family living in an empty store building out on the edge of town—a mother and half a dozen little children. I don't remember where the father was but he had probably joined that vast army of men who tramped over the country looking for work. The family was cold and hungry, and, to make things more acute, the mother had given birth in the night to a baby. She had stretched out on one of the store's old counters, after she had bedded down the children, and

20

managed to bring a new baby into the world alone and unattended.

I caught the streetcar and went out to see them.

My story that afternoon evoked a response that impresses me to this day. I don't recall that there was any effort to put the mother and baby in the hospital, but they seemed well enough, considering that they had no beds or stove or food in that old store.

The man who owned the store had not even known that they were there, but he made no objection when he found out, and I began to haul in furniture and mattresses, boxes of groceries, blankets, clothes. One man gave them a heater and installed it himself. There was a ton of coal waiting for somebody to pick it up. The paper gave me a truck from the circulation department and I went and hauled the coal. I went into basements and attics to get the gifts proffered by sympathetic Mobilians. Darkness had settled and I was making my last haul. Excitement over the response and the satisfaction of seeing the family taken care of had begun to pall. I was wet—my own shoes had cardboard over the holes in the soles—cold, and utterly exhausted.

One more stop, I said to myself, and pulled up in front of the home of a prominent lawyer. His wife met me at the door. She alone among all the people who gave me things had thought to prepare something the family could eat immediately. She had a big pot of hot soup on the stove.

Taking a look at me, she said softly, "My dear, *you* need to eat. Take off your coat and those wet shoes. Sit down. Warm a little and eat some of this soup."

The warmth of the kitchen, the first food of the day, and the kindness of the old couple were a moving end to what had been one of the momentous days of my life—an exhausting day in which pain and need had been met by an outpouring of concern and generosity. I sat there in my stocking feet and cried a little.

But those tears were nothing to the ones I would shed in rage and

21

frustration a few years later when I heard that the kind couple whose soup I had eaten had become victims of the first instance of anti-Semitism I had ever known about.

For years they had spent their summers at an ancient, sand- and windswept hotel on the eastern shore of Mobile Bay, and they assumed that they would continue to do so after the hotel was bought and re-placed with a far grander structure. They wrote to make their annual reservation and were turned down. Clientele, they were told, was "re-stricted," which meant no Jews.

As far as I know they made no protest, and if the gentle, grand-motherly woman who had warmed and fed me cried a little, nobody knew about it. But it was the first time I had encountered senseless prejudice against *white* people. We took segregation of our black friends for granted, not even suspecting that they minded it. After all, we had never heard of black people who considered applying for a reservation at any hotel, much less a fancy resort hotel. I think it was the first glim-mering I had of an idea that there were many wrongs in the world that a few published words of mine could not change.

No Jason seeking the golden fleece, no Ponce de Léon on trail of the fountain of youth was more charmed with the ex-otic and magical places they found than I was with At-lanta. The old *Constitution* newsroom seemed to me to be exactly what a newspaper newsroom should be—crowded and noisy, first, its splintery wooden floors caked with almost three-quarters of a century of old crankcase oil and dirt, its windows clouded from without by smoke from railroad trains and from within by the blue fumes of burning tobacco. AP and UP teletype machines clattered out news from dis-tant places, old manual typewriters under the touch of hunt-and-peck two-fingered virtuosos alternately sputtered and fizzed with local and state news.

The walls were plastered with yellowed news pictures going back to the days of Jack Dempsey, Man Mountain Dean, Clara Bow, and Marie, the Queen of Roumania. Mixed in the curling and dusty gallery was a picture of a typical movie-version reporter—snap-brim hat, trenchcoat, cigarette smoke curling up artfully from a butt caught in the corner of his mouth. "Don't Talk About Him," said the hand-lettered caption glued to the bottom. "He Works Here Now." I knew he must be the new Lee Tracy-type hot-shot reporter and I couldn't wait to meet him, but he must have come and gone pretty speedily because I never saw him or anybody in the motley assembly around the city desk who remotely resembled that glamorous photograph.

As the newest reporter on the staff, I had to work most Sundays and nearly all holidays. I happened to be off Sunday afternoon, December 7, and was sitting on the floor holding my arms out to Susan, who at eleven months was standing alone and trying to take her first tentative steps. Jim had the radio going in the bedroom and suddenly he turned it up and yelled: "Listen!"

Pearl Harbor had been bombed!

The details came pouring out. A surprise attack by the Japanese forces at 7:55 A.M. in Honolulu—eighteen ships sunk, 174 planes destroyed, more than 3,000 people killed or wounded.

It meant war, we told one another, as the horror story rattled out. Pearl Harbor, where so many of our Pensacola Navy friends were assigned, crippled, all but destroyed. The attack had gone on for two hours, and the roll of lost battleships—*Arizona, California, Oklahoma, West Virginia*—was especially shocking to Jim, who had an acquaintance with some of them.

We sat by the radio all night, and the next day I learned that as federal-beat reporter I was to cover the military, which suddenly became very big and very active in Atlanta. Recruiting offices were

23

jammed, lines of would-be volunteers flowed out into the street and around the block. Fort McPherson, the Third Army headquarters, became a reception center for enlistees. Colonel Stacy Knopf, the Third Army intelligence officer, who had an office in the old federal building and had been an amiable source of little stories about a pet cemetery he was establishing, suddenly became very hard to see.

Back at the office the staff collected around the teletype machines, whose bells jangled and whose keys clicked out President Roosevelt's speech to Congress asking for a declaration of war against Japan. He called December 7 "a date which will live in infamy."

Because the staff was depleted I got to cover a remarkable range of assignments, while filling that onerous gaping hole, assistant city editor's slot. There was a trunk murder and I asked to go. A sailor had reported his wife missing. I handled the picture, suspecting, as did the police, that the young woman had left home voluntarily and would show up. Her body did—in a trunk in a rain-flooded basement after some days of evil and mysterious smell. A little widow, suspecting the sailor's wife of being after her handsome son-in-law, had done her in with a sash weight and pushed her into the trunk.

The afternoon a black man hired to clean the basement came upon the body and called the police, the little widow was coming home on the bus from shopping downtown and saw the police cars in her yard. She rode past her stop, wondering what to do, and then apparently making up her mind in the space of a block, she got off the bus and walked back home and confessed.

I went to see her at the jail—a neat little old lady who looked lonely and bewildered. I began by asking her if I could do anything for her and she smiled on me warmly.

"Yes!" she said. "Would you bring me some bananas?"

While I fed her bananas through the bars of her cell, she told me how she had been persuaded that it was necessary to eliminate the

24

buxom girl named Mildred she suspected of breaking up her daughter's marriage. Later her defense attorney got her life sentence commuted to the state mental hospital with a device I, when I became a columnist, found offensive. She had a "plunder room" filled with stacks and stacks of boxes jammed with clippings of Dorothy Dix's columns. Proof, said the famed defense counsel and former congressman William Schley Howard, that the poor woman was mentally incompetent.

There was a lot to do—other murders and fires; a daily military column; a weekly Victory Garden page, which I wrote, edited, and made up; politics; air-raid alarms and blackouts; vicissitudes of rationing; bond-selling campaigns by such luminaries as Bob Hope, Dorothy Lamour, and our own Margaret Mitchell. Fortunately, it took some of the onus off assistant city editing, which I loathed. Not a piece of copy passed through my hands that I didn't tackle it with the wistful notion that I could have written it better, and why wasn't I out there covering the story instead of being office- and deskbound? I think it became clear to everybody then that I was not made for command but was by instinct and inclination a member of the ground troops.

The First Book

On one of my trips to Hollywood I had started a book. It was really busywork, done because I had a roomette on the Super Chief and found it lonely being shut off from the day-coach crowd. On all previous trips to the West Coast I had flown, but it began to seem a waste to me—all the country I was passing over and not seeing. So on one fall trip I took a train to Chicago, spent a wonderful day sightseeing there at the direction of a woman I had picked up on the train, went to a matinee of *Guys and Dolls*, and boarded the Super Chief for Los Angeles in the late afternoon. It was a novel experience and seemed totally glamorous to me for a day and a night. Then it began to pall. Reared a day-coach traveler, I missed people—holding wet babies, sharing shoebox lunches, the whole sociable business of journeying poor folks. On the Super Chief every passenger was hermetically sealed from every other passenger, some of them in roomettes, some of them in drawing rooms, and all of them, I reflected bleakly, isolated and cut off from the human race.

It happened that I was taking a small snake to actress Jean Peters, the gift of our movie editor, Paul Jones, who had learned of her affection for snakes while she was in Georgia making the Okefenokee swamp movie, *Lure of the Wilderness*. This reptile was small and innocuous, I suppose, but I was terrified of him just the same. Not wanting to admit it, I stuck the glass jar with ventilating holes in the lid down in a narrow, covered basket to be sure I would not have to look at the snake. So he was no company, except for the fact that dining-car waiters learned about him and came in two or three times a day with flies they had caught in the kitchen for him to eat.

Lacking anything else to do, I started a murder mystery. I opened up my portable typewriter and between looks at the wonderful, fearful scenery of the desert and bare-bouldered West, I plugged along on a story about death in an Atlanta newspaper office. It wasn't *Gone With the Wind*, but it kept me happily occupied until I arrived at the Los Angeles train station, where I was met by a publicist from 20th Century–Fox, Miss Peters, and the studio's herpetologist.

One look at the gift snake and the studio publicist decided he was too puny and unimpressive to warrant any attention from the Los Angeles newspapers. Right away somebody was dispatched to rent a *real* snake, and presently the herpetologist, Miss Peters, and I were posing for newspaper pictures with a boa constrictor draped over the herpetologist's shoulders. After some debate the experts agreed that Miss Peters's fans might be offended if she got *too* cozy with the snake, so she merely patted his head. I, the supposed donor, was caught fearfully backing into the woodwork.

Sometimes I wonder what happened to that scrawny, fly-fed little snake who, probably against his wishes, was hauled from Georgia clear across the continent on a glamorous movie-star railroad train and then, like many another film hopeful, found inadequate.

The murder mystery I started probably had a happier fate. I took it one night to read to a group of writing friends, who met occasionally to read their deathless works, exchange great dollops of praise, and encourage one another to newer and loftier endeavor. The group had started out at our Sunday magazine, under the maternal eye of a prodigious writer named Wylly Folk St. John. Wylly was always looking for story ideas, and she found a small item in the newspaper one day that appealed to her as a plot germ. She persuaded five of us, co-workers, to take the bare bones of the story and try our hands at writing something around it. We turned out a variety of prose, including a short story, a novelette, a dog story, a magazine interview, and a television play. After work one afternoon we adjourned to Wylly's old-fashioned, tree-shaded front porch in Kirkwood with beer and sandwiches and read aloud.

It was so much fun, so really stimulating, we made a regular thing of such meetings, and our group expanded to include some already-successful published writers. Among these was a delightful woman named Nedra Tyre, whose first novel, *Red Wine First*, had been critically acclaimed before she turned to writing murder mysteries.

Nedra was present when I read the eight opening pages of my Super Chief opus.

"Go on with it, Celestine," she said. "Finish it."

"Oh, I don't have time," I said. "You know I don't have time."

Nedra leaned over and touched me on the shoulder.

"Just fifteen minutes a day, Celestine," she whispered. "Just fifteen minutes a day."

It was the best writing advice I ever received. Nedra knew what I

27

was to learn, and that is if you force yourself to sit down and write for fifteen minutes every day you might find that you stick to it for an hour or two.

Even with a shortage of writing time I got about thirty pages written and saw it off to Doubleday. David Creviston, that publisher's Georgia representative, was a friend of mine and he volunteered to take my manuscript to New York and give it to Isabelle Taylor, who presided over the company's output of murder mysteries, called the Crime Club.

To my amazement and delight Mrs. Taylor wrote me right away that she liked the story, except for a flaw I didn't perceive—it was smart-alecky in spots. If I could remedy that, she would offer me a contract and a nice cash advance. For days to come I couldn't be separated from that dog-eared manuscript. I read it on the bus, when I went to bed at night, when I awakened in the morning. I couldn't see how it was smart-alecky, but I was determined to find out.

Wylly came to the rescue. We had lunch one day and she went over my opening chapters carefully, pencil in hand. When she finished we had agreed to eliminate eight words.

Nervously, without much hope, I sent it back to Mrs. Taylor. Lo and behold, killing those eight words had been enough. She liked the start, wanted the rest of the book as soon as possible, and enclosed a check for $1,000.

28

The cabin at Holly Creek seemed the natural place to go for the necessary uninterrupted peace and quiet in which to work. It was summer and the girls were visiting Muv, so I took some vacation, and Jimmy and I loaded the car and headed north. The temptation to clean up the place, make improvements, and move in ferns and other wildlings to the yard was great, of course. But I managed to stick to the typewriter, which we set up on the screened porch. When the sun reached the porch and it was too hot to continue there I would take the portable and sit on a rock in the creek with my feet cooling in the icy stream.

Jimmy was in charge of the commissary department and fed us regularly, if monotonously. If I reached a pause in my writing and thought about it, I got tired of peanut butter and jelly sandwiches and sardines and crackers, but I mostly jogged along with what he provided, grateful for his help and the fact that the few dishes involved in Jimmy's cuisine could be set in the creek and presently the motion of the water and the swirling sand would scour them clean.

A welcome break in our fare came on those days when we looked out and saw the Tabors crossing the creek on the foot log. Frances invariably had a foil-covered dish containing freshly cooked vegetables from their garden, cornbread or homemade rolls, an apple pie or a chocolate cake.

With such friends, such a peerless retreat for working, I should have turned out a monumental work of the caliber of Maggie's *War and Peace* or, at the very least, a latter-day *Gone With The Wind*.

Instead, it was a pleasant, I think, but fairly slight murder mystery of Doubleday's "Damsel in Distress" persuasion.

In the spring of 1958 not everybody in the world had a new book out, as they seem to have at almost every season nowadays, so my first got a lot of generous attention. From everybody but the *New York Times*, that is. The *Times*'s reviewer gave it two or three paragraphs, pointing out that I knew a lot more about newspapers than I did about opera. (I used opening night in Atlanta to get some of my murders off the ground.) Anthony Boucher, the review king, was absolutely right, of course, but my feelings as a new author were young and tender, and since I admired him and his works so much I was wounded as many another author has been, to find him picky about my prose.

Other reviewers were uniformly kind, however. Our editor, Ralph McGill himself, did the *Constitution*'s review, saying, "a great many thousands...already know how well Celestine can write" and urging the book on them as authentic newspaper and good mystery. He explained the title, *The Malignant Heart*, which I took from the Georgia code's definition of murder: "The act of an abandoned and malignant heart." I was grateful because a lot of people thought it might be a medical tome about cardiac problems. There were parties and autographings and Isabelle Taylor came down from New York to see me through the first ones. The possibility that a store will buy up a lot of your books, throw a party to which no one comes, and there the store and you are stuck with all those unread, unwanted volumes haunts every writer, I suppose. I have had that experience but not with the first book, thank goodness. It would have thrown my fiction writing into permanent, traumatic arrest.

The kickoff for any book by a Georgia author used to be at Rich's and I knew the system. If the clamor of the reading public for a book was so faint as to be unheard, the book buyer would put hats on the clerks and walk them by the author. Not many authors knew that but I did, and I started out looking with suspicion at everybody who came toward me with a book to be autographed. Are you from hosiery or housewares? I wanted to ask. Fortunately, I was saved by friends, who rallied round spectacularly.

When you have had the mayor and the governor and half the legislature as well as all your neighbors and newspaper friends at the first party, then you start worrying about the second one. You are going to be, you reflect bleakly, *all alone with all those books.* Davison's department store, now called Macy's, gave me a gala celebration on its book mezzanine, but even as they set out the cookies and punch I worried that nobody would come.

Just as I reached the point of doing what I used to do at high school dances, retreating to the bathroom, I heard a commotion on the up escalator. Half the Atlanta police department, pals all, led by Chief Herbert Jenkins, was arriving. Before they had bought their books and moved away, the Salvation Army, trumpets, trombones, and tambourines, arrived. I couldn't see to autograph for the tears in my eyes.

Now I really have used up my friends, I thought humbly. There's nobody else left in the world to care that I've written this little book and to want a copy. But the escalator was bringing me a new and surprising wave of the faithful.

The summer before I had spent a week or ten days in the little south Georgia town Vienna, waiting out the death of the state's senior U.S. Senator, Walter F. George (the one, you recall, President Roosevelt tried unsuccessfully to purge because of his opposition to packing the Supreme Court). A *Journal* reporter, the late John Pennington, was also there, and we spent the long, hot days with Madge Methvin, editor of the local weekly, or visiting with her friends at the drugstore or the town's morning-coffee gathering spot. In that space of time I grew fond of the town and the people I met, especially Madge, who was the George family's spokesman and our contact with Mrs. George and the Senator's doctor. Because she worked so hard to help us, allowing us to use her newspaper office as our headquarters and taking us home to hot midday dinners, put on her table by a peerless black cook named Beulah, we volunteered to help Madge put out her paper as press time approached. It was my first experience with working on a weekly and I enjoyed it and Madge Methvin tremendously.

Now I looked out toward the escalator leading to Davison's book department, and there came Madge and a whole congregation of friends from Vienna.

I got up from the autograph table and tottered to meet them, gasping, "What on earth...?"

"Oh, we just decided to have a motorcade to Atlanta to get this book!" said Madge blithely.

There must have been fifteen or twenty of them, beautiful and unforgettable.

31

There were other parties and kind attentions from many quarters—I even got Sigma Delta Chi and Theta Sigma Phi awards, and me not a member of either group!—and it was a good thing because there's nothing like your first book. After that there may be a pleasant bustle here and there. You may get to go to New York to be on the *Today Show* or to book-and-author dinners around the country. (The one in Richmond, which the *Atlantic*'s Edward Weeks used to emcee, is a don't-miss if you're ever invited.) But there will be lulls, dry spells, times that the author Harnett Kane described as occasions of such isolation that you are grateful when somebody stops by and asks you the way to the ladies' room. I once had such an experience in his beloved New Orleans, selling but two books and I bought one of them.

So everybody who writes for a living probably does what I have just done and relives, fatuously, the triumph of that first book.

—from *Turned Funny*

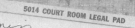

Girls' Friction Leads to Murder in Newspaper

By ELEANOR SMITH
Herald Mystery Book Editor

THE MALIGNANT
HEART, by Celestine Sibley.
(Crime Club, $2.95.) There
was friction between clever,
ambitious Paula Reynolds and
her straightforward colleague
Katy Kincaid. It could have
been office politics, or personal matters.

But whether this friction
was responsible for Paula's elegant form to be found draped
over Katy's desk with a copy
spike in her back is another
matter. Katy was in for a peck
of trouble as clues seemed to
be stacked against her.

And then the killer struck
again — as the saying goes.
Poor Katy!

The story has the bustle and
excitement of a big city newspaper office, a background in
which Miss Sibley is completely at home, being a columnist
and staffwriter on the Atlanta
Constitution.

THE
MALIGNANT HEART
A CRIME CLUB SELECTION

Celestine Sibley

malignant heart

Monday

Dearest Muv,

This has been slow a-coming but I've been so busy. Had a murder trial in Conyers last week and really needed you to help me handle the old men. They clustered around the courtroom like bees to sourwood. It was such a lovely case, too—a slob of a woman hired a couple of Negroes to beat her husband to death while he slept. Her 16-year-old son supervised the whole thing and then she got a taxi and they hauled the body out to the woods and abandoned it in the husband's car. She had a beau who allegedly offered the older Negro man $2,000 to get her husband "out the way." We made quick work of them, though. Gave the woman and the older Negro the electric chair, the beau and the younger Negro and the son life imprisonment. You should have been along. Took me all week to ~~~~ it.

Susan and Mary and Cornelia Hamond and I went up to the Saturday morning, taking along some cute red curtains to hang and cabinets out of the apartment kitchen. We spent Saturday afternoon up the place and putting up curtains ~~~~ keeper, bless h~~~ sisted some ~~~~ after ~~~~ you n nt and

Four delicate but deadly writers discuss tools of their trade. Genevieve Holden, Celestine Sibley, Medora Field Perkerson and Nedra Tyre have murder on their minds as they enjoy a spot of tea.

These Gentle Ladies Are Killers   By Patricia Noot LaHatte

Celestine Sibley joins Atlanta's amazing group of murder ~~~~ Pictures by Floyd Jillson

Chapter 2

MURDER

Celestine Sibley has an unfortunate affinity for telling the truth.

Even when she's writing lies, or "fiction" as some of us like to call it, she's telling the truth.

The first time she committed fiction, with her 1958 mystery, *The Malignant Heart*, Celestine gave herself clean away. The heroine of *The Malignant Heart*, as in all her subsequent mysteries, is Kate Kincaid, a savvy lady newspaper reporter. Very early in her fictional career, Kate admits to a fascination with criminal doings.

"Any of my colleagues on *The Atlanta Searchlight*, that great Southern newspaper, could have told you that murder was my favorite assignment," Kate confesses.

And any of Celestine's colleagues on the *Atlanta Constitution*, the very real Southern newspaper where Celestine has for decades covered "Dixie Like the Dew," first as a reporter, and then, for the last fifty-odd years as a columnist, could tell you that the lady loves a good, juicy crime yarn.

It's not that she loves murder. Celestine is a peace-minded citizen whose only strong dislikes seem to involve purple flowers, egg dishes, snakes, and anybody unfortunate enough to fall into the category of the mealymouthed or squinchy-faced. What Celestine loves best about murder is the lively and usually unforgettable cast of characters she's come to know intimately over the years in the courtroom, the newsroom, the squad room, and yes, the jailhouse.

If the courthouse is sagging, mildewed, or termite-ridden, so much the better. Give her a few ancient overall-clad gentlemen playing dominoes in the lobby, a Confederate War memorial out front, and a sharp-tongued spinster manning the clerk of court's office, and she'll stay all day.

My theory about Celestine's mystery-writing is that she took it up in the first place to give herself an excuse to hang around with cops and murderers, a much nicer class of company than she could find in any newsroom.

Thirty years after *The Malignant Heart,* her second murder, *Ah, Sweet Mystery*, was published in 1991. Readers were reintroduced to Kate, who, although widowed and retired from reporting in the intervening years, was still a columnist for a famous Atlanta newspaper. The sleuth lived in a restored log cabin near Roswell, and, amazingly enough, liked to hang around with cops and murderers.

While researching *Ah, Sweet Mystery*, Celestine took a tour of duty with the Atlanta Police Department's elite Red Dog antidrug squad. When she sat down to write *Straight As An Arrow*, her third Kate Mulcay mystery, Celestine finally figured out how to realize her lifelong ambition of piloting an airplane. She committed a murder or two and then put Kate at the controls of a tiny Cessna. And with the publication of *Dire Happenings At Scratch Ankle,* her fourth mystery, Celestine took Kate to her beloved north Georgia mountains, where research for her character required that she try her hand at rappelling and caving.

Through Kate Kincaid Mulcay, Celestine Sibley shares her own clear-eyed vision of good and evil. She tells the truth, and her legions of fans have the good fortune to go along for one hell of a ride.

Kathy Hogan Trocheck

—Kathy Hogan Trocheck

Photographs on page 34:

top right: Celestine's courtroom notes for the trial of James Earl Ray

top left: Isabelle Taylor (left) with Celestine. Taylor was the editor at Doubleday who bought Celestine's first book, *The Malignant Heart*, and also Larry Ashmead's mentor. (Photograph by Tom Arnold)

middle: Review of *The Malignant Heart* by Eleanor Smith for the *Herald*

bottom: promotional card for *The Malignant Heart*

Photographs on page 35:

top left: engraved dagger letter opener given by Kirk Douglas to reporters who attended the opening of his movie *The Land of the Vikings*

top right: letter from Celestine to Muv, hitting both the curtains she is making and the murder trial she is covering

middle: clipping about Atlanta's community of female mystery writers, from the *Atlanta Journal and Constitution Magazine*, March 30, 1958

bottom: Celestine's police press pass

Perspective

A murder trial was to me the purest form of drama: Shakespearean tragedy played out on the small stage of a courtroom with a couple of differences. The principals were playing for keeps, often for their lives, and far from being theatrical types made up to star they were frequently sad, sick, desperate men and women, whose stories opened doors on lives I had never known and could not visualize.

Sometimes going to a country courtroom was like going back to another century. There would be a water bucket and dipper instead of drinking fountains, spittoons for all the tobacco chewers (and they were numerous), the festivity of country-come-to-town for Big Court. An entrepreneur named Dock sold spring lizards to fishermen on the Blairsville courthouse lawn in the mountains, local church ladies offered gingerbread and cider for sale, there was a spirited traffic in coonhound trading, and in the courtroom an audience pitifully, acutely vulnerable to judgment and punishment, the real commodities of the day. I saw young mothers nursing babies, and one teenage boy, who had helped his mother kill his father, sit stoically at the defense table staring vacantly at the sunlight on the scarred old table top. He had good reason to want his father dead. The man was a drunkard who abused his wife and children monstrously. But I found that out by chance. Like his mountain forebears, the young fellow could kill, if he felt that he had to, but he stubbornly refused to say anything against his father. It created quite a problem for the court-appointed defense attorney.

Once I was covering a mountain trial in which an elderly man with Old Testament vengeance in mind had killed his daughter's suitor, a young wastrel who hung around the town's pool hall. The murder weapon, poetically, was a billiard cue, wielded with deadly accuracy. That trial went on for several days, and I began to notice that a regular,

39

front-row spectator was an old lady who looked like Grant Wood's *American Gothic*. She wore a neat cotton-print dress with a little white collar pinned by a small gold wishbone, cotton stockings and lace-up oxfords, and a rusty old straw sailor hat set primly in the middle of her head, with her thin gray hair pulled back tight and skewered in a hard little knot. She was in the same seat, early and late, and she impartially fixed stern and unloving eyes on the witnesses and court attendants, listening intently to every word that was spoken. Puritan conscience, I thought, here to see evil get its comeuppance, here to will punishment for the guilty.

A local friend slipped into the seat beside me during one morning's session and I pointed out the old lady to her.

"Carved out of hickory," I said. "Straight-laced, unbending, righteous."

My friend laughed back of her hand and whispered, "I'll tell you at recess."

The austere-looking old lady, she told me, had had a beautiful buxom daughter years ago. She came home from cleaning one of the town's more prosperous homes and found her daughter in bed with a city official. The man, a respected deacon in the church and a devoted husband and father, by all accounts, was distraught. He leaped into his pants, jabbering out apologies.

"I'll do anything on earth that I can to make this all right," he promised to the straight-laced mother. "If money would help, I'll pay whatever you ask."

The old mother took off her prim little sailor hat and skewered it with a hatpin before she answered.

"Just tell me what you want," pleaded the cornered adulterer. "I'll pay whatever you ask."

The mother fixed him with a gimlet eye.

"How does four bits strike you?" she inquired coldly.

The Floyd Woodward Case

At the office I was deep in the problems of a man named Floyd Woodward. The paper had had a big story about him when I first started to work there. He had been involved in the bunco racket in Atlanta back in the twenties and had killed a man. He was not arrested and brought to trial right away, and he disappeared, but not before he had written the rector of the Episcopal church where his family were long-time parishioners a shocking account of how many Atlanta police and court officials were also involved in the racket.

The state prosecutor in a Javert–*Les Misérables* turn became obsessed with the idea of finding him and bringing him back to stand trial. But he miraculously eluded capture until a postal inspector recognized him on a golf course in Monrovia, California, twenty years later. He was arrested and returned. The day he arrived in town Harold Martin boarded the train at the suburban Brookwood station to ride into town with him and interview him.

He said very little about himself and I had not been particularly interested in the story even when he was tried and convicted, until one day months later he tried to commit suicide in his jail cell. The city editor sent me down to talk to him, and I was surprised and overwhelmed with pity for the convict. He was a white-haired, blue-eyed man then in his fifties and one of the gentlest, most courteous people I ever met. Weakened by his suicide attempt and ill, he still got to his feet when I entered his cell and greeted me in a courtly, deferential manner.

He did not want to be interviewed but he seemed to feel that objecting was pointless, perhaps a little rude to a young woman who had gone to the trouble to look him up. He let me ask the usual run of questions and answered them politely, if briefly. He had been reading a letter when I went into his cell and I asked him about it.

41

He smiled and picked it up and turned it in his hand thoughtfully.

"It's from my wife, Blanche," he said after a moment. "Would you care to read it?"

Of course, I'd care to read it! It wasn't every day in the week a convicted murderer's letters were available to me. What I read to "Dear Tommy" (her name for him) was the kind of letter any good woman, any loving wife and mother might have written. She had been notified that he was ill—not precisely why—and expressed regret that she couldn't have been there to move a cot into his hospital room, as they always did for one another. She sent him tender admonitions about his health and then she got to family news. Their little girl, also called Blanche, had joined the Girl Scouts and was loving the experience. They had gone to choir practice the night before and she mentioned some of the songs they had sung. A man came to give them an estimate on repairing the roof...the roses were doing beautifully this year...she had to stop and put little Blanche to bed. They loved him, they missed him...do write.

I think I had tears in my eyes when I handed the letter back to Mr. Woodward, and he looked unspeakably sad.

"She deserves so much better than this," he said, looking at the narrow prison cell.

I asked him if I could do anything for him, get a minister or somebody to talk to him. He nodded. "I'd like that," he said. "Blanche and I are regular church members back home."

I thought about that letter all the way back to the office and for days to come. A man whose wife wrote him such simple homely things—choir practice, Girl Scouts, repairs to the roof, roses—couldn't be a criminal. My first impression of him had been that he was a good man, a gentleman. His wife's letter had confirmed it.

I went back to the jail again and again to see him, and I started digging into his case. He had shot, in self-defense he said, another

42

gambler who was looking for him with a gun in the corridor of a downtown hotel. The coroner's jury had held it was self-defense and he was free to go. Unfortunately, he wrote a letter back to the pastor of his family's church implicating police officers and the solicitor general's staff in gambling operations. The minister made the letter public and the solicitor general angrily reopened the case and launched a nationwide search for Mr. Woodward. Naturally, Mr. Woodward acquired an alias and by the time I got interested in the case I found that the coroner's jury report was mysteriously missing. I began trying to track down the jurors. In twenty years some of them had died, some had moved away. I could only find one or two but they said it was true; they had held that Floyd Woodward shot Ed Mills in self-defense.

I called and wrote to people in the little town of Monrovia, California, and what he and Blanche had indicated about their life was also true. He had changed his name to Tommy Thomas when he left Atlanta and changed his way of living. He met Blanche on a ferryboat, they fell in love and were married, and she never knew that he had a background of gambling or that he was wanted for murder. They bought a home and adopted little Blanche and became well-liked, well-respected citizens in the community, church members, active in civic affairs. One man I talked to said, "Our town had no more valued citizen than Tommy Thomas." He had a woodworking shop in his backyard and he invited in troubled and erring kids and taught them to use the tools and to make things of value.

I had begun to think of getting him a parole, and it was necessary to talk to him often. In the peculiar hierarchy of the imprisoned, he rated very high at the jail both with the other inmates and with the jailers. He was allowed trusty-like freedom and often called me at night after I got home.

One night we had as a houseguest the wife of a friend of Jim's. Jim had accompanied the husband on a business trip and they had asked

43

me if the wife, who had been ill, could come and stay with the children and me. I had put her to bed, but she was acting strange, turning restlessly and babbling senselessly, and I kept going in to see if she needed something or if I could somehow calm her down. The last time I went in the room she had hitched up her pajama coat and was trying to get something out of the fingers of a kid glove she had tied an a string around her waist.

Was it dope? I had heard that she was an addict. I was rocked with fear and consternation. Alcoholics I knew about. But dope addicts were an unknown quantity. I didn't know what she would do next and if it could possibly be dangerous to the children. While I stood in the hall puzzling over it the phone rang.

Mr. Woodward had a couple of things he wanted to talk to me about. And at that moment the basement door popped open and the deaf mutes [tenants in the basement apartment] came filing up with soap and towels. Their hot water was off!

I sagged weakly against the wall.

For the first time it occurred to me that my ménage might not be quite normal. A dope addict in the bedroom, deaf mutes erupting from the basement, a murderer pal on the phone...did other people live like that?

Mr. Woodward, the alleged murderer, was, of course, my favorite of the lot. His soft-voiced observations, his wry humor, delighted me, and, of course, I was determined to get him out of jail.

44

Mr. Woodward's case was shaping up. I had found some of the old coroner's jury members and had assembled some of the trial jurymen, who were sympathetic to the defendant and would be glad to have the parole board undo the life sentence. The prosecutor had died but the judge made no objection to a parole. The minister I had asked to visit him after his suicide attempt was Dr. Stuart Oglesby of the old Central Presbyterian Church a few blocks from the jail. He had become Mr. Woodward's friend and counselor, taking him books and newspapers and spending part of almost every day visiting him. He would be a witness before the parole board.

Ralph McGill, our editor, had followed the case as I wrote about it and worked on it, and he agreed to emcee the show I had lined up.

I had letters from people of Monrovia saying that Mr. Woodward had led an exemplary life there and my plea was to be that he had done what the prison system could not do, rehabilitate himself after a bad youthful start as a gambler, which had led almost inevitably to that shooting.

The hearing was quick and easy; the parole was granted without a dissenting vote. Mr. McGill and I walked back to the office together, and in my excitement and triumph I felt my stockings slip their moorings and start sliding down my legs.

I pushed my notebook and my purse into Mr. McGill's hands.

"Will you be embarrassed," I asked anxiously, "if my stockings fall off?"

"No," said our editor, courteously averting his eyes and examining the sunlit skyline. "But once I was dancing with a young lady and her underpants fell off. That *did* embarrass me."

There was a day's delay in Mr. Woodward's departure, and I found out later that he and his lawyer, my old friend Lawrence Camp, formerly U.S. district attorney, had arranged it so it would happen on my time and after the *Journal*'s deadline. They had a private plane waiting at the Atlanta airport to transport him to Memphis, where he would board an airliner for California, something the *Journal* never suspected. The whispered invitation to me to meet them at the jail came half an hour before takeoff time.

I waited in the car in the prison yard with Mr. Woodward's friends, who had supplied the plane, and watched as he came out into the light fall of rain. He stood a moment, feeling the drops on his head and shoulders. He was smiling.

45

"You forget what it's like in *there,*" he said to me, nodding toward the gray walls of old Fulton Tower.

At the Memphis airport he called Blanche in Monrovia, and when he came out of the phone booth he had a puzzled look on his face.

"She cried," he said wonderingly. "Do women always cry when they're happy?"

I nodded. I was crying, too.

Sometime later a policewoman friend, Frances Lykes, nominated me for the Pall Mall Big Story award for the Woodward case. The cash prize—$500—came in handy, and later when they turned it into a television show there was another $500 emolument.

I was thrilled with the money. We needed it. But our police reporter, Keeler McCartney, echoed my sentiments when he said, "They give you all that money because they're going to embarrass you." The whole pitch toward making me out a Brenda Starr–type reporter was embarrassing. The television crew was the most confounding of all. The facts in the case did not suit them and they rearranged things to conform to their ideas of what the story should be, including such small details as picking Christ the King Catholic Church as the church of Dr. Oglesby the Presbyterian minister.

"It *looks* more like a Presbyterian church," a cameraman explained to me.

For years my children could amuse themselves by doing imitations of the little dark-haired actress who played me, wearing ankle-strap shoes and purple lipstick. (I didn't see it. I took Mary and went to the movies.) But Susan and Jimmy watched, and they loved to lean against a wall with cigarettes hanging out of their mouths, smoke curling upward (it was, after all, sponsored by a cigarette company), saying huskily, "My name is Celestine Sibley. My friends call me Sib."

Some of them did, after that.

—from *Turned Funny*

The Murder of Mary Phagan

The morning of July 28, 1913, dawned hot and muggy in Atlanta. The sky was cloudy, a gray matched by the mohair suit and the silk tie of the neat little man who, escorted by Wheeler Mangum and several deputies, entered the makeshift courthouse at the northeast corner of Pryor and Hunter Streets to begin trial for his life.

Workmen were beginning to arrive on the site of the new courthouse, which was being built across the street, and a crowd was already gathering in the street.

That was the reason Sheriff Mangum had got his prisoner out of Fulton Tower, three blocks away, by 6 A.M. and into what was really the city hall before he had a chance to eat any breakfast.

The crowd of the curious was sleepy and good-natured at that hour, but by the time the sun climbed and the thermometer reached for the 100-degree-mark it had held the week before, Fiddlin' John Carson, the lanky mountain minstrel, would be on the steps tuning up and singing the new ballad that was making the rounds that summer. And the crowd might become dangerous.

Fiddlin' John wailed:

Little Mary Phagan, she went to town one day.
She went to the pencil factory to get her weekly pay.
She left her home at eleven.
She kissed her mother goodbye.
Not one time did that poor girl
Think she was going to die.

The second version was a month ahead of the jury with a pre-trial verdict:

Leo Frank he met her

With brutish heart and grin;
He says to little Mary
"You'll never see home again."
She fell down on her knees
To Frank and pled.
He picked up a plank from the trash pile
And beat her o'er the head.

The neat little man in the gray suit was, of course, Leo Frank.

And the trial which began that July morning and lasted 29 days was one which would be heard around the world, one which would make and break political fortunes, attract the attention of sociologists and scholars from all parts of the country, precipitate the writing of books, articles and theses still coming off the presses 65 years later, and give impetus to the reactivation of the Ku Klux Klan and the organization of the Anti-Defamation League.

Many murders have been committed and many defendants have gone to trial in Georgia since that summer of 1913, but none has stirred the population, none has had the far-reaching effect of the death of Mary Phagan and the trial of Leo Frank. It has been said by some students to have brought about the South's first disillusionment with, and first protest against, that industrialization Henry Grady had worked so hard to bring about. It certainly set off a conflagration of anti-Semitism hitherto unknown in an area where Jews were in short supply but valued and respected.

At a glance, it seems strange that Mary Phagan, a nondescript child of poor tenant farmers turned mill workers, should have become the cause célèbre. So few people knew her. So few people cared about her. But those are exactly the elements which made her death a tragic drama that was heartbreakingly

48

personal to thousands upon thousands of poor Southerners.

They *knew* what life had been like for Mary and her folks. They hated and feared what had happened to her and the man from the class of rich, northern, factory-owning Jews they believed had brought it about.

Mary was a child, a month away from her 14th birthday, when she met her death.

She was one of John and Fanny's six children, born on a tenant farm outside Marietta in 1900. Marietta would later loudly proclaim that it was Mary Phagan's hometown and erect a monument on her grave in Citizens' Cemetery. But it hadn't offered her refuge a few years earlier when five-cent cotton had caused her father to be dispossessed from the land he had cropped on shares.

John and Fanny, hearing of jobs in the textile mills in Atlanta, had taken their children and walked the 15 miles from Marietta to Bellwood, where the Bankhead Highway branches off from Marietta Street.

The Bellwood mill provided them with a three-room house and let them charge food at the mill store, until, working 14 hours a day at 20 cents an hour, they could get a toehold. It was hard work, and John Phagan wasn't a strong man. He died in 1911, and Fanny married a carpenter named J.W. Coleman.

By that time some of the children were old enough to earn five cents an hour in the cotton mill and Mary could go for the big money—12 cents an hour—at the downtown plant of the National Pencil Co. It was a five-cent street car ride away and, because most of the workers were young girls, Mary had social life such as the farm in the country had never provided.

Four feet, ten inches tall but, as her mother later said, "heavy set," she looked older than her 13-plus years. She was pretty, with dark

49

reddish blonde hair worn long, blue eyes, and a dimple in either cheek. She even acquired a beau or two, one a man many years older who would be questioned in her death and the other a barefoot boy of 14— he claimed "15-going-on-16"—who would be remembered chiefly for his pipe dreams about the case.

Mary's job at the factory was to put the metal caps on the pencils. On April 21, 1913, the metal ran out and Mary was laid off with only one day's labor to her credit. The Saturday after her enforced layoff was Confederate Memorial Day, April 26, and Mary decided to go to town to collect the $1.20 she was due for Monday's work and to see the big parade that would be moving down Peachtree Street at noon.

A minister from Macon was to make a speech from the reviewing stand at Five Points when the procession of bands, school children and some 200 Confederate veterans got that far.

Mary ate some cabbage and bread and dressed herself in her holiday best, a lavender dress, lace-trimmed, with gunmetal stockings and shoes. She picked up her new, brightly colored parasol and caught the English Avenue streetcar.

She got off the car at Broad and Hunter Streets at 12:10 P.M., walked to the pencil factory at 38 Forsyth Street (today the site of a hamburger palace, a record shop and part of Rich's Store for Homes). She went straight to the office on the second floor of the building and asked Leo Frank, the superintendent, one of the few people on duty that holiday, for her pay.

Frank said, as was the custom, that she gave her payroll number and he was not sure of her name until he looked it up later. He gave her the envelope containing her $1.20 and she started to leave, pausing and turning at the door to ask if the new metal had come. He said he told her "No" and turned his attention to the financial report he was compiling for his uncle, the New York owner of the factory. Then, he said, he heard the girl's footsteps moving off down the hall.

The next morning at 3:30 A.M., the factory's night watchman, a black man named Newt Lee, found the child's body, bloody and dirty with a rope and the ruffle from her petticoat pulled tight around her neck, dead on the basement floor.

The police medical examiner said she had been dead between 10 and 15 hours—of strangulation.

The first newspaper extra off the press was the *Atlanta Constitution*'s—by a fluke. The newspaper's police reporter, a brilliant young man named Britt Craig, was sleeping off a session with ardent spirits in the police patrol wagon. The wagon jounced over the cobblestone streets and he awakened at the scene of the crime.

But the *Atlanta Journal* and Hearst's *Atlanta Georgian* quickly hit their stride, and for days black headlines on extras trumpeted each new development in the Mary Phagan case. The *Georgian* called it "the greatest news story in the history of the state, if not the South."

Newt Lee, the night watchman, was arrested almost immediately and the crowds around the police station cried, "He ought to be lynched!"

Two notes found by the body didn't impress Atlanta police in that day, before the science of handwriting was so important in crime detection, but they struck cold terror to Lee's heart. One was apparently a rewrite of the other, and they read:

"Mam that Negro hire down here did this i went to make water and he push me down that hole. long tall negro black...was long sleam tall negro. i wright while play with me. he said he wood love me and play lie like the night witch did it but that long tall back negro did it by his slef."

Lee was a "long tall black, sleam (slim)" Negro, and they all thought "night witch" was meant to be night watchman. Not until much later did a lawyer named Henry Alexander study the notes carefully and come up with the theory that negro superstition was involved. A "night witch," according to African lore, supposedly rode the dark skies and if a sleeping child was not awakened from a nightmare he would be strangled to death with a cord around his neck before daybreak.

There was another Negro—not tall or slim—who was to be the most important witness in the case: Jim Conley, sweeper.

Conley wasn't heard from at first, but after the nervous, myopic 29-year-old superintendent of the factory, Leo Frank, was arrested, Conley came into his fame, and some say, his fortune.

Frank was taken into custody three days after the murder.

Five feet, six inches tall, with protruding eyes behind thick glasses, Frank had been very cooperative with the police. The morning Mary's body was discovered, they had awakened him at the home where he and his wife, Lucile, lived with her parents, Mr. and Mrs. Emil Selig, on Georgia Avenue. He had dressed immediately and gone to the undertaker's to view the body and then to the plant with the officers. Because it happened at their plant, he had persuaded the owners to employ the Pinkerton Detective Agency to help with the investigation. (In the meantime, the *Constitution* had started a public subscription to hire William J. Burns, "the world's greatest living detective," to do the same.)

52

At the behest of the police, Frank had even talked to Newt Lee and tried to persuade him to "tell the truth"—confess to the crime.

Now Frank was in jail himself, the last of seven suspects arrested.

Almost unique in Southern history up until that time, Frank was a white man whose fate rested in the hands of a black man.

—from the *Atlanta Journal* and the *Atlanta Constitution*, February 27, 1978

The Murder

Johnny Pace, the music editor, found Paula slumped over on my desk with a copy spindle through her heart the night last April that the Metropolitan Opera opened in Atlanta.

I was in the news room writing what they call the color story on the opening and I saw Johnny go in my office in search of his opera encyclopedia. Johnny is a good newspaperman, but Serious Music came into his life late and he is no Olin Downes yet. He couldn't review a first-year piano recital, much less the Met, without that encyclopedia in hand. He is sensitive about his source book and keeps it out of sight of concert press agents and the music-club ladies by hiding it in my office between reviews.

When I saw him heading for my office, looking a little like a dressed-up poodle dog in his white tie and tails, I knew what he was looking for. And I was dimly conscious of the fact that Johnny had flicked on the light in the little cubicle where, under Paula's ladylike lash, I'd come to labor. I hated that office. It gave me claustrophobia to work in there away from the muted hum of the news room where I grew up. I slipped out every chance I got and, although Paula liked her minions to stay put, a city-side assignment like opening night at the Met was legitimate excuse for working in the news room and I seized it.

I was sitting there at my beat-up old Royal, savoring the sound and the smell of the news room, exchanging flippancies with the boys ranged around the copy desk, and enjoying the prospect of being back on page one again. And that, pallid as it may seem, was a moment I remembered in the weeks that followed as the last lovely interlude before insanity set in.

I saw Johnny put on the light and then I heard him yelp. Nobody noticed that. People are always making uninhibited noises in the news room. But when he stuck his head out we couldn't help noticing.

53

He still looked like a poodle dog except pale green.

"My God, Shep," he whispered in the direction of Shepherd Willis, the night city editor. "You better look here."

There was something about his tone that forestalled any bright answers or horseplay from the Desk. I didn't think about it at the time, but Shep got right up and walked toward Johnny in a grave manner usually reserved for third floor executive conferences. And the rest of us, pulled to our feet by the urgent quality or maybe just the *queerness* of the situation, trailed after him.

Paula Reynolds, thirty-two, "wife and homemaker *first*," as she would have insisted and then allowed you to add, "and the South's outstanding newspaperwoman," sat at my desk with her back to the window and her face down on the stack of papers which are indigenous to my desk. Her arms hung limply off the edge of the desk. The café-au-lait stuff of her new spring suit (bought at a fashion editor's discount to bring out the amber of her eyes and the startling snow white of her hair) stretched smoothly across her narrow shoulders. And between the shoulders, so neatly placed, so shining it might have been a bauble worn backwards, was the lead base of an eight-inch copy spike.

The Body

I saw the crowd of railroad workers and pressmen, truck drivers, and mail-room workers, before I saw the police cars. I jammed on Elwood's brakes as I came up behind my car, and then I saw the Grady hospital ambulance, its stretcher out, and on the stretcher...the strangest, most terrifying object I have ever seen!

An object the size and shape of a human body but trussed up in newsprint and baling wire like a mummy.

Beside me Mary Jean made a strangled sobbing sound.

"Hush," I said faintly. "It's nothing. A joke maybe."

Then I saw the blood. A patch of blood, dark red in the sunlight, seeped through the ivory white of the paper.

"It's a joke, Mary Jean," I babbled desperately, feeling ill but unable to take my eyes from the thing on the stretcher. And then a pair of broad shoulders moved between it and me.

Mulcay.

"Don't look, Katy," he said. "Go on upstairs, you and Mrs. Daniel. We've got to find out who it is. But you go on."

Both of us climbed out of the car on Mary Jean's side, not looking back. Lieutenant Mulcay took each of us by an arm and propelled us toward the basement of our building.

I stole a glance at his face.

"Is it...dead?" I asked haltingly.

He nodded.

"Where?" I asked, dreading the answer.

"Your car." He said it with a total lack of expression, but the words were heavy as hammer blows.

I stopped.

"You go ahead, Mary Jean," I said, suddenly overwhelmed with a sick knowledge. I *knew*. But I had to be sure. "You go on," I repeated senselessly. "I've got to wait and see."

Mary Jean was pale but she was game. "If you've got to stay, Katy, I'll stay with you," she said. "Go on back, Lieutenant, we'll wait right here. You don't have to *see*, do you, Katy?"

I shook my head dumbly. I'd take Mulcay's word. I'd take *anybody's* word, because now I was convinced.

It was Garrity.

Garrity trussed up in winding sheets of paper and bound around with wire. Dead...in my car.

The Danger

I turned toward the end of the building which ran along the railroad siding with boxcars drawn up alongside to unload the mighty rolls of newsprint. There was little room between the boxcars and the building, and I thought hopelessly that it looked like a good place for Miss Treasure to hide if she was trying to hide.

The doors on that side seemed to be closed, and I was about to turn back and try for the elevator again or, at worst, brave those iron steps, when something—noise or a flicker of light—attracted my attention.

I stopped. Opposite a great dark empty boxcar, a sliding door in the side of the building was open, and although the lights were off there was noise in there—a machine running, somebody working.

I moved closer and then I heard another train coming and felt its headlights reaching out for me like a giant searchlight. I cowered against the side of the building.

Inside there was the whine of a labored machine—one that moved about. A swish of paper and then a low, human moan!

Crouching, I crept up under the doorway and then raised up enough to peer in. It was the paper warehouse where all the newsprint is stored. Even in the darkness I could see the giant rolls of paper towering like ghostly white columns to the ceiling. And down in there somewhere one of the little tractors they use to lift and haul the paper about was running.

Behind me on the tracks beyond the boxcar the train was coming, even at its slow, railroad-yard speed pounding the rails with a thunder that drowned out the busy little tractor inside. I crouched there, waiting, pinioned against the wall by the light, scared to move and scared not to move.

The diesel engine squealed, and for a brief instant as it thundered past its light illuminated the doorway and I saw just beyond arm's reach in the warehouse—two silly, tasseled boots!

"Miss Treasure!" I whispered, and then without thinking any more I was scrambling into the warehouse on my stomach and crawling toward her.

Light from somewhere in the building, maybe the pressroom, filtered through the tall stacks of paper, making an eerie kind of visibility within the warehouse. As I reached Miss Treasure's side I saw the tractor lift bearing down on her.

"*No!*" I cried. And then I screamed. As loud and as hard as I could I screamed.

A white-coated figure, face lost in shadow, rode the tractor—a monster who must have been startled and momentarily thrown off its deadly course by my scream, because the tractor veered off to the side.

Seeing an advantage, I grabbed Miss Treasure under her arms and dragged her up close to a bale of wastepaper. Something was humming close by. I searched the gloom and then I saw: the red eye of the wastepaper baling machine!

The Thing on the tractor had been about to lift Miss Treasure into the baling machine where with one flick of a switch a monstrous weight would have come down on her and she would have been crushed and then efficiently wrapped and wired into a bundle of wastepaper!

I shuddered and drew Miss Treasure farther back into the shadows.

The tractor was still running. Somewhere out there...Then I saw! The lift was coming toward us, a roll of paper I knew weighed nearly a ton lifted high, poised to drop.

I couldn't scream, I couldn't move. Hanging over Miss Treasure's limp little body, I simply watched, knowing it would crush us both in a matter of seconds.

But mercifully, because the fingers were awkward and unsure on the controls, the giant claw that held the roll of newsprint dropped it...*before* it reached us! It fell with a force that shook the building and

57

then it rolled harmlessly away.

I knew there would be another try—maybe a successful one. I had not to be there. Half dragging, half lifting Miss Treasure, I started for the doorway. Ahead of us in the darkness I heard the tractor engine, heard the faint squeak as the lift climbed upward, and saw another roll of newsprint lifted in the air.

I stumbled over something and Miss Treasure moaned. I stopped. Suppose she were badly hurt, her back broken or her skull fractured, and I was dragging her around this way? I peered anxiously at the weird little bundle and lost the second's advantage I had.

The tractor was bearing down on us. We were right in its path with nothing to stop it.

I closed my eyes and screamed and then darkness engulfed me.

The Conclusion

Good evening, Katy," she said coolly. "I've come to kill you." "Why, Bets?" The words were wrenched out of my parched throat. I could only think that as long as she was interested in me she wasn't pointing that gun at Papa, who sat there in his wheel chair, unable to move.

"You're a common, trashy little meddler!" she said venomously. "You'll associate with anybody—old carnival hoodlums, policemen, anybody!"

"You mean your aunt?" I asked.

"That's a lie!" she screamed. "She's not my aunt! I hate her, I hate them all. I've made something of myself. I'm Somebody. Why, did you know, my daughter is going to marry one of the richest men in the South?"

She leaned over and asked the question in a hoarse whisper and then I noticed her eyes. Mad. Bets was mad.

"Yes," I said placatingly. "I knew. I think it's wonderful, Bets. You've really done wonderfully by your children."

A self-satisfied smirk twisted her face, and I noticed with relief that she had lowered the gun. A little.

"Yes, I have, haven't I?" she said smugly. "Tennant would have stopped me. He wanted a divorce. He wanted to bring somebody else into that house where my children and I had a right to be. But I showed him. He knew I was right at the last, poor fool. So he acted the death-bed gentleman. He told the police it was a *burglar!*"

She laughed. "The precious Warrens weren't sure, but they didn't want me around after that. They would have kept my children if they could have proved anything. But I've been careful, mighty careful. I said I could do better by them than the Warrens and I have. You knew Betsy was engaged?"

She asked the question of Papa with a kind of social archness that was almost as terrible as the rest of it.

"I heard about it," said Papa, sounding impressed.

Bets turned back to me.

"Oh, Paula would have scotched that, if she could! Yes, sir. She had the nerve to suggest that I killed my husband. She said, 'What will the Coulters think of Betsy when they hear that?' And I said, 'They won't hear it.'"

She laughed again, a wild abandoned sound.

"She won't tell the Coulters! And old Mr. Garrity won't tell them— and you won't either, Miss Nosy Kincaid!"

The room was very quiet. I prayed Betsy was asleep, I prayed Papa wouldn't do anything to make her swing that shining, lady's-sized little gun toward him.

"Garrity wouldn't have told, Bets," I suggested politely, more to keep her talking than anything else.

"Oh, not about Tennant," she said airily. "But he would have told about Paula. He came in at the wrong time. I hit him with the other

59

copy spike but you know"—her voice held childish surprise and petu-
lance—"it didn't kill him? When I came in from the opera and found
Paula was the only one I killed it upset me."

"Oh, I imagine," I said solemnly.

"Yes," said Bets, "so I looked all over the building while you all
were so busy with Miss Paula. I found him. I knew he couldn't be far
and he wasn't. Right there in the mail room. You'll never know how
easy it was."

"I guess not," I said, feeling a little ill. "But why me, Bets? Why my
car and my desk and my gloves?"

It was a mistake, because something about my tone offended her.

She raised the gun again and her face was the color of ashes and I
noticed her hand was trembling.

She'll shoot this time, I thought dispassionately. There's nothing
to stop her. If I move it'll be over that much faster.

"Miss Nosy Kincaid!" she said again scornfully and in the childish
epithet there was the pent-up poison of a lifetime of well-behaving.
And something more: A kind of end-of-her-rope looseness. She didn't
care. She had nothing else to lose. And somehow in my bumbling way,
mostly through my friendship with Miss Treasure, in her mind I had
set myself against her.

60

She walked a step closer. The light from the desk gleamed along
the gun's short barrel, and it was pointed at my chest.

The room was so quiet I could hear the kitchen clock ticking and
the shallow rise and fall of Bets's breathing. Or was it my own?

Suddenly in the room behind Bets a dog howled, a sharp, mourn-
ful, agony-ecstasy sound.

She spun around, but on the other side of the room a tugboat
whistle blew a mighty blast and she turned again, trembling, frantic,
breathing faster. The dog bayed again and she searched the ceiling and
the walls desperately. From the other corner the tugboat screamed.

The noises, first the boats and then the hound, rose and fell in the little room, bouncing from wall to wall, screaming from the ceiling, howling from the floor.

Bets whirled this way and that, her head frantically turning, her eyes rolling from side to side—the gun in her hand forgotten.

Suddenly there was a barely audible click and a man's voice, deep, rich, close at hand, intoned intimately, sonorously:

"Come lovely and soothing death,

Undulate round the world, serenely arriving, arriving,

In the day, in the night, to all, to each,

Sooner or later..."

There was a faint cry from the woman in the middle of the room, and although I saw it happen I'll never be sure if she aimed the gun and pulled the trigger or if, as she sank to her knees, spent, it accidentally went off.

Papa turned off the record player and the tape recorder, pushed aside the extension control panel he had rigged up for his wheel chair, and wheeled to her side.

The front of Bets's smart suit was stained bright red.

She was dead.

—from *The Malignant Heart* 61

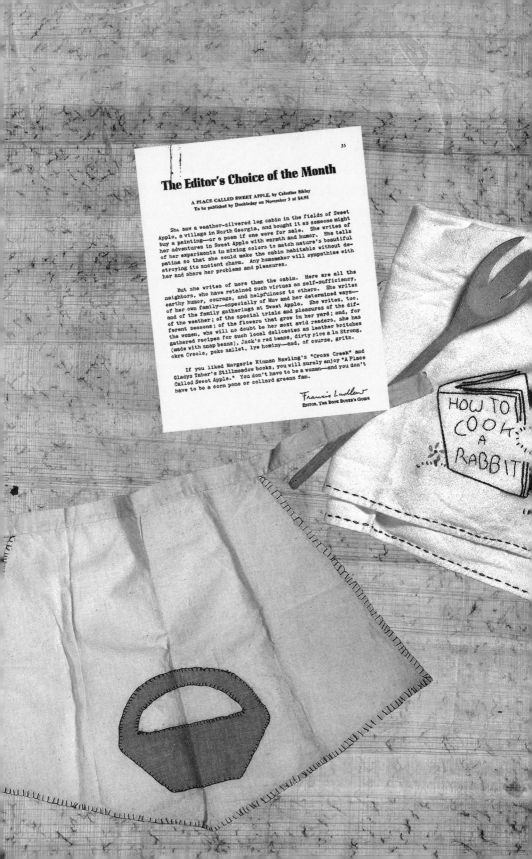

33

The Editor's Choice of the Month

A PLACE CALLED SWEET APPLE, by Celestine Sibley
To be published by Doubleday on November 3 at $4.95

She saw a weather-silvered log cabin in the fields of Sweet Apple, a village in North Georgia, and bought it as someone might buy a painting—or a poem if one were for sale. She writes of her adventures in Sweet Apple with warmth and humor. She tells of her experiments in mixing colors to match nature's beautiful patina so that she could make the cabin habitable without destroying its ancient charm. Any homemaker will sympathize with her and share her problems and pleasures.

But she writes of more than the cabin. Here are all the neighbors, who have retained such virtues as self-sufficiency, earthy humor, courage, and helpfulness to others. She writes of her own family—especially of Muv and her determined ways—and of the family gatherings at Sweet Apple. She writes, too, of the weather; of the special trials and pleasures of the different seasons; of the flowers that grow in her yard; and, for the women, who will no doubt be her most avid readers, she has gathered recipes for such local delicacies as leather britches (made with snap beans), Jack's red beans, dirty rice a la Strong, okra Creole, poke sallet, lye hominy—and, of course, grits.

If you liked Margerie Kinnan Rawling's "Cross Creek" and Gladys Taber's Stillmeadow books, you will surely enjoy "A Place Called Sweet Apple." You don't have to be a woman—and you don't have to be a corn pone or collard greens fan.

Francis Ludlow
EDITOR, THE BOOK BUYER'S GUIDE

HOW TO COOK A RABBIT

A HAPPY HOME

THOMAS BROTHE

Country

Ham

Cured With Salt, Sodium Nitrate, Sugar, Sodium ...

PACKED FOR

THOMAS BROTHERS

ASHEBORO, N.C.

27203

NET WEIGHT

U.S.
INSPECTED
AND PASSED BY
DEPARTMENT OF
AGRICULTURE
EST. 1498

LBS.

OZS.

Chapter 3

FOOD

The Mistress of Sweet Apple
...in which our heroine
takes us into the kitchen
for a little smackerel of something.

In all the amazing magnitude and wondrous diversity of Celestine's writing, nothing gives her—or the rest of us lucky souls—more entertainment and pure satisfaction than stories about the rituals of cooking, serving, and eating in the company of family and friends. Here we encounter the beloved and redoubtable Muv in all her glory, a veritable amalgam of Fannie Farmer, Mary Poppins, and Mother Teresa. And here is our ever-charming and humorous Celestine at her self-deprecating best, slipping us little nuggets of wisdom like fortune-cookie notes hidden in the yeast rolls or tucked under the custard cup.

The focal point for many of these stories is the snug and aromatic Sweet Apple kitchen, which serves as the equivalent of a stage setting for a Greek drama. Celestine has written of it often in her columns, and most especially in *A Place Called Sweet Apple*, her 1967 book of country living and Southern recipes from the cabin in the Cobb County woods.

"There's nothing lonesomer than an unused kitchen," she declared in a reflective rumination a while back:

> For more years than I care to remember, the kitchen has been the center of my life. When I was a child we ate in the kitchen, dried clothes and took baths by the big wood range, rocked and did homework and read poetry there.

My mother started plants in the kitchen window, and I brought in first-blooming violets and yellow jessamine to fill pitchers and glasses.

The dining room was for Sunday, the living room for company and Sunday nights in winter when we ate off the tea cart by the fire and listened to Fred Allen and the "Bayer Aspirin Hour" on the radio. Summer evenings we ate on the screened porch, where it was all right if watermelon dripped a little. Day in and day out we lived in the kitchen—and so did kittens and baby chicks in blankets under the stove.

My mother started me cooking there—grits first, and eventually country fried steak and chocolate layer cake and, off and on, such specialties as banana pudding and ice cream custard.

It was a fine place, the kitchen was, but I know now that it owed its charm to the activity that went on there. An inactive kitchen is a dreary, lonely place.

My Sweet Apple kitchen has had a vital role in our family. Once I had my sewing machine there. Many times I have moved jam jars over to make room for my typewriter. The children did their homework there. We rocked and soothed and fretted babies there. And food, everything we knew to cook, everything we yearned to eat, we put together there.

A Place Called Sweet Apple is a charming book about a time (the sixties), a place, and a particular group of people—Celestine with family and friends. Listen as the story unfolds.

—John Egerton

Photographs on page 62:

top: Francis Ludlow's review of *A Place Called Sweet Apple* for *The Book Buyer's Guide*
middle: Celestine's hand-embroidered kitchen towel
bottom: apron made by Celestine in Vacation Bible School

Photographs on page 63:

top left: Celestine's daughter Mary Little's artwork from Vacation Bible School
top right: Celestine's Thomas Brothers Country Ham bag ("also makes a great dishcloth")
bottom: publicity photo of Celestine at Sweet Apple for the release of *A Place Called Sweet Apple,* c. 1967 (Photograph by Floyd Jillson)

Corn Meal

The garden is at its productive best now [c. 1965], and by galloping at full tilt we can harvest the tomatoes, great green bell peppers, and beans before the weeds take them. The okra really gives you a race for your money. You have to cut it every single day or those tender little pods that we enjoy boiling whole and dipping in lemon juice and butter will be big pods and too tough to eat whole.

Pleasure in our home-grown vegetables is slightly marred for Muv, however, because of the sad situation with corn meal. Muv feels about corn meal the way some people feel about wine. The wine bibber, tasting and smelling, seeking a "bouquet," turning his glass between his fingers in the light, examining the color of the wine, and then making his pronouncement as to the very region, the exact vineyard in France where it grew, hasn't a thing on Muv and corn meal.

She, too, uses all her senses on meal, rubbing it between her fingers for texture, shaking out a little the better to see the color, smelling for freshness, and tasting for whatever it is you taste in raw meal.

And I have it on Muv's authority that the world is in a bad way for decent meal.

"Bought meal!" she scoffed when she saw the package in my cupboard. "Honey, have you come to this?" She read the label and gave me that dark, bright-eyed glance which said as plain as words that her own flesh and blood was betraying her. "Self-rising!" She threw the word at me as if it were a moral indictment.

I promised her that we would go up to Aubrey Chadwick's store on Saturday morning and remedy the meal situation. Chadwick's store is on the site of an old grist mill and I felt sure Aubrey had a proper feeling about corn meal. But it turned out that his shelves held only what Muv dismissed scornfully as "Mixes and 'additive' stuff!"

"You don't need anything in meal except good corn properly

ground," she told him.

He was apologetic. He said he had made arrangements with one of the neighbors to get some good corn and get it ground and it should be in within a few days.

"We're having beans and corn and okra for supper," Muv said severely. "How can we wait?"

Then I had an inspiration. Mr. and Mrs. Lum Crow had mentioned having to take their corn to mill. Maybe they would lend us some meal.

We went by their house and while Mrs. Crow got the meal Mr. Crow showed us his corn patch—"roas'n' ears" for now and "bread corn" coming on.

Muv was soothed and reassured only temporarily. It alarms her to think that corn bread eaters the world over haven't Mr. and Mrs. Crow to borrow from and are at the mercy of those who slip baking powder and salt and maybe worse into honest meal.

Vegetable Soup

As long as I can remember one of the delights of the first wintry day of the year was coming home from school to find a pot of vegetable soup simmering on the back of the stove. That soup started in November—or October, if it was cold enough—and, with certain artistic additions and subtractions, lasted almost till spring, always getting better.

When Muv came to visit at Sweet Apple a week or so ago we had one of those sudden cold days and we both thought simultaneously of soup. Not a casual soup out of a can or a package, although they are nourishing and tasty and handy to have, but a start-with-the-bone, lovingly assembled poetry of a soup.

Fortunately for our soup-making rite Chadwick's is the kind of country store where they *give* you soup bones. None of this weighing and wrapping in cellophane and stamping with a price roughly equivalent to a sirloin steak for them.

You say to the young butcher, "Alonzo, have you a good knuckle bone for me today?"

And Alonzo retires to the cold-storage room and emerges with half a cow, sets it down on the block, and with a profligate hand chops you off a great meaty joint. This, simmered all day long, gives forth gelatin, marrow, flavor, and an aroma that reaches out into the cold air and brings hunters, tramps, and random motorists to the door.

After a day of simmering, the bones are lifted out, stripped of any bit of lean meat that hasn't cooked off, and along with most of the suet, bestowed on Brownie. Then begins the gradual addition of goodies to the broth. I fling what I have into the pot. Not my mother, Muv. She has a timetable.

Carrots and onions first—they take a lot of cooking. Snap beans at some time when the broth is cool. (Never start snap beans in hot water.) She will use corn freshly cut off the cob but canned corn never. ("Clouds the broth and the soup doesn't keep as well.") Potatoes and tomatoes go in and sometimes a handful of spaghetti or rice and after that I lose track.

The first day of the soup nobody can stay out of the kitchen. The young folks come in from cutting wood or tramping through the woods to the lake and lift the lid on the big pot and inquire if we need them to taste the soup for us. Toward midafternoon they don't ask but get out mugs and cups and ladle out a little "to see what it needs."

Little hot corn cakes go with the maiden meal of the season's first pot of vegetable soup, but after that French bread with sweet butter from Artie Cox's cows suffices. (With second or third-day soup you don't have to make a ceremony of stirring and browning those little baby hoecakes. Ceremonies are for first days.)

If William Makepeace Thackeray had ever pulled up a chair to a

69

good slow-burning oak log and dipped a spoon into Muv's vegetable soup, he would have written a poem far better than his "Ballad of Bouillabaisse."

Red Beans and Rice

Dried red kidney beans strengthen and sustain us at Sweet Apple. They are not indigenous to north Georgia, I'm afraid, where all dried beans are unjustly associated with lean fare or wash day. They are particularly beloved in New Orleans, where no restaurant is too elegant to feature red beans and rice at least once a week. Most of them, particularly the plain ones patronized by working people, offer red beans and rice every day.

One Saturday after hours of roaming around the French Quarter a friend and I were exhausted and hungry and had our minds set on dropping by that wonderful old delicatessen, Solari's, and lunching on red beans and rice. To our disappointment, they weren't on the menu that day. We were about to order something else when a gentleman two seats down the counter interrupted with the easy New Orleans familiarity and hospitality.

"You want red beans?" he asked. "You get 'em to da Roosevelt *Saturdays.*"

The waitress understood our need and graciously waved us off to the Roosevelt Hotel dining room.

There are many ways of serving red beans and rice but we are partial to Jack Strong's recipe at Sweet Apple. Reared on the Mississippi coast and in New Orleans, he abhors the makeshift inland way of using canned beans and has shopped around until he knows the more reliable sources of packaged dried beans. Not surprisingly these are usually stores in the poorer sections of town where a pound package of beans for thirteen cents is still an important bargain.

Jack's Red Beans

1 1-pound package dried red kidney beans
3 medium Bermuda onions (others will do)
3 cloves garlic
3 medium ham hocks (lean)
2 teaspoons salt
1 tablespoon oleo or salad oil for sautéing

Wash and put beans on to boil in a large heavy bottom pot of iron or aluminum with a cover. (A 4-quart pot will be a bit crowded but will suffice.) Dice onions and sauté until they are transparent. Mince garlic and sauté separately from the onions—this to make sure the garlic gets sautéed. Scrape onions and garlic directly into the water and beans. Place the ham hocks in the pot with the beans and add the salt after the water has started boiling. (Salt keeps the beans whole. If it is not added early beans may cook to pieces.) Use lean ham hocks whole but trim most of the fat from fatty ham hocks. After the beans have begun to boil turn down heat and simmer for about 4 hours or longer until beans are tender. Additional water may be required as ingredients cook down.

Some cooks stir the beans and have a reddish gravy with them. Jack prefers no stirring and liquid that remains clear.

The accompaniment for red beans is, of course, rice. It is not a north Georgia specialty either but a staple of my childhood. We ate it at least once a day in south Alabama—always as a vegetable at dinner, which was our midday meal then—sometimes with cold milk for supper and now and then in pudding. One of the first tasks I learned to perform in the kitchen as a child was that daily rite: "Put on the rice."

This was done by washing a cupful of rice in cold water until it ran clear and then putting it on to boil in a cupful of water with a teaspoonful of salt. When it comes to a brisk boil, turn the heat low, cover, and let simmer for about twenty minutes or until dry and fluffy.

A more foolproof method, I have found in recent years, is to put the rice on in a quart or more of rapidly boiling salted water and cook until the grains are soft but not mushy. Drain, rinse in a colander with cold water, and set back over a pot of boiling water to steam. (If you let this process go on too long—hours, that is—the top grains of rice will dry out and harden, which gives my method a bad name among Gulf Coast friends. Otherwise, it strikes me that the rice is lighter and dryer and there's the additional advantage of not having a lot of it stick to the pot.)

Either way you cook your rice you will want a plateful of it when you ladle on red beans with their rich juice and the chunks of lean ham. Some people enjoy further spicing their plates with a lacing of Louisiana red hot or Louisiana green hot, that condiment of liquid fire which can be purchased at most grocery stores.

The meal can be more sophisticated with a tossed green salad, a loaf of crusty French bread, and a bottle of French table wine.

I have heard of people using leftover beans in salad but I can never bring myself to tamper with perfection. Cold red beans eaten with a spoon out of a refrigerator dish at midnight set well with me and one of my favorite midmorning snacks, after fishing on the Gulf from before dawn, was a sandwich made of Julia's leftover beans and French bread. Other members of the party contended that the ham from the beans and hot mustard made an even better sandwich but I never could relinquish my hold on beans long enough to try.

To show you in what esteem the dried bean is held in New Orleans, the *Picayune Original Creole Cook Book* earnestly points out that "In the colleges and convents where large numbers of children are sent to be reared to be strong and useful men and women, several times a week there appears on the table the nicely cooked dish of Red Beans, which are eaten with rice.... The Creoles hold that the boys and girls who are raised on beans and rice and beef will be among the strongest and sturdiest of people."

It is certainly one of the ways we keep up our strength at Sweet Apple.

Okra

An unending surprise to me in cooking is that you never know when you are plagiarizing. Just as two or three great minds hit upon major discoveries in science and invention almost simultaneously, so several people may discover the same new way of cooking an old staple at the same time. Okra grows well in Southern gardens and is standard summertime fare on Southern tables.

In fact it is so essential to soups and seafood gumbos that our late friend, Frank Gutierrez, used to tell of an old neighbor of French extraction whose standard greeting was: "How's yo' okras, Frank?"

Not how are you, how is your wife or your business, but how is that minimum requisite to life and well-being, your okra patch.

73

The first garden we had at Sweet Apple was a prodigious producer of okra and in order to keep up with it we devised many ways of eating okra. A favorite way is to gather the pods with a bit of stem attached while they are in mere infancy—three inches long at most, preferably less—and then run with them to the kitchen where a pot of salted water is already boiling, plunk them into the pot, and check the time. Meanwhile, in an ovenproof ramekin have half a stick of butter melting, to which add the juice of half a lemon. When the okra has boiled five to seven minutes, depending on its size, lift it out with a slotted spoon to avoid piercing its tender young skin, of course, and arrange in a circle around a dish of butter and lemon juice. The nubbin of stem left on the end makes a handy holder for the people on the terrace who will dip the okra in the butter and lemon juice and eat it as an appetizer.

We had been eating this delicacy a full summer before we discovered almost the exact recipe in Marjorie Kinnan Rawlings' *Cross Creek Cookery*. I believe she served hers as an appetizer, too, but had the additional information that you best allow twelve pods of okra per person—a detail I had to learn by experience.

The tendency of okra to sliminess kept me from valuing it as I should for years. This failing is avoided in the foregoing recipe by keeping the okra skin unbroken and not overcooking it. I find that the addition of lemon juice to the water in which okra is boiling also helps.

A few pods of young okra are a great addition to a pot of field peas and butter beans in the summertime. They should be added ten or fifteen minutes before the peas are ready to serve—not longer or they'll cook to pieces.

Other uses of okra which we have enjoyed:

Fried Okra

Wash the pods and slice in rounds, salt, lightly dip in corn meal, and fry in just enough fat to keep from sticking. Brown lightly, turning often to keep from burning. Drain on paper towels. If you happen to like a less crisp okra you may add a few tablespoons of water and finish the cooking with the okra covered.

French Fried Okra

Select young pods leaving stem end on, wash, dry on paper towel, salt and dip in beaten egg and milk, then flour, and fry in deep fat.

Drain on paper towel but only briefly. They should be eaten while they're hot and crisp.

Greens and Corn Bread

Southerners are inclined to make a good deal over having been "raised po'ah." I suppose joking about it, which invites the participation of even the more affluent, made the reality of scant rations less harsh. In the country particularly you hear frequent references to hard times. There is even a road near Sweet Apple which memorializes tough going. It's called Hardscrabble.

One day up at Chadwick's store some of the old-timers were discussing Depression days and one raconteur sought to overreach them all.

"Shoot, I remember," he said, "when things was so tight you prayed every fall the persimmons would hold out till the poke sallet come up in the spring."

Things probably weren't literally that bad with many people but the most graphic lesson I ever had about the rigors of Reconstruction days following the Civil War was given to me by my Great Aunt Dilly, who was a teen-ager in 1865. I remember as a child seeing her eat cold corn bread and cold collard greens for breakfast when I was delicately toying with my orange juice. Caught between distaste and awe I asked her how she could stand such fare so early in the morning.

"I say, how can I 'stand it'!" she repeated, cruelly mimicking my finicky tone. "If you had been raised when I was you'd be mighty glad to get any kind of food. You et it when you got it—lest somebody else beat you to it!"

Except for the timing, Aunt Dilly's dish of collards and corn bread, like so many items of plain country fare, had a great deal to commend it to the attention of gourmets. I don't recommend cold collards and

75

corn bread and I especially don't recommend them for breakfast, but there are certain seasons of the year when nothing tastes so good as collards which have been touched by frost, gathered while they are still young and crisp, and cooked with smoked bacon.

Naturally they must have hot corn bread to go with them—to my taste a plain hoecake of corn bread cooked in an iron skillet on top of the stove with only water, salt, and bacon drippings to season it. There are many kinds of corn bread and they all have their place. The place of plain skillet corn bread is, I submit, at the side of collards or, at the very least, mustard or turnip greens. Corn muffins, egg bread, crackling bread, or the little crisp corncakes may be happily wed to any vegetable dinner.

Collard Greens

Select the tenderest leaves and wash them well, nipping off the tough stems. Cut the leaves crosswise into ribbons about an inch wide. (I use kitchen shears for this.) Put on in just enough cold water to cover with a chunk of smoked bacon scored deeply or a lean ham hock. (A three-inch square of bacon is about right for the usual market bunch of greens.) Boil slowly an hour or longer until the greens are tender and most of the water is cooked away. A bottle of hot pepper sauce is a must in the household where greens are a staple. Each diner dribbles it on his greens at his own discretion—or risk.

Turnip Greens

Turnip greens are available in Georgia almost year-round. They are among the first things up in the garden in the spring, along with lettuce and English peas, and they reappear again in the fall, surviving light frosts sometimes almost until Christmas. A really killing freeze, however, will get them. After they are no longer available in local gardens we stop by the Municipal Market in Atlanta and buy greens that have been trucked up from south Georgia or Florida.

Being a working woman I make full use of my pressure cooker and never more happily than with turnip greens. For one thing, the picking and washing of turnip greens is such a time-consuming task I'd be in the kitchen all night if I didn't have something to speed up the cooking. I learned from Muv to take one leaf at the time, inspect it carefully for bugs or wilted spots, and break off its stem. (Some cooks use the stems but Muv contends they are bitter and stringy.) Every leaf must be lovingly washed, starting with tepid water and working up to cold water. I once heard of a woman who washed her greens in her washing machine but I haven't had the nerve to try that.

While the green picking and washing process is going on I give a chunk of smoked bacon or two or three slices of breakfast bacon and the turnip roots, peeled and sliced, a three-minute headstart in the pressure cooker, using as little water as possible. The greens are added, relying mostly on the water that sticks to them to keep them afloat. It is seldom necessary to add water to turnip greens and the less the better.

Five minutes is enough time in the pressure cooker, perhaps twenty or at the most thirty in an ordinary pot or your Dutch oven. (Overboiling greens makes them dark and slick and tasteless.) When you have sampled a leaf and find it tender and done, drain the liquor off and reserve for dunking with corn bread at some time when your spirits and energy are low. Chop the greens fine, using two knives, and adjust the seasoning. Sometimes it is necessary to add salt—if your bacon wasn't salty enough—and a tablespoon or two of bacon drippings.

Greens without corn bread, as I may have suggested once or twice, are like spring without violets, a fiddle without a bow.

Oven Corn Bread

Oven corn bread is foolproof and I bake it almost every day in the summer when we're having a vegetable dinner and always at Thanksgiving or Christmas when a big pan of it is needed for Muv to make her celebrated corn bread dressing.

For an 8-inch square pan of bread I use:

1 cup corn meal (preferably water-ground)
$^{1}/_{2}$ teaspoon salt
3 teaspoons baking powder
1 egg
3 tablespoons cooking oil
1 cup milk

Grease the pan and set the oven at 375 degrees before sifting meal, salt, and baking powder together. Add cooking oil. Beat egg slightly and add to meal with milk. Bake until brown and springy.

This is meltingly good with Artie Cox's country butter. Sometimes, as at Christmas and Thanksgiving, I have to double the recipe. The important thing is to always use as much milk as you use meal. The mixture will be soupy but it turns out fine in the end.

Skillet Corn Bread

1 cup corn meal

$^1/_2$ teaspoon salt

Enough boiling water to make a rather thick batter
that will hold its shape when turned into skillet

Enough bacon drippings or cooking oil to grease the
skillet well

Mix salt and corn meal and stir in boiling water. Turn in to hot but not smoking skillet or griddle and cook slowly. You will need to upend your skillet over a plate to turn your hoecake but a couple of spatulas will do if you are using a griddle.

Thin this batter slightly to make little corncakes. Slightly richer, crunchier ones may be made by adding 3 tablespoonfuls of melted butter to the basic meal and salt mixture and cooking on a cookie sheet in a 375-degree oven for about 20 minutes.

Grits

I n these days of calory counting we don't have grits every day but when there's company or time for a leisurely breakfast and especially when there's grief or trouble in the family, I find myself turning automatically to grits. There's something comforting about grits—hot and creamy and bland, resting beneficently on the tired and troubled stomach.

A few years ago I embroiled myself in a controversy by referring to grits as "they." Readers chose up sides and bombarded me with letters on the subject. When the tumult and the shouting died down and I had sorted over the letters I came to the conclusion that those who saw grits as a singular noun were perhaps more knowledgeable about grammar. But those who regard grits as plural were the true grits fans.

Among the authorities cited for "they" are Marjorie Kinnan Rawlings, a woman with both a flair for food and some little success with the language, and the *Picayune Original Creole Cook Book* which calls *them* "Du Gru Bouilli" and rhapsodizes: "In any manner in which they are served, they are always palatable."

When I was a child grits cooking was a long and slow process. Sometimes we soaked them overnight. They had to be washed, as Muv always directed me, "until the water runs clear." Nowadays I buy the quick-cooking kind, obey the package order not to wash, and can't tell the difference.

The standard package directions for instant grits are about one cup of grits to four cups of water and a teaspoon of salt. Cook five to seven minutes.

On Sunday mornings I keep the grits hot in a double boiler and enhance their creamy consistency by stirring in a little butter and, if no dieter is watching, a dash or two of coffee cream.

Once we had a friend from New York who tried valiantly to enjoy our breakfast grits, served, of course, with bacon and scrambled or fried eggs. He never became a bona fide grits fan until one night he discovered cheese grits. Then he was hooked. He simply couldn't have cheese grits too often and I remember coming home from work to find him in my kitchen grating cheese and leading my children in singing—to the tune of the "Toreador Song" from *Carmen*—an aria he had composed to grits. Half a cup of grated cheese is about right to stir into a potful of grits just before serving.

Nowadays when I have leftover grits I feed them to the birds. Muv used to sauté an onion in a couple of tablespoons of bacon fat, mash up the grits with a fork and heat them through in the skillet with onion and fat and sprinkle liberally with black pepper. This was a hot and doubtless nourishing supper dish but it never really caught on with me.

Some better is the method of slicing cold cooked grits into wedges, dipping in egg and milk, and frying until brown in bacon fat or butter. With a dollop of Mrs. Walter Geer's May haw jelly, with which I am endowed occasionally, and a glass of milk this makes a good Sunday night snack.

A rather more fancy breakfast dish is:

Baked Grits

Boil one cup of grits in two cups of water and two cups of milk with a teaspoon of salt. Cool slightly and turn into a baking dish, mixing in two beaten egg yolks. When egg yolks are well blended add two egg whites, which have been beaten quite stiff, and a half cup of cream. Bake in a medium oven for ten or fifteen minutes, until golden brown.

This is also a pleasant Sunday night supper dish if you were planning to have only leftover roast and feel the need of something hot or have unexpected company. It is a cousin to the Southern spoon bread of song and story.

Gumbo

For years shrimp gumbo was one of my company recipes and then I lucked into Julia's shrimp and crab gumbo recipe which is even more of a good thing. Its secret, I believe, is the roux, dark and rich and of creamy consistency. I made it for my shrimp gumbo but Julia uses it for a great many of her fragrant, spicy "pots"—shrimp and crab gumbo, chicken stew, and duck and turnips.

Roux

¹/₄ cup corn oil or meat drippings
²/₃ cup plain flour

1 medium onion, chopped

2 cloves garlic, chopped fine

Heat oil in heavy skillet, add flour, stir until brown. Add onion and garlic. Cook about 2 minutes.

Shrimp, Crab, and Okra Gumbo

$1^1/_2$ pounds cleaned and deveined shrimp

$^1/_2$ dozen fresh crabs, cleaned and cracked

$^1/_2$ pound okra, chopped

$^1/_4$ cup corn oil

1 medium onion

2 cloves garlic, chopped

$^1/_4$ pound ham, chopped

1 teaspoon Ac'cent

7 cups water

Salt and pepper to taste

Heat oil in Dutch oven, add okra, onion, ham, and garlic. Cook over low fire until okra won't rope. Add water, salt, pepper, and Ac'cent. Make roux, omitting onion and garlic since you have already added them to the vegetable mixture. Cook 1 hour. Sauté shrimp and crabs in oil in a heavy skillet a few minutes and add to vegetables. Cook about 20 minutes. Serve over rice. (Omit ham on days of abstinence, Julia advises.)

Sausage

For years I wondered why country sausage wasn't as good as I remembered it from childhood when my Great Aunt Babe always gave it to us. She made her own, seasoning with herbs out of her garden, shaping it into patties, which she cooked and packed down in fruit jars filled with hot grease to keep it through the winter. I had about attributed my disappointment in present-day sausage to the prejudice and possibly the superior digestive equipment of childhood, when I happened to breakfast with the Tabors one winter morning.

Along with hot biscuits and grits Frances served the best country sausage I had eaten since Aunt Babe's. The secret lay in an old recipe which has been in the Tabor family for probably a hundred years or more. Frances buys the sausage makings at the market and has them ground to her specifications, doing the seasoning herself.

Tabor Sausage

12 pounds of pork shoulder; 8 lean, 4 fat
2 tablespoons salt
2 tablespoons red pepper
1 tablespoon sage

Have the butcher trim the shoulder and grind once. Season and grind again. Frances freezes the sausage in small lots and brings it out before she is ready to shape it into patties, brown it quickly, add a little hot water, cover, and simmer until done.

83

Biscuits and Rolls

The natural accompaniment for sausage or ham is, of course, hot biscuits. For a party we make the biscuits and the sausage patties small—about bite size—taking the biscuits from the oven, breaking them in the middle, sticking a sausage patty in them and serving them immediately. Ham and hot biscuits are wonderful hors d'oeuvres. Thinly slice enough of the ham to start the guests off and then they will take over and serve themselves and all you have to do is have a relay system for running biscuits from the kitchen as fast as they come out of the oven.

In this, the hot bread belt, it is considered unpardonable to serve a guest a cold biscuit. There's an old story, probably apocryphal, of the northern visitor who spent months in the South and never got to taste biscuits because every time he would reach for one his hostesses would cry, "Let me get you a hot one!" and snatch them away.

That might very well have happened in the Jarrett House in Ellijay, an old-time mountain boardinghouse famous for its food. Miss Kitty Jarrett, one of the granddaughters of the founder, who with her sisters ran it until their recent retirement, circulated around the table with a plate of hot biscuits, making frequent runs to the big wood stove in the kitchen. The Jarretts are good company and I wondered once why Miss Kitty would never pull up a chair and sit with us.

"Oh, she wouldn't put the biscuits down!" somebody explained.

It was true I had never seen a plate of biscuits stationary on that laden table and I learned that Miss Kitty not only eschewed the practice of having biscuits wait on the diners, she eschewed diners who caused the biscuits to wait. City people driving through the mountains often tried to reach Ellijay at mealtime but if they got there five or ten minutes late Miss Kitty wouldn't admit them to the table.

"I'm not serving cold biscuits to *anybody!*" she said.

The Jarretts grew their own vegetables, raised their own meats, and cooked on a wood stove until the day they stopped taking boarders. City water comes to the big white two-story house by the railroad tracks but they still have a pipe running from the spring on the hillside out back, bringing in cold sweet "natural" water for coffee.

My own biscuits, which Muv started me to making when I was eight or nine years old, were a matter of pride with me until my ungrateful children once asked if we couldn't have canned biscuits "like other people." It was a real case of casting pearls before swine, I thought, wounded. But I bought some canned ones and liked them fine. Now I only make biscuits if I'm out of canned ones or am having a party and want little cocktail-sized biscuits.

There are two kinds—the light fluffy ones and the short ones. The ingredients vary slightly.

Fluffy Biscuits

2 cups flour
5 teaspoons baking powder
2 tablespoons shortening
1 cup milk
$^1/_2$ teaspoon salt

Sift dry ingredients together twice. Cut shortening in with a pastry blender or the fingers. Add milk gradually, working it in, roll dough to thickness of about half an inch, handling it lightly. Cut with small cutter, jar lid, or glass, place in 400-degree oven, and bake about 12 minutes.

Short Biscuits

2 cups flour
4 teaspoons baking powder

$^3/_4$ *teaspoon salt*

6 tablespoons shortening

$^3/_4$ *cup milk*

Sift dry ingredients, as for fluffy biscuits. Work in shortening until the flour is mealy. Add milk, turn out on a floured board and roll out to a thickness of about half an inch. Cut and cook in a very hot oven, 450 degrees, for about 10 minutes.

Frances makes hot rolls with less to-do than anybody I ever saw. Once while vacationing at Holly Creek we arrived at the Tabor house in the late afternoon to put a young guest, Margaret Leonard, on the bus for Atlanta. The bus was late and Frances said it was imperative that we feed the child before sending her forth. The Tabors had eaten their dinner at midday but there was plenty of cold sliced roast, Frances said, and she was just going to pop some rolls into the oven. The young people, six or eight strong, pulled up chairs in the Tabor kitchen and as fast as Frances brought the rolls out of the oven they vanished—along with mounds of country butter and several jars of honey and home-made jams and jellies.

I was busy eating and didn't notice the progress of my progeny and friends until out of a happy silence, broken only by the sound of the butter dish being passed, I heard Margaret say to Jimmy: "You know how many rolls you've eaten? I've kept count—fourteen!"

Frances's Rolls

1 package yeast

1 quart milk

1 cup sugar

1 cup lard

Mix yeast in $^1/_2$ cup of tepid water. Add to above. Add enough sifted flour to make a stiff batter. (You're on your own here. I guess about 4 or 5 cups.) Let rise 2 hours. Work down and add:

5 teaspoons baking powder

3 teaspoons salt

1 teaspoon sugar

Flour to make dough. (Several cups, says Frances.)

Roll out on floured board, cut into rounds, and let rise 20 to 30 minutes. Or if you want to, put in refrigerator and bring out and let rise another day, as when a swarm of hungry children descend on you.

Cakes

The fact that Muv always arrives for her Christmas visit with a full quota of holiday cakes beautifully browned or iced, as the case may be, without a crumb out of place, is an indication to me of some pioneer spirit. I believe she could have journeyed across the continent fighting off the Indians with a melodeon tied to the back of her covered wagon and arrive without a single key out of kilter.

Muv feels strongly about nearly everything but when she undertakes Christmas cakes she becomes a martinet. Her neighbors, realizing that Atlanta is a big metropolitan center with a full complement of fine bakeries, have suggested on one or more occasions that it isn't necessary for Muv to make her Christmas visit armed to the nines with cakes.

"Bakery cakes!" sniffs Muv. "Chalk and sugar."

And she preheats her oven and gets out her special cake pans, the

87

ones she uses for absolutely nothing else and will not even lend. (To keep from hurting her neighbors' feelings she maintains a separate collection of cake pans to lend. These are not kept as bright and untarnished as her private stock.)

Then I don't know what all goes on in her kitchen in Alford except that she considers it a poor "do" if she isn't feeling strong enough to do all the beating by hand and has to rely on an electric mixer.

"I can tell an electrically mixed cake," she maintains. "The texture is all wrong. If you haven't got the gumption to beat a cake yourself you shouldn't call yourself making a cake."

(I never have confessed this to Muv but I not only can't tell if it's a hand-beaten cake but I stoop to use cake mixes and have been known to eat boughten cake with some pleasure.)

When her cakes are ready Muv has to fight negativism in the members of her "crowd"—ladies named Miss Minnie, Miss Josie, Miss Pearl, all of ripe years and experience and an unshakable conviction that lemon cheese will fall to pieces on a 250-mile bus trip.

"No such a thing," says Muv. "I know what I'm doing."

And she takes off the closet shelf a big hat box, acquired months earlier at a haberdashery for this specific purpose and well reinforced with heavy cardboard. Into this box, one on top of the other, go the cakes: Pound cake (real butter, ten eggs), lemon cheese, and finally that triumph of all Christmas cakes, the Lane cake. (Until I begged her recipe for this book I never was sure what went into a Lane cake except that the layers are put together with a heavenly mixture which includes pecans from Muv's own trees, fresh coconut, and something which smells deliciously and suspiciously like brandy.) Between the cakes are acres of tissue paper, paper towels, and foil. And the whole thing is then tied together so securely it would be easier to assault Fort Knox than to get past Muv's knots.

From Alford to Atlanta Muv has to fight off the well-intentioned assistance of bus drivers and fellow passengers. In Alford, as in many small towns, everybody knows the bus drivers who pass through twice a day, taking them to the county seat and to do their shopping in neighboring small towns. And these men are solicitous about helping ladies carrying big hat boxes.

Muv will not allow anybody else to touch her box of cakes but if the bus is crowded she will give some young and limber-legged traveler the privilege of standing in the aisle while her cakes ride in state in the seat next to her.

After all, as Miss Minnie, Miss Pearl and Miss Josie say, lemon cheese *is* delicate.

I have never tried to bake Muv's lemon cheese and her fabulous Lane cake, which she brings us for Christmas and sometimes bakes for a birthday if the birthday person has had a hard year and needs something special and festive in his or her life. I don't think that the recipes given here are particularly difficult but I have a perhaps superstitious fear of falling short of what Muv brings off with perfection.

Lemon Cheese Cake

1 cup butter

2 cups sugar

4 eggs

3 cups flour

3 teaspoons baking powder

1 cup milk

1 teaspoon vanilla

Cream sugar and butter and add beaten eggs. Fold in sifted dry ingredients alternately with the milk. Add vanilla. Bake in 3 layers at 350 degrees about 30 minutes.

Filling:
2 lemons, juice and rind
3 egg yolks
1/2 cup butter
1 cup sugar

Combine ingredients and cook in double boiler until thickened. Cool and spread between layers.

The Lane cake recipe is an old one, named for a south Alabama family where it originated. The recipe calls for bourbon or brandy in the filling and although Muv's town is dry and her church and her immediate circle of friends frown on spirits in any form, she feels so strongly about the Lane cake that she will go to almost any length to get the proper seasoning for it. Once this resulted in a harrowing experience in a Panama City bistro. Muv rode down to the coast after church one day with one of her friends and while the friend was on another errand she slipped into the first place she saw with a neon sign blinking "Bar."

"It was a nice sunny day," Muv reported to us, "but dark as the inside of a cow in that place. I had on my good church clothes, hat and gloves and all, and this creature came slithering up to me wearing...I don't know what."

"Probably a cocktail dress, Muv," one of the children suggested.

"Maybe so," said Muv. "Anyway she looked half naked and she was downright impudent. She said, 'Madam, this is a cocktail lounge.' So I just drew myself up and said, 'My dear, I didn't *think* it was the Methodist parsonage! I'll have half a pint of Early Times please.'"

However the habitués of the bar may have felt about it, *we* thought the cake was well worth Muv's expedition.

Lane Cake

8 egg whites
1 cup butter
1 teaspoon vanilla
2 cups sugar
3¼ cups flour
2 teaspoons baking powder
1 cup sweet milk

Cream butter and sugar until light. Add flour, baking powder, and milk a little at a time. Add stiffly beaten egg whites and vanilla. Mix well and bake in 4 layers.

Filling:

Beat well together 8 egg yolks, 1 cup sugar, and ½ cup butter, stirring all the time. Add 1 cup raisins, 1 cup chopped pecans, a wine glass of bourbon or brandy, and 1 teaspoon vanilla. Spread between layers, sprinkle top with freshly grated coconut, add candied cherries for decoration. Store a few days before serving.

—from *A Place Called Sweet Apple*

Talmadge Asks Law Limiting Aid to Illegitimate Babies

By CELESTINE SIBLEY

Gov. Talmadge wants to put an end to "illegitimate baby-having as a business in Georgia."

The Chief Executive late Wednesday dispatched to the House, for introduction under administrative colors, a bill calculated to cut 2,000 illegitimate babies off State Welfare rolls at an estimated savings of $444,000 annually.

The measure would amend the 1937 "Aid to Dependent Children Act" and provide that no grant of assistance should be made "for more than one illegitimate child of a mother by any County Welfare Department or the State Department of Public Welfare."

"Should a mother have more than one illegitimate child," the Governor's bill provides, "then the one grant of assistance or money payment shall be made for the first-born or eldest, if eligible."

State Welfare Director Alan Kemper said 70 percent of the cases of multiple illegitimacy in a family were to Negro families. He hailed the Governor's proposal as a step to halt what he said was a "growing tendency" to regard producing illegitimate children "as good business."

The estimated 2,000 children whose ADC grants would be cut off are second, third, fourth and

even fifth illegitimate children in their families.

The grants of an estimated 42,000 other children would be unaffected by the measure.

Welfare Director Kemper said Aid to Dependent Children rolls were boosted by an average of 900 new children each month. Eleven percent of these are illegitimate according to a study made by welfare workers two years ago.

Under State law a mother of five children may collect $99 a month for the support of the children, if their father is dead, disabled or missing. The grants have served in many cases as bonuses, Welfare officials said, and provide incentive for mothers who are already kept at home by one or two small children to increase their income with additional children.

The Governor's bill, however, posed new problems for welfare workers. In case of twins and triplets of illegitimate birth, which one would be entitled to ADC grant?

Atty. Gen. Eugene Cook's answer: "That's a medical problem, not a legal one. The bill says 'first-born or eldest' and I suppose the attending physician could tag the baby delivered first."

ACCEPTANCE SPEECH
BY
GOVERNOR JIMMY CARTER

DEMOCRATIC NATIONAL CONVENTION
NEW YORK CITY
THURSDAY, JULY 15, 1976

pt your nomination.

pt it in the words of John F. Kennedy: "With a full
rt -- and with only one obligation -- to devote eve
dy, mind and spirit to lead our party back to victo
on back to greatness."

ll not be a year of politics as usual. It is a yea
and of quiet and sober reassessment of our nation'
purpose -- a year when voters have already confo
experts.

e a year of inspiration and hope.

arantee you, it will be the year when we give th

media
'77 inaugural

PARTY-
SHOREHAM

AFFILIATION:

Chapter 4

POLITICS

Among all the reporters who have covered Georgia politics over the years, few understood and delighted in the foolishness and foibles of its colorful participants as did Celestine Sibley.

What's more, she plainly liked us. She liked us and you could see it in her writings. We unanimously loved her. She was always fair, reporting what she saw without fear or favor, but also without ridicule or rancor.

She has never acted like she was superior in intellect or character. Of course she is, but she never wore a sign around her neck proclaiming it as many reporters do.

In the past, she has especially liked the great storytellers and raconteurs like Cheney Griffin, George Bagby, and Bobby Rowan and sometimes would break into a cackle over some silly stunt or outlandish remark. At the same time, she has always been able to cut through the rhetoric and showmanship and get to what was most significant.

For many years, Celestine Sibley has written about the ridiculous and the sublime with equal skill. But this shrewd sister always knows the difference and separates the two as well as anyone who has ever covered Georgia politics.

Once Celestine and I were doing a book signing together and no one was there when it was supposed to start. She smiled and said, "The worst thing in the world is to have a book signing and no one show up." To which

I replied, "No, the worst thing is to have a political rally and no one show up."

Knowing a great deal about both, Celestine knew exactly what I meant.

—Zell Miller

Photographs on page 92:

top: left to right: Speaker of the House Tom Murphy, Celestine, and the late Representative John Greer
middle: sample of Celestine's reporting, from the *Atlanta Constitution*
bottom: Celestine's invitation to the dedication of the Carter Presidential Center

Photographs on page 93:

top: Celestine's press copy of Jimmy Carter's acceptance speech at the 1976 Democratic National Convention, with her notes
middle: publicity photo taken upon Celestine's receipt of the Christopher Award in 1952 (Celestine had a previously unnoticed tumor on her neck that showed up in the photograph when it ran in the newspapers. Spotted by her mother, the tumor was consequently diagnosed and removed.)
bottom: Celestine's media pass to one of President Carter's inaugural parties

The Double Governor Controversy

In the mid-1970s Celestine Sibley wrote a four-part series that ran in the Atlanta Constitution. *In the series, she looks back to the year 1947, when Georgia became the first and only state in the nation to have a plethora of governors in office at the same time. The Double Governor controversy won worldwide attention and markedly changed some political careers in Georgia.*

Part I

They called him "The Wild Man from Sugar Creek" and many other things—both better and worse.

To his followers, who elected him governor of Georgia four times, he was "Ole Gene," the farmer's friend, a red gallus-wearing St. George fighting the dragon of integration, a tobacco-chewing saint standing between them and those twin evils, Yankees and "niggers."

To the national press he was a "turkey-necked, rabble-rousing" demagogue in whose obituary *Time* magazine tucked this line: "No contemporary politician except Louisiana's Huey Long and Mississippi's Theodore (The Man) Bilbo appealed so successfully to ignorance and bigotry."

Nevertheless when Eugene Talmadge, at the age of 62 years, slipped from a coma into death at old Piedmont Hospital four days before Christmas in 1946 he set off what until Watergate was rated by observers as "the biggest and oddest political row in U.S. history."

It was known locally as "the Double Governor fracas" and "the 63 days with TWO of 'em...THREE of 'em...you count 'em!'"

The world looked on and laughed. Radio comedians of the Sen. Claghorn stripe enjoyed a field day. *Newsweek* magazine noted that Georgia politics had hit the front pages of every major newspaper in the country "as the state finds itself in a mixup so fantastic that it made

97

the historic gyrations of the Balkans sound sedately sober in contrast."

Time said the South historically loved "buffoons, corny oratory and the smell of violence" but this latest political escapade was "like something conceived late at night by three unemployed radio writers."

At home a dazed electorate, not sure WHO was Governor and bewildered by early morning shenanigans in the Capitol, fistfights, broken locks, protest rallies, court suits, and ultimately, the word that tombstones were voting in Telfair County, could only ask feebly in the slang of the day: "Wha' hoppen?"

What happened was maybe not so simple or colorful as *Time* put it, calling it a Caesarian operation by which Herman Talmadge, now Georgia's senior U.S. senator and lately in the national eye for his service on the Watergate committee, was "jerked out of obscurity, blessed by the General Assembly, bathed in publicity and installed in the Governor's Mansion in his Pappy's place."

But it was pretty simple and plenty colorful at that.

The day Eugene Talmadge died—7 A.M. December 21, 1946—Georgians didn't even wait a tactful 10 minutes before they started asking, "Who'll be governor now?" Politicians, as a matter of fact, had started kicking that question around when "ole Gene" first began to feel pains in his stomach back in the summer before the general election in November.

98

General elections in those days weren't much excitement unless the candidate failed to get a clear majority in the Democratic primary—and Talmadge had that. His opponent, James Carmichael, a young Marietta attorney, had piled up the biggest popular vote ever accorded a gubernatorial candidate in Georgia but it was the county unit vote that mattered and Talmadge had it. He had waged a rough and tumble campaign to get it, promising over and over again to restore the white primary to the state, and maybe, his supporters felt, he had partaken too often and too liberally of campaign barbecue because his digestion seemed to be suffering. Anyhow, he checked into a hospital in Jacksonville where his wife, "Miss Mitt," kept vigil; reporters were barred and doctors acted secretive about their diagnosis.

All this must have set Gibson Greer Ezell, clerk of Superior Court in Monticello, thinking. He looked up the law and found that if, in the classic phrase, "anything happened" to Talmadge the new state Constitution seemed to provide that the legislature choose his successor from the next two highest candidates in the general election. Ezell called the old governor's campaign manager, his son Herman, who in that day was more often called Hummon.

The word went out: Scratch Eugene Talmadge's name on the ballot and write in Herman Talmadge's. It wouldn't take many write-in votes, since there were no other candidates, everybody figured, but there were a couple of hitches. Die-hard Carmichael supporters wrote in his name and that rare animal, a Republican, showed up. He was D. Talmadge Bowers, a North Georgia tombstone salesman, and he too had friends with pencils.

The elder Talmadge's condition worsened. He was in hospitals and out. He went home for Thanksgiving, went bird hunting, ate heartily, and checked in again at Piedmont hospital November 29. There were days when he rallied and on one of those he saw the *Constitution* editor, his arch political enemy, Ralph McGill, and talked to him about writing his biography. Then he suffered stomach hemorrhages and city firemen and policemen lined up to give him blood transfusions. Family and many of his friends were at his bedside when he died.

Cause of death was given as hemolytic jaundice and cirrhosis of the liver.

Some around the state began in effect crying, "The king is dead! Long live the king!" and rallying support for his successor.

Death came on Saturday, the old Governor's body lay in state in the capitol on Sunday, drawing thousands of faithful and sincere

99

mourners, many of whom followed it in a long cortege back to Telfair county, the seat of the Talmadge home, Sugar Creek farm, for the funeral on Monday.

Christmas and New Year came and then the General Assembly came to town and by that time the battle lines were pretty clearly drawn. Gov. Ellis Arnall, who was going out of office, contended publicly that he should stay put and serve as governor until the newly elected lieutenant governor was sworn in and could take over as acting governor. Melvin E. Thompson, a former school teacher, assistant state school superintendent, revenue service commissioner and at one time Arnall's executive secretary, had been elected Georgia's first lieutenant governor and he agreed with Arnall's contention. So did Atty. Gen. Eugene Cook.

On the other hand, old guard Talmadge men were strong in the General Assembly and they had a gifted and resourceful leader in Roy Harris, former Speaker of the House from Augusta. Harris set up headquarters on the 14th floor of the Henry Grady Hotel, rallying place for lawmakers in those days, and "began plying them with bourbon, cigars, veiled threats and glittering promises," as one political writer put it.

By midafternoon on January 15, the two Houses assembled in joint session and began the business of canvassing votes in the gubernatorial race. Robert Elliot, fiery Columbus attorney, now a federal judge, served as floor leader for Talmadge. Thompson forces were led by Sen. W. D. Trippe of Cedartown and Sen. Everett Millican of Atlanta. There was parliamentary jockeying and skirmishing with Rep. A. N. Durden of Albany trying to get the General Assembly to admit that it did not have the authority to elect a governor. The Durden resolution went down to speedy defeat. Instead, the members passed Elliot's resolution providing that a governor would be elected from those receiving the most write-in votes.

The votes were brought up from the secretary of state's office in a waste basket and two big cardboard boxes and they were counted.

Talmadge supporters had apparently miscalculated. Herman was running third.

James Carmichael had 680 votes, D. Talmadge Bowers had 637 votes, and Herman Talmadge had but 617 votes.

Apparently his home county of Telfair had given Herman only 29 votes. There were protests from the Telfair delegation and suddenly a new batch of votes arrived—77 of them, kiting Talmadge's total to 694. They had been misfiled in the lieutenant governor's envelope, it was said.

The gallery and the corridors were jammed with spectators who sent up a cheer. Herman, who had been waiting at the Henry Grady Hotel, materialized with his 23-year-old blonde wife, Betty, and his mother, "Miss Mitt" at his side.

He was not only elected governor at that moment but he was inaugurated immediately. It was by this time nearly 3 A.M. but the 33-year-old heir even made an inaugural address.

"It is my regret that my election could not have been by the people of Georgia," he said. "Unfortunately, there was no precedent in Georgia's history for this situation." He added that his first objective would be to restore the Democratic white primary and he would "seek to protect the county unit system at all hazards."

Judge C. W. Worrill of the Pataula Circuit of Superior Court administered the oath of office and the march to the governor's office began.

One of Talmadge's aides who now works for Lt. Gov. Lester Maddox remarked the other day that his assignment that night in 1947 had been to stand at a door to the House chamber and "try to keep the boys from leaving the chamber and running to the bathroom for a drink."

"There was plenty of drinking going on," he recalled, "but if they got too drunk they wouldn't be any use to us."

News stories at the time said the toilets were full of broken liquor bottles. The crowd had been noisy and now it became boisterous. It swirled around Herman on his march down the stairs to the second floor and took charge when the door to the chief executive's office turned out to be locked. The door was battered down.

Gov. Ellis Arnall and his executive secretary, Benton Odom, occupied the office. For all this excitement boiling up in the spectators the principles in the drama seemed remarkably calm.

The dialogue for a couple of quick quippers was almost colorless.

Talmadge said, "I presume that you have been informed that I have been elected governor by the General Assembly."

Arnall replied, "The General Assembly cannot elect a governor. I refuse to yield the office to you, whom I consider a pretender."

"Do you defy the General Assembly?" asked Talmadge.

"I do not," said Arnall. "But I uphold the law."

At this point, according to all accounts, Talmadge executed a turn on his heel and muttered noncommittally, "We'll see."

And Arnall, demonstrating a flare [sic] for showmanship, grabbed the last line. Waving genially he said, "You were nice to come in."

Meanwhile, fights were breaking out all over the capitol. John Nahara, a 300-pound Syrian wrestler and ex-body guard of "Ole Gene's" punched Arnall's chauffeur Buck Buchanan in the jaw, breaking it. The faithful were clambering over desks and chairs and threatening to oust Arnall bodily.

Roy Harris, walking beside Herman, whispered to him and then addressed the throng: "We will let Gov. Arnall keep his office in there for the time being and Gov. Talmadge will set up his out here in this room." (The lobby.) I know you're happy over this great victory but we want you to leave quietly now. We do not want disorder or trouble."

Marvin Griffin, later to become governor himself, was in a dual position that night. He had been Ellis Arnall's adjutant general but Arnall, of course, wasn't running for reelection that term so Griffin lined up with Eugene Talmadge and had been notified by Herman that he would be asked to stay on as his father's military chief. That night Herman swore Marvin Griffin in as his own adjutant general and Griffin promptly went to work to protect his erstwhile boss from his new boss' more zealous followers. He urged restraint and he walked shoulder to shoulder with Arnall when at 3:30 A.M. he finally left the capitol.

Georgians who had been at home in bed asleep while their state house roared and throbbed with excitement, were beginning to awaken and face the freakiest phenomenon in all their colorful political history. They now had two governors—or was it three?

—from the *Atlanta Journal* and the *Atlanta Constitution*, Sunday, June 30, 1974

Part II

Whether or not possession is actually nine-tenths of the law may be something to check with your lawyer someday. But in January 1947 the forces of the new, General Assembly–named governor, Herman Talmadge, didn't fool around with lawyers.

They got a locksmith!

Gov. Ellis Arnall, thinking he had successfully repulsed what he called The Pretender and had battened down the hatches of the chief executive's office and gone home at 3:30 A.M., arrived at the capitol to find the locks changed on the door, his staff evicted, and Talmadge's troops in full charge.

It was, cried Arnall, a "military coup d'état," pulled off by "thugs,

103

hoodlums and storm troopers" in behalf of "an interloper, usurper, dictatorship."

Bewildered Georgians, who had gone to bed with one governor and awakened with two, couldn't believe what they were witnessing— a spectacle described by one writer as "two raccoons snatching at a piece of cheese."

There was Ellis Arnall, 39-year-old Newnan lawyer who had just wound up four years as a progressive, liberal governor, hanging on to the office until, he promised, his legal successor, the new lieutenant governor, could be sworn in. And there was Herman Talmadge, 33-year-old Telfair county lawyer, claiming that on the basis of a hand-ful of write-in votes the legislature in a wild, highly alcoholic post-midnight session had properly elected him as the lawful successor to his father, the late Eugene Talmadge, who had died a few weeks be-fore he could take office. (Herman actually only had 25 more write in votes that James Carmichael, the man his father beat with the county unit vote but Carmichael announced early that he would not be a contender in the fracas. He had run under the rules of the Demo-cratic primary, he said, and he would abide by them, refusing to ac-cept the governorship from the hands of the General Assembly if by some fluke it were offered him.)

104   Nobody knew who was right but most citizens knew who they thought was right and hundreds of them flocked to the capitol to see what was going on.

What was going on was a comic opera.

Arnall, unable to get into the office so lately his, set up shop in the information booth in the rotunda. He had no sooner settled in when he had to move over for a 237-pound member of the legislature, the late Representative Jimmy Dykes of Cochrane, a Talmadge stalwart from a way back.

Since he was himself a man of boar-like proportions the press to this day considers Dykes' remarks at the time as memorable.

"Ellis," he said to Governor No. 1, "you remind me of a hawg. Did you ever slop a hawg? The more you give him, the more he wants and he never knows when to get out of the trough!"

Meanwhile, back in the governor's real office the staff of Governor No. 2 had spun into action. "Hummon," as the "wool hat" following called him in those days, was busy with appointments. He was already in possession of the chief executive's "No. 1" automobile license tag and one of his aides was busy telling somebody on the telephone that Ellis Arnall no longer worked there.

"We think he's selling insurance or something," remarked this comic.

For three days the capitol was bedlam. Reporters became schizophrenic trying to cover the legislature and both governors. Gov. Arnall divided his time between his law office in the Candler building and a desk in the rotunda, arriving with a retinue of reporters one rainy afternoon as a throng of his supporters milled around waiting. He had just seated himself at the desk when an explosion like a gunshot rang out and the area was filled with smoke. One female reporter picked herself up off the floor and ran for the telephones prepared to shout, "assassination" just as someone picked up fragments of a firecracker which had been thrown from the floor above.

Word came forth from Governor No. 2 that such capers should cease.

"I do not object to Ellis Arnall hanging around as long as he wants to," said Gov. Talmadge.

But he clearly didn't mean he wanted him hanging around the chief executive's house. Gov. Arnall invited reporters out to the Mansion in Ansley Park for lunch and found that he had been supplanted there. The Talmadge First Family, young Betty and their two little boys, Gene and Bobby, had moved in. Gov. Arnall reiterated that it was another "expert pincer movement by Herman, the Pretender...part of the infiltration that has been going on ever since the illegal election of The

Pretender." And then he shrugged and smilingly took the press to a nearby soda fountain to lunch.

"I bet he knew we weren't going to be able to get in when he took us out there," Photographer Bill Wilson remarked the other day, after thinking about it once or twice in the twenty-seven years.

Being evicted from the Mansion was slight inconvenience to Arnall. His family, Mildred and their small children, had already gone home to Newnan and on January 18, the event he had been waiting for took place. Melvin E. Thompson, forty-three, the quiet, dry-witted ex-school teacher who had been elected Georgia's first lieutenant-governor, was sworn in by both House and Senate of the General Assembly.

Here, proclaimed Arnall, is the rightful, legal successor to the late Eugene Talmadge—and, as he had promised, he withdrew from the field of battle.

Thompson now become not Governor No. 1 or 2 but Acting Governor. The problem was that Talmadge was in full command and he had nowhere to do his "acting." So he went to court. He and Arnall and State Atty. Gen. Eugene Cook filed three separate suits in Fulton Superior court seeking to oust Talmadge from the office they contended he held illegally.

Young Herman felt secure about his legal position. In fact, he said he didn't consider it any business of the courts but a matter which the General Assembly had already neatly and properly handled.

But he had other problems. State Treasurer George Hamilton was one of them. As confused as most Georgians about who was governor, he declined to pay ANYBODY in the executive department until the courts acted.

And Secretary of State Ben Fortson, the whimsical history-minded gentleman across the hall, was the other. By law the Secretary of State is custodian of what is called "the Great Seal of Georgia." This little artifact is not really great in size but about the size of a smallish pocket watch. But to Ben Fortson particularly it symbolizes the power and the glory of the office of Governor since it is required on most major documents issued by the executive department. Talmadge was up to his elbows in documents but Fortson wasn't sure he was entitled to the power and the glory. He declined to take the Great Seal out of the safe.

Comptroller Zack Cravey had arrived with something requiring the seal.

"We can't use the seal," objected Fortson. "I don't know if Herman is governor or not."

"Let that be on your conscience," said Cravey. "Trouble was," remarked Fortson, looking back, "that's where it was. Herman and I understood one another and he didn't send for the seal again but some of his people told some of my people that they were going to get it. I was afraid they might break into the safe at night and get it and so I got it out and hid it." Where he hid it is one of Georgia's school children's favorite stories today. Crippled in an automobile accident when he was a young man, the Secretary of State has been confined to a wheel chair since but he is an agile and intrepid wheel chair operator and he knew there was room in his vehicle for him and the Great Seal. "I sat on it by day and slept on it by night," the Secretary of State said recently. "If you don't believe it leaves a lasting impression—try that for 63 days."

107

—from the *Atlanta Journal* and the *Atlanta Constitution*, Monday, July 1, 1974

Part III

A month of the so-called Double Governor controversy in Georgia in the winter of 1947 was funny to most of America—one more example of how those hot-headed originals, southerners, served up their politics.

Radio comedians led the laughter, lampooning the Georgia capitol with the verve they once used on such classics as "Grand Hotel" and "Lost Weekend."

The nationally famous cartoonist Mergen dipped his pen in acid and sketched Herman Talmadge wearing a crown and lolling on a throne which rested squarely on the back of a sweating fellow labelled "Georgia."

His colleague, Herblock, depicted the really tall and handsome young Talmadge as a little shrimp blinded by a big hat, ostensibly wool, and the Georgia legislature as a crude big-mouth telling off "The People of Georgia" with these words: "We don't want none of your outside interference."

In Georgia it wasn't funny.

Those people who weren't going to court seemed to be marching on the capitol.

Two thousand college students bristling with signs calling the man in the governor's office "Herr Herman" and comparing him to Hitler and his election by "drunken legislators" to the German dictator's beer hall putsch, assembled in Plaza Park and paraded to the capitol. As they swarmed over the lawn Governor Talmadge ignored their demands that he come out and face them.

The students quickly parodied a popular song of the day, lifting their young voices in the cold winter afternoon air with the chant, "Open the door-r, Herman."

Finally, one of their number, proclaimed spokesman, was admitted to the chief executive's office where Herman received him but was adamant in his refusal to address the crowd.

Indignation meetings sprang up over the state. Many legislators who had helped to elect Talmadge governor that night of January 15, to take the post of his late father before Lt. Gov.–elect M. E. Thompson could be sworn in, were publicly censured. In some places they called themselves Aroused Citizens of Georgia. In Atlanta a mass meeting at the Woman's Club drew more than 2,000, far more than the auditorium could hold, and they gave Ellis Arnall, who had tried to stick in there as governor until Thompson could take over, a roof-shaking ovation.

"Tell 'em about it, Ellis!" they cried, borrowing a line that had been coined and polished in usage at old Gene Talmadge rallies.

A woman Talmadge supporter who took to the stage to rebuke Arnall and the Episcopal Bishop John Moore Walker, who was presiding, booed. Boos and shouts of "No! No!" drowned out Rep. J. Julian Bennett of Barrow county, who attempted to explain his vote for Herman Talmadge.

And then the courts acted.

Judge Walter Hendrix of Fulton Superior Court ruled that Talmadge was the legal claimant to the office and dismissed a suit by acting Gov. Thompson. Three days later a three-judge opinion handed down in McDonough also ruled, two to one, in favor of Talmadge, giving him access to approximately $95,000 in public funds left in the executive department account by retiring Gov. Arnall.

Atty. Gen. Eugene Cook promptly appealed the decision to the Georgia Supreme Court.

While they waited for the high court to act, Secretary of State Ben Fortson sat on the Great Seal of Georgia and along with every other Georgian watched each new unfolding act in the tragi-comedy.

Recently he recalled one of the funniest lines delivered by any actor on the stage the state capitol had become.

109

The late C. E. Gregory, portly political editor for the *Atlanta Journal* for many years, walked into Fortson's office in a lather of excitement.

"Do you know," Gregory said, "that they rose from the dead in Telfair county, marched in alphabetical order to the polls, cast their votes for Herman Talmadge and went back to their last repose?"

Secretary of State Fortson has never heard of such a thing and to this day he and the other principals in the drama insist that they never thought Herman Talmadge knew about it.

That afternoon the streamer across the front page of the *Journal* read: "TELFAIR DEAD WERE VOTED."

Acting Gov. Thompson said recently that the tip to Gregory originally came from him. He heard there were "voting tombstones in Telfair" from a Baptist preacher and a county commissioner. He told Gregory, who called his office and George Goodwin, then a *Journal* reporter, now a public relations man, was dispatched to the scene with Photographer Bill Wilson.

A check of Helena precinct records showed that of 103 persons listed as voting, thirty-four on the list appeared in alphabetical order, starting with A and ending with K. Not all of these were dead. Some were alive and said they had not been to the polls that day because they felt they had done their all for Eugene Talmadge in the primary. One man said it was raining and his windshield wiper was broken and he stayed home. Many of the persons listed as voting could not be found, some were said by their neighbors to have moved out of the county years before and then there were the amazed comments from kinfolks of the dead.

"Papa didn't vote. He died seven years ago," said one. "Why, old Mr. Hankey couldn't have voted. Old gentleman passed away two or three years ago."

Governor Talmadge called it "yellow journalism" at the time and told his press conference: "That's the *Journal's* story, not mine."

Recently on his way home from Washington for a weekend at his farm at Lovejoy, a mellow and relaxed U.S. Senator Talmadge said the same thing: "That's the *Journal's* story, not mine. My friend Stanley Brooks could have gotten hundreds of votes for me down there, all alive."

Nevertheless, the *Journal's* Goodwin won a Pulitzer prize for the exposé and Aroused Citizens multiplied and became vociferous in their demands that Talmadge move out and give the seat of governor to Acting Gov. Thompson.

A little more than two weeks after the tombstone voting exposé the Supreme Court decision came through. By a vote of five to two the high court over-ruled the Superior Court and declared that M. E. Thompson was governor of Georgia.

In the Georgia House Representative John Lewis of Sparta shouted, "There always were two statesmen and five politicians on the Supreme Court!"

Such excitement prevailed in the General Assembly that Speaker Fred Hand recessed the House from 11 A.M. to 2 P.M. because it was impossible to preserve order. Rep. Charles Gowen, then of Glynn county, now an Atlanta attorney, had been a Thompson supporter from the first and he introduced a resolution calling for a joint session of House and Senate to hear a message from "His Excellency, Acting Gov. M. E. Thompson."

Some Talmadge supporters would have fought it but the young governor-for-sixty-three-days cleared out his desk and departed the capitol within forty-five minutes.

Representative Frank Twitty of Mitchell county, a Talmadge supporter who would later serve as Herman's floor-leader in the House, pleaded for the adoption of the Gowen resolution and a polite audience for Thompson.

He said of Talmadge, "He accepts the decision. So should we."

Talmadge did accept the decision but not for long. Two years later he appealed it to the voters of Georgia and won, handily unseating Thompson and returning to capitol and mansion for a four-year term.

—from the *Atlanta Journal* and the *Atlanta Constitution*, July 2, 1974

The Most Disfranchised City in America

For generations students of government came to Georgia to behold democracy's anathema, election by the few, treated locally as a sacred tribal rite. Professor Albert B. Saye of the University of Georgia called Atlanta "the most disfranchised city in America."

The county unit system was born of the conviction that electing state officials and representatives in the U.S. Congress by popular vote would put political control in the hands of what Tom Watson called "a few city bosses...using corporation influence, the job-lash, money, whiskey and log-rolling." The rural counties were where virtue and honor resided, Watson and many of his successors firmly believed.

From the 1880s to 1917, the system existed informally, urgently defended and upheld by people like Watson. In 1917 with the enactment of the Neill Primary Act, it became law—a system whereby all candidates for congress, governor, state house officials, and justices of the state supreme court and court of appeals were elected according to the number of counties they carried and not the number of votes they received. A candidate receiving the highest number of popular votes in a county was considered to have carried the county and to be entitled to the full vote of such county. The weight of that county's influence was measured on a unit basis, two votes for each representative it had in the lower house of the General Assembly.

Under that system, the smallest county in the state, little Echols in south Georgia, with a population of 1,876 people, had one unit representing 938 voters. Fulton County (Atlanta), with a population of 556,326, had six units, each representing 24,183 voters.

Naturally, the people of the cities, most of whom had come from the country originally, railed out against this disfranchisement, but it wasn't until 1962 that they had any real hope. When the U.S. Supreme Court ruled early in 1962 that the Federal District Court had power to

113

grant a group of Nashville citizens more representation in the legislature, Georgia politicians—wrote *Constitution* political editor Reg Murphy—"knew the jig was up." Governor Ernest Vandiver called the legislature back in to special session in the spring of 1962 in a bit of window dressing which was supposed to show the rural areas that the politicals still were fighting for them. But Vandiver and the legislature both knew well enough that they could not be successful.

While the legislature sat through the twelfth day of that grim special session, a three-judge Federal Court sitting half a mile away in the third-floor courtroom of Atlanta's old post office building began tearing into the system.

The legislature made minor concessions—a few more units for the cities. The courts said it wasn't enough. The state Democratic leadership decided any further granting of units to cities was impossible. The Democratic Executive Committee met and decided to hold the first popular-vote elections in about fifty years.

Ex-Governor Marvin Griffin, making a bid for a comeback, panicked. He asked the committee to hold the election on a plurality basis, figuring a split vote would help him if there was no runoff.

The committee, dominated by the outgoing Governor Vandiver, wouldn't have it. It said there must be a majority vote. Griffin's chances ended with that decision, but it wouldn't be proved until the hot summer's campaign was over and the votes were in on September 12. Griffin, a tough old veteran of the "hog-and-hominy" school of politics and an arch-segregationist, was defeated by Carl Sanders, a young Augusta lawyer called a moderate by his supporters. (Sanders said of himself, "I'm a segregationist, but not a damned fool.")

The attacks on the county unit system continued. The legislature was pushed into another comer by a three-judge Federal Court decision during the summer, saying there must be reapportionment. The General Assembly came back into session in late September and

114

boosted the Atlanta metropolitan area's representation in the Senate from one to twelve senators.

This brought on another election in a summer so election-ridden that people joked they couldn't go home to dinner any day until they had dropped by the polls and voted. Everybody got into the race for the senate—old-timers in city and county jobs who hadn't dared to aspire to the state senate as long as there was only one seat, fresh young lawyers, housewives, Negros, and Republicans.

When the smoke of battle cleared, Atlanta hadn't elected any women (one came close), but it had included in the round dozen the first Negro since the turn of the century, a lawyer named Leroy Johnson, and a white Republican, an insurance man named Dan MacIntyre, III.

Too Busy to Hate

Atlanta was probably the least turbulent of the big cities involved in the civil rights movement, and almost immediately its black leaders were turning to politics.

The day of Dr. King's funeral a young black lawyer named Maynard Jackson was at the hospital awaiting the birth of his first child. The solemnity of the "life-death cycle" engrossed him for long moments, and he made up his mind then that entering politics was the way to go for his country's good and for the future life of his newborn baby.

Jackson was a member of the "black aristocracy." His great-great-grandfather Andrew Jackson was a slave who bought his freedom and founded the Wheat Street Baptist Church in Atlanta. His maternal grandfather was John Wesley Dobbs, a railway postal employee who despite being a Republican in a predominantly Democratic town was a power in politics and one of the "summit" Negro leaders who had worked diligently for the improvement of housing and health facilities for blacks long before the civil rights movement. He believed in education—higher education. One of his daughters, Maynard's mother, received a doctorate in French at the University of Toulouse in France and returned to this country to head the modern languages department at North Carolina Central University in Durham. His aunt was the famed Metropolitan soprano, Mattiwilda Dobbs.

Born in Dallas, Texas, in 1938, Maynard was brought to Atlanta at the age of seven when his father became pastor of the Friendship Baptist Church. He was graduated from Morehouse College at the age of eighteen and went on to obtain a law degree at North Carolina Central, where his mother taught, graduating *cum laude* and being designated as one of the outstanding debaters in the United States by the New York Bar Association.

His first bid for political office was almost a fluke. Twenty minutes before the deadline for qualifying, he borrowed three thousand dollars and entered the race for United States Senate against the powerful, oft considered invincible Herman Talmadge. He lost but not before piling up twenty-five percent of the statewide vote—a feat for an unknown black.

"Georgia has told the world," declared Jackson as he conceded defeat, "that any American—black or white, rich or poor, liberal or conservative—can run for public office in this state."

116

Spur-of-the-moment in his decision to challenge Talmadge, Jackson carefully planned his campaign for vice mayor of Atlanta—and he won with one-third of the white vote and ninety percent of the black vote. Next he went for mayor, entering the race in a field of eleven candidates, including the incumbent Mayor Sam Massell, Atlanta's first Jewish mayor, who had been elected as a liberal with the backing of blacks and the support of organized labor. Jackson was second in the eleven-man race and won the runoff against Massell with fifty-nine percent of the vote. He became the first black mayor of a major Southern city and, at thirty-five years, the youngest in Atlanta's history.

At his inauguration in January 1974—a gala in the Kennedy tradition with music by the Atlanta Symphony Orchestra—his aunt Mattiwilda Dobbs sang. She had previously refused to sing in Atlanta because the audiences were segregated.

Jackson served two terms and was succeeded by Andrew Young, a black preacher, son of a New Orleans dentist, who had been with Dr. King when he faced fire hoses and police dogs and was with him when he was slain. Young won by a landslide against the late Sidney Marcus, a long-time member of the Georgia legislature. Young had helped to draft the Civil Rights Act of 1964 and the Voting Rights Act of 1965, and his name was well-known to Atlanta voters. Unsuccessful in a bid for Congress in 1970, he came back in 1972 and won, the only black member at that time to be elected from a predominantly white district, north or south.

A Carter supporter, Young was called by the president "the finest elected official I've ever seen." He was named ambassador to the United Nations by Carter and is credited with having brought new luster to the United States with the African nations. Unfortunately, when he was found meeting with representatives from the PLO, the tide of public opinion against him caused him to resign, although the president had not asked it.

Nearly a quarter of century since Mayor Bill Hartsfield called Atlanta a city "too busy to hate," blacks have found it what Maynard Jackson called it, a city "*not* too busy to love." Blacks occupy many of the posts in the Georgia General Assembly and hold positions of authority in Atlanta from police and fire chief and sheriff to chairman of the school board.

It may not be what one writer called "a black Camelot," but it is a far cry from what they used to call the home of "the darker third." As of 1986 the population of Greater Atlanta was still predominantly white, but the city itself was sixty-seven percent black.

117

And the birthplace of Dr. Martin Luther King, Jr., almost alone among Atlanta leaders, has been designated an historic site, along with his grave and the memorial Center for Nonviolent Social Change, which has daily tours and a library where his papers are preserved.

Beginning in 1986 Georgia joined the nation in observing his birthday as a national holiday.

—from *Peachtree Street, U.S.A.*

'ETERNAL MATRIARCH'

Celestine Sibley's 'Muv' Dies at 83

Mrs. Evelyn Sibley died in her sleep Thursday at about 5 p.m. at her home in Alford, Fla. She was 83.

Mrs. Sibley was the mother of Constitution columnist and author Celestine Sibley and had become well known as "Muv" to thousands of readers through her daughter's writings.

Relatives said Mrs. Sibley received large amounts of mail from readers during her illness and was thrilled to hear from them. Letters addressed simply to "Muv" were delivered to her.

"She was the eternal matriarch, strong and wise, merry and brave, and at the same time warm and loving—holding things together through times of trouble," said former Constitution columnist Harold Martin.

Martin, who worked for many years in the same office as Miss Sibley, said, "The passing of 'Muv' will leave a lonely place not only in the lives of Celestine and her children, but in the lives of all of us who came to know and love her through Celestine's column."

"Muv' came to be a favorite of Constitution readers because she seemed to represent the spirit, strength and sometimes oneriness of mothers of any age, of any time.

From some of Miss Sibley's columns were gleaned these vignettes:

"I'll never forget my sainted mother's attitude toward an old lady who was said to have killed her son-in-law with a potato rake," Miss Sibley once wrote.

"What did they do to her?" I asked, flabbergasted.

"Nothing,' said Muv calmly. 'He NEEDED killing."

In another column, Miss Sibley gave us this cameo of her mother, the cook:

"She is absolutely certain that nobody else in this world brings out the best in her oven.

"'You have to know its peculiarities,' she insists.

"To have her granddaughter, Susan, able to assemble the makings and turn out a delicious cake with the disloyal oven cooperating all the way is an irritation to Muv.

"'Susan does very well,' she says, grudgingly. 'But she doesn't have to paint the porch furniture. I didn't have any place to sit for two days.'"

Another insight into a mother's feeling toward her [daughter] —happy to see them on [a visit,] happy to find peace afte[r they] have left—is reflected i[n ...] ... Muv finally

got all of her friends and relatives out of her house—at least temporarily—and it suits her fine. A neighbor brought her mail to the door and he reported to me that she said, 'I'm alone at last—and I LIKE it'

"Lately, when I remarked that I knew how she felt and that I was trying to arrange to have a neighbor look after her on a come-and-go basis, Muv professed not to know what I was talking about.

"'Why I LOVE having you all with me,' she said with a sweetness I didn't trust. 'I can't imagine having said that. I wanted to be alone. It must be that old medicine the doctor makes me take that causes me to talk like that.'"

Mrs. Sibley was a native of Pearson, Ga., and was the widow of Wesley R. Sibley, a Creola, Ala., lumberman. She had resided in Alford on the Florida Panhandle for 35 years.

Services will be held at Alford Methodist Church at 2 p.m. Saturday. Maddox Funeral Home of Marianna, Fla., is handling arrangements, and the family has requested that [no flowers] be sent.

Survivors a[re ...] Celestine Sible[y ...] James W. Litt[...] Mrs. Richard [...] mis of New [...] Edward (Susa[n ...] Atlanta, and [...] children.

Chapter 5

FAMILY

Miss Louise Murphy is a triumphant symbol, in my memory, of the word *family* and what it means in the South. She was born a Culpepper, a condition in our county from which a female was never known to recover in one lifetime. She married Mr. Dean Murphy and they lived to marvel at and enjoy what she called "a long tail of grandchildren stringing out behind me." She is the one who taught me with firmness and Culpepper asperity, when I fumed to her about some recently acquired in-laws, "Sambo, if you want to hang on to this, you have to put up with that." There was no doubt that she loved her family, but it was also a certainty that her vision was clear and her judgment accurate. She was a grand, a glorious matriarch, and everyone who met her respected her. Me? I adored her.

I also adore Celestine Sibley. What a matriarch she is! Her Southern roots, her appreciation of blood, and her acknowledgment of kin, her observation of bonds and ties in families other than her own, have been shared and spread delightfully on the printed page. She understands with great good humor that no family is sacrosanct, that pomposity will be justly rewarded, that the very word *family* immediately levels the playing field so that all members can meet, cavort, compete, weep, and laugh. She understands that most American humor is based on some father-figure taking a pratfall. She knows it is better to laugh than to cry.

We have exchanged many stories, she and I. She likes the one my grandfather told on Will Sams, his nephew. Will

Sams was a hardscrabble child, born during the desolation of Reconstruction, and reared in a clan determined to maintain its values and its pride, neveryoumind the poverty engulfing the region. He grew up and married a Hodnett, a gentle lady of unblemished lineage.

They both held their heads high; they knew where they came from, and they knew who they were. Part of the creed they had each learned in their respective families was "Blood will tell." They believed that.

They had also learned, "Money isn't everything." It was good that they also believed that, for there surely wasn't any.

There was, however, plenty of homemade whiskey in the area, and Will Sams on occasion drank with more enthusiasm than discretion. This was strictly a male activity, since no lady of breeding, certainly not Cousin Mamie Hodnett Sams, would tolerate its presence in her home.

One evening, very late, Will Sams stumbled up the porch steps and sagged against his front door, entreating, "Mamie! Mamie! Let me in! I'm dying!"

Cousin Mamie hurriedly opened the door and supported him as best she could while he lurched down the hall and collapsed on their bed. "Help me, Mamie, help me. I've never been so sick in my life. For God's sake, help me, Mamie!"

Cousin Mamie was trying to undress him as fast as she could, but gently replied, "Yes, Will, I know you don't feel well. Let's get you to bed so you can sleep."

"Mamie, I'm worse than 'don't feel well,' I'm sick unto death. Mamie, I think I'm dying. Mamie, I want you to pray for me, you hear?"

"Yes, darling, I hear," she soothed. "I'll pray for you."

"Mamie," Will Sams raised his head and proclaimed, "leave my socks alone and pray for me. You don't understand. I want you to pray for me now. I mean right now!"

Cousin Mamie Hodnett Sams dutifully dropped to her knees and in her soft voice began, "Dear Lord, we thank Thee for the day that is just gone and for the many blessings you have bestowed upon us in the past, and we ask Thee, dear heavenly Father, to look with favor and have mercy upon my poor drunken husband."

Will Sams raised his head again from the pillow and roared most piteously, "Hell, Mamie! Don't tell Him I'm drunk."

Celestine, like a proper lady, always chuckles when I start the story of Will Sams and his wife Mamie (she was a Hodnett). Then with defensive skill, she aborts the retelling by saying she remembers.

Celestine always remembers. She remembers what is important. She knows that money isn't everything. She knows that to hang onto *this*, you have to put up with *that*. She remembers what family means. And she acts on it.

In her late eighties, Miss Louise Murphy, still the controlling matriarch, was convalescing in a hospital bed when Boots, one of her daughters-in-law, called her. "Muur," she said, "what do we do when a Stell dies?" Miss Louise's reply was crisp, authoritative, and realistic, "We get in the kitchen and cook!" Which one was it?

When Jennifer, our oldest granddaughter, died, it was a grievous family wound. Celestine was in the midst of chemotherapy for her cancer. She had discussed with me in matter-of-fact acceptance how intensely ill the treatments made her and remarked with deprecating laughter that she was as bald as an ostrich egg. In shock at Jennifer's death, I had not called Celestine. When we filed out of the country church at Jennifer's funeral and lined up in cars to go to the cemetery at Woolsey, I looked out at the crowd.

I briefly felt like Oral Roberts when he saw an eleven-story Jesus. Then I thought even more briefly of Joe Camel in drag. It was Celestine. She stood out from the mob looking at least ten feet tall. Her skin was translucent and lemon-yellow. Her head was wrapped in a turban and crowned with some improbable hat. My wife gasped, "She has no business being here in this heat, as sick as she is."

But she was there. Her recognition of my family bonds and my grief was a greater goad than her nausea, her weakness, her obvious physical exhaustion. In addition to the other things she knows about family, Celestine knows that grandparents aren't supposed to outlive their grandchildren.

I leaped out of the car and embraced her. We wept. Together. She was totally beautiful. And remains so.

Celestine triumphed over her illness, as she has everything else in her life. Today she sparkles, laughs, regales others with anecdotes, thinks of her friends and helps them.

Her marvelous writing reflects that she is fully aware that life is a mixture of joy and sadness, that families are mixtures of virtue and vice. I know of no writer who evokes that more vividly. Enjoy.

—Ferrol A. Sams, Jr.

Photographs on page 120:

top left: Vincent and Wolfie Schaum, Celestine's first great-grandsons
top right: Susan Sibley Hall Bazemore, Celestine's fifth grandchild
middle: Celestine's youngest granddaughter, Betsy Vance
bottom right: Celestine's grandsons David and John-Stephen Vance with a neighbor child
bottom left: Muv's obituary in the *Atlanta Constitution*
bottom center: Muv at Sweet Apple with her poodle, Jackie, and country dogs

Photographs on page 121:

top left: Celestine's dog, Kazan (Photograph by John Bazemore)
top right: Celestine with her first four grandchildren—left to right: Ted Bazemore, Sibley
    Fleming, Byrd Fleming, and John Bazemore
center: back row, left to right: Celestine, daughter Mary Little-Vance, daughter-in-law Marie
    Little, daughter Susan Bazemore. Front row, left to right: grandson Edward "Ted"
    Bazemore, son-in-law Richard "Cricket" Fleming with grandson Charles "Byrd"
    Fleming, son Jimmy Little with grandson John Bazemore, and son-in-law Edward
    Bazemore with granddaughter Sibley Fleming (Photograph by Floyd Jillson)
bottom: Celestine's grandson John Bazemore with her third great-grandson, John Conor
    Bazemore

Young'uns

A few years ago there lived in the north Georgia mountains a man I sometimes think of when the subject is children. Our friend Herbert Tabor told us of this gentleman, and, looking back, I wonder if it was mere coincidence that he usually thought of the story when he would see my children and their friends swarming over his strawberry patch like a plague of locusts or with their feet under the table in his kitchen wolfing down hot rolls and Mrs. Tabor's homemade preserves.

According to the story, Mr. Tabor's father, judge of the Court of Ordinary of Gilmer County, walked home from the courthouse to lunch every day and often got in a little work in his garden before he returned to his office. He was hoeing his beans one day when a countryman from up in the hills walked up, dragging in his wake a string of dirty, runny-nosed little children.

"Jedge, I want to talk to you," the visitor said.

"Well, make haste," said the judge. "I got to finish this row of beans and get back to the courthouse."

"What I want to ask you, Jedge," said the man, "is, Do you want some of these young'uns?"

"No, much obliged," replied the judge, continuing his hoeing. "I got about all the children I can clothe and feed and send to school."

"I figgered you'd say that!" the man shouted, triumphant in his disgust. "I been to the mill and the mine and the lumberyard, and there ain't a soul that wants any of my young'uns. All I got to say"—he raised his voice and shook his fist furiously—"all I got to say is it's a damned sorry place where you can't give away a young'un!"

The desire to give away a young'un may have struck me from time to time, but only fleetingly. My three and their nine, counting two little ones who died, have been...well, I'll tell you: While I was in the hospital recovering from the birth of my third child, my employer, the late famed *Atlanta Constitution* editor Ralph McGill, sent me a lovely little cache of cologne and dusting powder, not for the baby but for myself. With the gift came a note inquiring, "Haven't you found out what's *causing* 'em yet?"

Mary and M.L.K.

The civil rights storm broke over the country in the 1950s, and although I was alternately interested and shocked, sympathetic and frightened, it was from the position of a spectator. I took no part in it. My fourteen-year-old daughter did.

She had joined forces with a group of older teenagers who were meeting on campuses, picketing lunchrooms, marching down the streets of Atlanta carrying placards, boldly confronting the Ku Klux Klan which, placarded and berobed, came out to meet them. Proud of her idealism and her bravery, I was also terrified. Later, when she ran away from summer school, where she was making up a history course she had flunked, I was wild with apprehension and anxiety.

She had gone, I learned from her friends, to join Dr. Martin Luther King, Jr., in Montgomery—headed as surely for Mississippi's Parchman Prison as if she were an old and hardened criminal, I thought.

Years later, when she was grown and married and had two children, I was to recall that time with pain and a sharp sense of poignancy.

My five-year-old grandson John and I were driving across Alabama and Mississippi to Shreveport, Louisiana, to make an Easter visit with her, his aunt, and his cousins. It was a dark rainy night, and after a hamburger stop in Montgomery, John went to sleep on the back seat. We had reached Mississippi, and the rain was beating against the windshield and the lightning was flashing wildly across the sky. Static had made me turn off the radio, but it was lonesome in the black rainswept night, so I fiddled with the dial, hoping for news. I got a fragment or two about a shooting somewhere, before the crack of lightning and the roar of the wind and rain let the whole story through.

Dr. Martin Luther King, Jr., had been shot in Memphis!

The lights of a truck stop were just ahead, and I pulled off and sat there. The impulse of all newspaper reporters is to call the office when news of great moment happens, to ask, "Do you need me? Shall I come in?" But I was more than three hundred miles away with a sleeping child on the back seat and other children ahead waiting for me. The need for any services of mine would be over by the time I could get back, so I sat there by the Mississippi truck stop, watching the rain make mud of the parking lot, watching the big trucks pull in to wait out the rain and thinking about Dr. King, that kind man, that eloquent man. Gone.

My personal acquaintance with him was slight. He had done me a favor once. That day Mary had left school and caught a bus for Montgomery, I had called Dr. King.

I was frightened, I was frantic. With his own people being beaten and killed, my concern for my little white child might well have amused him. It didn't.

"She's got to *learn* history before she can *make* it!" I wailed. He agreed. He said he would find her and talk to her, and within a few hours one of his aides took her to the Montgomery airport, boarded a plane with her, and brought her home.

129

Sitting there by the truck stop, I wished that I had been as eager to do something to help his cause as my child had been. I wasn't even sure I had said thank you to him.

Everybody Needs a Ten-Year-Old Boy

From time to time I hear from my children about the age child I like best. Little babies because you can tuck them in their beds and go dig in the yard. Toddlers because they are responsive; hold out your arms and they run into them. (Sometimes. If you try to take them shopping with you they disappear under dress racks or behind soft-drink displays and you can't find them until you hear a crash.) Teenagers because they can bring in fireplace wood, cut grass, and change tires and will eat absolutely anything you decide to cook.

Some ages are more interesting than others, some more exhausting. Just to look at runabout children makes my back hurt. And then in the cool of the evening take one of that age, all bathed and powdered and ready for bed, out to swing in the hammock under the maple tree, and you forget the spillings and breakings, the chasing and lifting that went on all day. The squeak of the hammock chains, the sleepy sounds of the birds, the gradual onset of darkness suddenly seem endowed with magic. Baby hands that pulled the cat's tail, banged the screen door a thousand times, broke plates, and tipped over flower pots are still and somehow as appealing as starfish or open roses.

All ages have their charm. But there have been times when I was convinced that everybody needs a ten-year-old boy. That's the age, I'm certain, when a boy young'un is more company, more pleasure, and more help than at any other time in his life.

He's old enough to be housebroken, of course, and although he may not be meticulous about bathing and dressing himself, he can slough off a layer or two of the muck while playing with boats in the bathtub with no bother to anybody else. Who cares if he has cockleburs in his hair and hasn't combed it since some time last month?

He's also self-reliant about food. If it isn't cooked and set before him, he'll find it and eat it anyhow. He can, if it interests him, even fry up something for himself, usually something Euell Gibbonsish like daylily buds. He certainly isn't bound by Julia Child standards about what is suitable for certain meals. If there's watermelon to be had, it tastes as good to him for breakfast as at any other time.

A ten-year-old boy is old enough to eschew the childish prattle of his earlier years and talk about important things like books and how to make an outrigger boat out of bamboo or did you ever eat alligator eggs?

He's a contemplative being, the ten-year-old boy, who can hang by his knees from the limb of a tree, looking at the world upside down for long moments without breaking the silence of a summer evening. He can sit on his spine with his head tilted back and look at the sky for hours, as quiet as a cattail in a placid pool or a leaf on a windless night.

A ten-year-old boy is a chivalrous fellow, appreciative of his elders and uncritical of his peers. He's patriotic. Unlike his elders, he sees very little that's wrong with his country and a lot that is gloriously right.

He knows the Boy Scout oath, the Pledge of Allegiance to the Flag, and can sing nearly all of the "Star-Spangled Banner," no more off-key than anybody else. His favorite word is "neat," although he isn't, and his only expletive is "Neat-o!"

A ten-year-old boy isn't self-conscious about telling you that he likes you, hugging you hard with skinny all-elbows arms or crawling into your bed at night because he's afraid you got cold or lonely. He'll say now what he'll never say later: "You're the best grandma in the whole world."

And when he is driven away from you, he hangs out the back window throwing you kisses with a grubby paw.

At the age of ten a boy is, maybe for the last time in his life, eager to please you, enthusiastic about helping you. Take him on a trip to Disney World, and you don't find out until later that he was too old to ride on the merry-go-round but hid his embarrassment and boarded it anyhow because you were crazy to do it.

Mention to him that you have a burning desire to mulch your flowerbeds with old sawdust and maybe sprinkle a little on your compost pile, and he whirls into action. Older boys would find the sawdust pile troublesome to get to, a snarl of honeysuckle roots, and not worth the trouble. A ten-year-old boy finds it a challenge, a gold mine in the jungle, and joyfully figures out a complicated system whereby he can transport the rich dark mulch up the hill to the wheelbarrow, transfer it to the red wagon, and tow it by riding mower to the garden. What does it matter that he makes work for himself, that pushing the wheelbarrow all the way would be easier? He's helping you, isn't he? That's not work but high adventure.

If you have a ten-year-old boy in your family, you'd better hold him close and cherish him. Above all, know what you have—for the age isn't forever.

And Then There's Sweet Sixteen...

To a child, of course, sixteen is a milestone. There was the January when my daughter Susan attained that auspicious age. The rain dropped off the trees and whispered in the gutters and made a singing noise as it ran into the sewer under the street outside. And in the house she sat hunched over on the sofa with tears, big fat silver tears pouring from her eyes and running off the end of her freckled nose.

"What's the matter?" I cried, dropping raincoat and umbrella and pocketbook. "Are you hurt?"

She shook her head miserably.

"Are you sick? What's wrong?"

She gulped and brushed her eyes with the back of her hand, making great smears across her face.

"I'll tell you," she said. "I've been sixteen years old for *four* days, and I still haven't got my driver's license!"

132

I wanted to laugh, but in the face of such calamity I couldn't. I wanted to make soothing noises about oh, well, you've got the rest of your life to drive a car and it's not such a high privilege anyhow.

But that wouldn't do either. When you've been counting the days until your sixteenth birthday for about two years, four extra unallowed-for days of delay amount to a lifetime.

"I'm sorry," I said. "You know how it's been—something every afternoon. I haven't had time to take you to State Patrol headquarters."

She understood that the license bureau's hours were not necessarily going to jibe with my free time but still...the tears, the disappointment. So I agreed to let her be late for school and to arrange for myself to be late for work so we could make the momentous journey to the bureau the next morning.

Then I went to bed to pull the covers over my head and try to forget all the new anxiety, all the family squabbles, all the tensions attendant upon having another teenage driver in the family. But you cry peace, and there is no peace.

She came with that little book the State Department of Public Safety puts out and sat on my feet and asked me questions. How much visibility must a public carrier have before stopping to unload or take on passengers on the highway? How many days do you have to report an accident to the director of public safety? How many feet does it take to stop a vehicle traveling at a speed of thirty miles an hour? (She called it "vee-hickle.")

"Look," I said, "I've got my driver's license. I've been driving by ear since I was fourteen years old—and I can't worry about all that stuff now. It makes my head hurt."

"Mother!" She was shocked. "You mean you don't know the *rules?*"

"Comes the time when I need a rule, I know it," I said with dignity, putting a book up before my face. "I've never had an accident or had to go to traffic court in my life. See if you can do as well."

She finally went to bed, clutching the Safety Department's bible to her heart, and we did get up early and head for the State Patrol headquarters. I stood around with a lot of other mothers, yawning and drinking vending-machine coffee and praying that she would pass. She hooked her loafered feet around the rung of a chair, scratched her head with her pen, and labored over the written test. Then, beaming proudly at a grade of ninety, she went off with a trooper for a road test.

When she finally emerged, license in hand, she was smiling radiantly.

"Would you like me to drop you off at the office?" she asked graciously, beating me to the driver's seat in our car. And then, when we were under way, quite seriously: "Mother, you really ought to study up on the rules. That's one of the dangers on the highway today—middle-aged drivers."

Rolling Up My Hair

Sometimes a mother gets tired, and if there is anything more exhausting than exhaustion it is having children to help you rest. My own were teenagers, and I came home from the office after a long day, wanting nothing so much as bed. They had had their dinner, and mine was all ready. I was to take a hot bath, climb right into bed, and they would bring me a tray. You don't really need a tray for a hot dog, but they fixed one anyhow, with a flower on it in a teetering bud vase and a cup of very strong coffee—to keep me awake while I was resting.

Any woman who has had children as long as she can remember knows rest in the midst of the family is not pure and unadulterated. You have to put a hem in an urgently needed dress, eat soupy custard they saved for you, listen to a new Elvis Presley record, and talk to somebody's mother over the phone about a birthday party. All this before the ritual known as Rolling Up My Hair begins.

It seems to me that girls don't roll up their hair nowadays, and I count that progress for the human race. When my daughters did it, it was just the prelude to an interminable period of loving, ceremonious attention to the whole body and minute searching of the soul.

Questions like "Mother, do you think I ought to paint my toenails?" and solemn paeans beginning "I *wish* I knew what to do about my duck!" (a hairstyle, not a barnyard fowl) were easy to ignore. I could even listen to them puffing and blowing and beating their bottoms on the floor in an effort to look trim in the new-style pants. But then the Serious Talk starts.

"At last, Mother, I know your secret," was the way Mary began it.

"What secret?" I asked casually. Not that I had one, but you never know.

"I'm adopted," she said.

"Pooh," I scoffed, trying to wiggle the foot she was sitting on. "Get off my feet and go to bed."

"No, really, Celestine," she said, "it's time we were realistic about this."

"You call me 'Mother'!" I said automatically.

"If you insist," she said with an indulgent air. "But I know the truth. You and Daddy—I mean your husband, Jim—you all adopted me from a famous Hollywood producer. My true mother was a famous actress. You were sweet to take me in, but now I know."

"Ha," I said morosely. "Pure soap opera. You stop watching that stuff."

She was examining herself in the mirror on the closet door, raising first one eyebrow and then the other, sucking in her cheeks to make Katharine Hepburn hollows and letting a look of haughty languor half close her brown eyes.

"Just look at me," she said. "All your other children are redheaded. I always did think it was tacky," she mused, watching her sister coping with the bright red ends of the unhappy "duck." "Now I'm glad to know that I'm not a bit of kin to any of you."

She smoothed her hair and widened her eyes.

"My poor famous actress mother died before I was…I mean *when* I was born. And here I am with you people." She sighed. "It explains why you have never really loved me."

"Now look here," I said, sitting up in bed so fast the hot-dog tray, my own supply of murder mysteries, boxes of bobby pins, and unfinished sewing tumbled to the floor. "I'm tired of this lousy joke."

"Really, Celestine," she interrupted, giggling. "Do let us be realistic about this."

From her position on the floor, her sister settled the matter for both of us with the classic line from *Born Yesterday*.

"Leave us," she said languidly, "not conduct ourselves like a slob."

It was no way to spend a restful evening at home.

Hit Him Back, Stupid!

It wasn't necessary for the children to teach me to value children. As an only child myself, I grew up envious of big families and with a high regard for all young'uns. Not so my daughter Susan. She had to learn to like children from her own.

Susan was a kind and competent baby-sitter whose services were always in demand among our friends, although they recognized that unlike her sister she baby-sat for money, not out of an o'er-weening affection for little ones. Even when she went to the hospital to have John, she stoutly maintained that it would be cheaper, easier, and more fun if they got a cocker spaniel instead. John changed her.

She took up children, loving and admiring them and enjoying not only her own baby but the babies of others, marveling at their swift development, their various abilities and charms. In fact, she may have been in danger of swapping her youthful detachment for real mushyheadiness if it hadn't been for Ted.

Ted, who became the most amiable and companionable of teenagers, was born on Election Day, an act I considered sheer perversity. Why couldn't he have let his mother vote before he decided to come? For a few years he was a model of perversity, the reddest of our redheads, the angriest of Angry Young Men. He scorned baby talk. In fact, he scorned communication of any kind until he was over a year old. Then his first words came in a clear, well-rounded imperative. His mother was playing the piano and she sprang a song on him.

"Don't sing!" Ted ordered.

The only time I, his loving grandmother, was ever allowed to hold Ted was when he was debilitated by illness, suffering a raging fever, and due at the doctor's office momentarily. The rest of the time he brushed off babyish cuddling and devoted himself to such enterprises as putting sand in the piano or dropping the family silver down the sewer.

With a child like that I fully expected Susan to revert to her old attitude that babies are more trouble and less pleasure than puppies. But she doted on Ted. She really liked him, and occasionally I'd catch her viewing him with a mixture of awe and incredulity.

One day she reported to me that he had been watching bumblebees on television. She was pleased to see the depth of his concentration and hopeful that it was the beginning of a happy association between Ted and the great baby-sitter. Then she heard him say, loud and clear, "Hit him back, stupid!"

We were all staggered. Where, oh, where, did a two-year-old get such talk? Was television to blame, his older brother, or some bad companion like an aggressive three-year-old?

Secretly, I felt a little set up to behold that new and vigorous blood in the family. As a longtime pacifist and exponent of turn-the-other-cheek, it cheered me that we had a fighter. Nobody admires spirit as much as the mealymouthed. I didn't want Ted to know it, but I said hooray for "Hit him back, stupid!"

Three years later Ted became an author, pasting up, writing, and illustrating a volume with the title "Hate at All Times."

What's the Score?

John introduced me to football. I met it briefly when I was in school, of course, but when I stopped knowing the members of the team I stopped paying any attention to the game. John loved it from the time he was eight years old, and I began to go with his mother to watch him play when he was twelve or thirteen. I found all that tumbling around on the ground, the heaps of flailing bodies, confusing and a little frightening.

"Don't play that dumb game, honey," I begged him out of my vast prejudice. "They'll knock out your teeth and break your bones. Pay attention to English and history and forget football."

"Let him alone, Mother," my daughter Susan advised. "As long as he's interested in football he's not drinking beer or smoking pot. He's jogging and lifting weights to take care of that old body."

Beer drinking and pot smoking were real problems in some of our schools then, even some of our elementary schools. It was disturbing and heartbreaking and I wanted no part of it for our children, so I subsided. It was true that his physical well-being was important to John— as a means of getting on that rough turf on Friday afternoon and knocking down what appeared to me to be nice young fellows who had done nothing to antagonize him except that they wore muddy, grass-stained uniforms of a different color from his and showed an inordinate interest in gaining possession of a very commonplace-looking little ball.

Still, I went to games in preference to other forms of social activity. Friends asked me to parties, sometimes to meet celebrities like Erma Bombeck and a Saudi prince and princess.

"I'm so sorry," I would regret automatically. "We're playing Westminster Friday night."

That "we" shows you. I wasn't playing anybody. I was sitting on a hard bleachers seat, sometimes in an electrical storm, sometimes in sleet or record-breaking heat, worrying myself to death over things I didn't understand, like "first downs" and "conversions," which had nothing to do with either failure as I knew it or religious experience or exchanging your foreign money.

John's parents and brother and sister moved away to New Jersey when he was a high school junior, but he stayed behind in boarding school, not because he couldn't bear to be separated from his beloved school and dear relations but because be held varsity status here. If he went to New Jersey he couldn't play varsity football for a whole year!

"For goodness' sake," I said when I heard. "That's nothing to determine where you're going to live and go to school. A game!"

John didn't deign to argue against such ignorance and insensitivity, and I was, of course, glad that he stayed behind because he spent weekends with me, moving in when football season was over. The presence of that big boy in the house at night was comforting and cheering. His humor brightened my days, the logs he cut and hauled for the fireplace brightened my nights. As a result, I went to a lot of his football games by myself when I couldn't round up family or friends to go.

A man friend was with me the night John was injured while playing. An old football player in his youth, he kept up with the game far better than I did, and before I saw it, he said quietly, "John's been hurt."

John's lessons to me kept me in my seat. I had long since learned that female relatives were not wanted many places but especially on the football field or hanging over the fence behind the players' bench. With remarkable self-control I did not go plunging down on the field but sat very still watching coaches and a doctor moving with deliberate speed toward a great muddy hulk of a boy who lay on the ground, looking, from where I sat, awfully quiet and very vulnerable.

They leaned over him while the clock on the scoreboard stopped, and then two of his teammates hauled him to the bench and stretched him out there, using his helmet to elevate his right foot and a spare football as a pillow for his head. I was so caught up in the devices they

139

were using for succoring a fallen comrade that I didn't worry for about a minute.

"I hope John hasn't broken his foot," Jack said.

Suddenly the antiquated business of no-place-for-a-woman outraged me.

"Go see," I said desperately. "Go down there and ask the doctor. You can go; you're a man."

It was gall for me to say it, but I had to know.

The report was slow coming back. My friend spoke to the coach and the doctor and leaned over and said something to John. He signaled to me, an airy wave of the hand I knew was meant to reassure, to say John was all right. But looking at my big young'un stretched out in that ludicrous arrangement of helmet and football, I didn't see how he could possibly be all right. He was out of the game, wasn't he?

Jack didn't come back to his seat, and I had to know more. I packed up that gear you take to games—cushion, raincoat, thermos jug—and worked my way down to the fence.

"Is John hurt bad?" I asked Jack.

It wasn't easy getting his attention. He mumbled something about an intercepted pass and I realized he was doing the unthinkable, paying no attention to John but *watching the game!* I looked at John, and he had lifted his head from the football pillow and was doing the same.

140

Settled For the Night

Women should have known centuries ago that they could do absolutely anything, become editors, engineers, inventors, soldiers, sailors, surgeons, prime ministers, miners, scientists, because they had trained on something tougher—getting young'uns settled for the night. The trouble is that it's like childbirth or climbing Mount Everest. When the struggle is over, you forget what it was like.

The early part of the evening lulls you into thinking you've got it made. The late-day capers over the grass in pursuit of a ball or the dogs, suppertime and bath time and hammock time, are all velvet. You prepare a bottle (his comfort, his soporific, although he is now eighteen months old and can drink out of a cup) and you bear him up to bed, bathed and powdered and drowsy (you hope) at 8 P.M.

At first all is quiet and, glowing with self-congratulation, you clean up the kitchen and plan a leisurely bath. Then you hear the bottle hit the floor, followed by the soft plunk of the teddy bear. The slats of the crib creak complainingly. The air is rent by howls. The house is either on fire or he is being attacked by bears and alligators.

"Let him cry it out," my daughter had instructed me. So I hovered at the foot of the stairs, wringing my hands and listening. The tone changed. He was no longer frightened of demons. He was angry. He hollered and screeched, and there was accusation in every note. You know you have done something wrong, and you plod up the stairs to see.

Yep, his diaper needed changing and it was all my fault. He wriggled with delight over the operation, kicking me playfully in the stomach, whooping with pleasure at the sight of me.

Once more you put baby and bottle and teddy bear in the bed and return to your listening post on the bottom step of the stairs. All goes well for a while. He sings and rocks the bed. Then he lets out an experimental cry. You are unmoved. He cries again, neither in anger nor in censure but because he is sad and lonely, a neglected waif, an orphan, Oliver Twist crying in the night. You swallow hard and dry your damp hands on your apron. Maybe he's winding down. Maybe in a minute he'll go to sleep. He doesn't. The piteous wails tear at your heart.

Once more, up the stairs.

He was jubilant at the sight of me. He wound his arms around my neck, nestled his head against my shoulder.

"Bocka, bocka," he said softly, and I knew "rocker" when I heard it. I obediently took him to the old Brumby chair on the porch.

Darkness was beginning to settle on the woods. The birds made sleepy sounds. We rocked, we sang, and finally I filled a fresh bottle and stuck on a fresh diaper and hauled him up the stairs again. It was an uneasy quiet for a time—but it was quiet. Waiting, listening, I found my back aching, my clothes drenched with sweat. It seemed hours before I dared to tiptoe up the stairs to check.

He was a rose and gold Botticelli angel, the most beautiful thing in the world—a sleeping baby. It was 9 P.M.

—from *Young'uns*

Turnip Greens and Jelly Cake

Before my mother died in early summer of 1976 she wanted to talk about it. The subject of her own death fascinated her, and the long-unremembered details of her childhood and the lives of the relatives who reared her came back to her mind with undimmed freshness.

"Come, sit down and let's talk," she would say as the twilight deepened around her little house in the northwest Florida town of Alford, where she had lived in her girlhood and to which she had returned in the early 1940s.

I couldn't bear to. I didn't want to believe she would not recover from the pains that had begun to rack her eighty-three-year-old body. I didn't want to know where she had put the deed to her house, the only thing she owned, or the name of the man to whom she had been paying her burial insurance for nearly forty years. The stories of the hard times through which her family had lived were painful to me.

"I'll be there in a minute," I'd lie and tackle with renewed frenzy cleaning out the utility room, where she had been saving brown paper bags since World War II. I scrubbed her oven and cleared out kitchen cupboards and replaced shelf papers. In the daytime I dragged the ladder around the house and washed windows with a mindless, obsessive fury.

She sighed and turned her attention to any neighbor who might be passing the gate.

"Come in," she would say hospitably, "and tell me the news."

While two old ladies talked, I cleaned madly, relieved that I didn't have to sit still and listen. Now I grieve that I didn't listen. Now I know there's nobody left to tell me things about my family in general but especially the things about my mother, who was the most important person in all our lives for as long as she lived. When she died, I believe in her sleep, one hot afternoon in June, I was overwhelmed with guilt

143

that I hadn't been with her.

She had called Atlanta to tell me, I think. At least she said "that pain" was back in her chest.

"Get Bessie to take you to the hospital," I said, referring to her next-door neighbor and unfailingly kind friend, Bessie Powell. "I'll be there as fast as I can."

"No, I'll wait for you," she said.

"Muv, I'm six hours away," I said, exasperated. "I'll get there as fast as I can but go on to the hospital."

"I may and I may not," she said obstinately and hung up.

Four of my grandchildren were spending time with me in the country and I had obligations at the *Atlanta Constitution*, where I worked, but I made arrangements as fast as I could, and my son, Jimmy, and I took off for Muv's house. We stopped for gas in Columbus and I called her. No answer. I called her neighbor, Bessie.

"She's asleep," said Bessie. "I was just over there and she seems to be resting."

Three hours later we drove up to her gate to find a police car parked under one of the big oak trees and neighbors standing about on the porch and in the yard. Stupidly, I didn't realize what had happened.

"What's going on?" I asked Buck Barnes, who lived across the street from her.

"Your mother has died," he said. "About an hour ago, they think."

It took me a long time, months, maybe years, to realize she had done what she wanted to do. She had no stomach for going back to the hospital and putting up with tubes and needles and the hideous exposure of tests and examinations. She had loved life but she knew she had death coming to her, and she was ready to claim it. I think she walked into her room and got in her bed and willed herself to die.

She may even have been sure the day before that death was imminent because when I went into the kitchen I found that she had

done what she always liked to do when she knew that we were coming—"prepare" with turnip greens and a jelly cake, fresh cooked and
waiting for us.

—from *Turned Funny*

Bernard
Lavery's
Choice
seeds for
GIANT VEGETABLES

MARROW
Kingsize
Contains:
A Minimum of 7 Seeds
Packeted for Year End AUG '96
Sow by: AUG '98
SEC rules and standards Standard Seed

Chapter 6

GARDENING

Celestine Sibley is my kind of gardener and my kind of writer. She knows that gardening is always an iffy proposition; sometimes you win, sometimes you lose. But you always enjoy the process. As Celestine says, "The doing is the thing."

Her stories about her adventures—and misadventures—in newspapering and life have left me amused, amazed, and admiring over the twentysome years we've been friends and colleagues. She once wrote, "I have seen—and sometimes joined—fighters for everything from planned parenthood to banned fireworks." But as my own passion for gardening grew during the last decade or so, her gardening tales began intriguing me most of all.

Celestine's vast knowledge, cloaked in self-deprecating humor, always gets a day off to a good start. And, while she mercifully uses mostly common plant names, her enjoyment of language spices her conversation and writing with seldom-heard but forever-admired words and phrases: "a crisp green ruching of leaf lettuce" comes to mind, as does her expression, "putting in my oar," for inserting herself into a conversation.

Celestine's doings in the garden, shared with friends, colleagues, and leaders of her books and newspaper columns, comfort. They are as familiar as those of a sister or a mother. As familiar as our own doings in our own backyards. When she talks and writes about her less-than-impressive tomato crop at Sweet Apple, every gardener yearning for (but failing to get) big, red fruit by the truckload understands that he is not alone.

Since I plant very little food and reap even less, I take great solace in Celestine's observation that "the measure of success in gardening, like the measure of success in some other endeavors, is not always in the harvest."

Not wishing to dwell on the heartbreak of food-growing, I always feel a lot better when our gardening chats head toward flowers, shrubs, trees, and other growing things that feed the soul if not the body. When we talk about Carolina jessamine and boxwoods and azaleas and dogwoods she's grown and loved over the years, Celestine's passion always inspires me to go to my own garden and take a long, appreciative look. So it is with her writing. My own jessamine never looked or smelled better than after I read about hers, blooming beautifully in the spring, spilling over a trellis.

She speaks to gardeners everywhere when she writes: "For me spring comes when I kneel on the ground with a trowel in my hand, feel the sun on my back, and breathe in a special earthy smell that promises warmth and life."

Sharing the joys—and the failures—is only part of any gardening relationship. Like all who dig and plant in dirt, Celestine and I love sharing plants. I've always enjoyed her reports about how a fern or some thyme from my garden was faring in hers. And I couldn't wait to show her how the mullein she gave me grew to Jack-and-the-beanstalk height, inspiring countless memories of grandmothers who made teas to fight colds.

What started as a little sprig of variegated English ivy, known around my place as "Celestine ivy," now tumbles happily out of an old half-barrel and grows along the walk, longer and fuller each year—like our gardening times together.

Lee May

—Lee May

The Gardener

For the moment I am blessed among women—a gardener, a rich and successful gardener.

A mockingbird swaying high on the old apple tree melodically assures me it is so. The July flies, properly called cicadas, thrumming their tune of summer's ending in the woods, confirm it.

The fact that the beans I'm snapping came from a neighbor's garden casts not the slightest ripple on the deep pool of my content. My own beans just came in earlier, that's all, and not so profligately. Some gardeners grow beans, some button zinnias. Some grow spectacular watermelons, some exult over a volunteer vine that sprang up where the old compost pile was and has now climbed hand-over-hand to the top of a very tall pine tree, hanging swags of white bloom and tiny green pendant gourds all the way up.

Its not what you grow that makes you a rich and successful gardener, unless, of course, you are a pro, doing it for your livelihood. Some of my neighbors at Sweet Apple, farm-reared and still sustained all winter by what they produce in summer, regard my efforts as transient and grasshoppery.

To them that basket of tomatoes my six plants yielded up is not impressive—clearly not enough to can whole or convert to soup mix, juice, or ketchup. But to me those tomatoes not only look like the crown jewels straight out of the Tower of London, blazing rubies of flawless texture and matchless symmetry, they will provide great dripping tomato sandwiches for lunch and a bountiful salad for the twenty people who are coming to supper. And there are more where those came from, burgeoning green or slowly reddening on the vines.

It's inconceivable to me that there should be people in the world who are not attracted to and fascinated by the great natural laboratory of earth, water, sun, and seeds. It's as if there were children who didn't like Christmas. I'm sure such people exist somewhere, just as there are

151

probably children who sleep late on Christmas Day, but they are alien and exotic creatures beyond my experience.

It has little, if anything, to do with the fact that I am a Southerner and the South has been a predominantly agricultural area until the last few years when sidewalks and paved roads began to catch up with row crops.

The Edifice

My great-aunt Babe, one of the first gardeners I remember noticing, lived in a small town. It's true that she and her husband owned a farm on the outskirts of the town, to which she drove a horse and wagon to gather fresh vegetables several times a week. But the small, town-sized lot on a street corner is what I remember. It had not a handful of dirt that wasn't sternly and lovingly commissioned to grow *something*.

Water oak trees, put out as striplings, outlined the fence and shaded street and sidewalk. Azaleas screened the foundation of the porch and eventually reached up to meet the overhang of the roof. Rosemary and sweet basil, bachelor buttons and old maids, spice pinks and verbena spilled over the walk. They didn't have plumbing in that little town when I was a child and the privy presented to Aunt Babe a real challenge in landscaping, although she wouldn't have called it that.

The idea was to hide what was euphemistically called "the garden house" and the approach to it from the street. So Aunt Babe built a corridor of loveliness to The Edifice—trellises and fences freighted with rambler roses, morning glories, and the dainty little cypress vine with its lacy foliage and star-shaped red and white flowers. Honeysuckle cascading over the roof served the double purpose of camouflaging the sturdy utilitarian building and perfuming the air—a useful service in those days before aerosol air fresheners.

The path to the privy was a delight to a child. The gate leading from the yard to the garden area was weighted to swing shut by an iron pot suspended on a chain between the gate and a post set in the ground. Some people further weighted the cracked pots they used on gates by filling them with horse shoes and rusty railroad spikes and other scraps of metal. Aunt Babe put dirt in hers and planted petunias—not the bright, rich-toned hybrids we know today but an old-fashioned kind that looked as if they had been faded in the wash— pallid bluish white and wan bluish lavender. They came back year after year, growing paler all the time but blooming prodigiously and smelling heavenly, particularly after a rain.

Sage and peppers grew by the gate—a potpourri of hot reds and yellows and cool gray-green colors and fragrances, which would show up again at hog-killing time when Aunt Babe mixed and ground and seasoned her incomparable homemade sausage.

Strawberries outlined the walk to the outhouse, offering bouquets of white flowers and red fruit simultaneously. She had more room for them out on the farm but she could not trust Will, the hired man, to maintain constant and unflagging vigilance against the jaybirds. So she planted strawberries where she could personally protect them, rushing out many times a day to flap a dish towel or a broom in the faces of the feathered marauders.

153

All children knew that jaybirds tattled to the devil, going every Friday to take him fat pine splinters to keep his fire going and an inventory of all our sins. I wouldn't have crossed a jaybird for all the strawberries or figs in the world but Aunt Babe either didn't believe in the jaybird mystique or wasn't scared of the devil. She fought for her berries, feeding them the richest cow manure and mulching them with the dark moist "rakings and scrapings" from behind the washhouse. This was where leaves and chinaberries, weeds and sweepings from the yard were piled and the laundry tubs were emptied. I know now that it was a compost pile of sorts but Aunt Babe called it her fish-bait bed, drawing from it not only the rich black earth for her strawberries and pot plants but fat rosy earthworms she would take to the creek bank when she needed respite from her gardening.

Clearings and Fences

T ime was, I know, when aloneness was the condition of country living and not too desirable. My predecessors at Sweet Apple had to fight their way through a wilderness to get here and a symbol of home was a clearing—a little space where you could see the approach of enemy or friend, a swept area wild animals would be reluctant to cross, a clean spot where even the smallest snake track would be visible. The landscaping in those days didn't include foundation planting, which is to say flowers and shrubs around the walls of the cabin. Whatever ornamental bushes and trees the householder got were set off at a distance. Boxwood, if any, grew in the middle of the yard. The old clump of mock orange which was here when I came was up the slope and halfway to the garden.

The cabin itself was built close to the road—for company, I suppose, as well as for convenience. Transportation was difficult at best and people wanted to be as near to the public roads as possible. If anybody passed, the family with no telephone or automobile wanted to be at least within hailing distance. Even better, the passing traveler might stop and share a bed or a meal and relate all the news from the world beyond.

The need to be near passing traffic no longer exists but habit is strong. People who have small lots necessarily build cheek by jowl to their neighbors. But even with space to spare you'll see new houses going up, all barefaced and exposed, next to the paved road. And then when the craving for privacy hits, you'll see a redwood-enclosed patio

154

going up in the back.

The style for the "uncluttered" came along a few years ago and throughout the land you saw householders taking down picket fences and the wonderful old iron fences. They uprooted their hedges, whacked down their dark cedars and hauled away old and fat ligustrum bushes. (And a good thing that last was, too!) The fashion was for sweeps of unblemished lawn and maybe a few low-growing hollies around the eaves to sort of anchor the house to the land. (I had a friend who planted the thorniest holly she could find under all her windows to repel burglars.)

Everybody in the world went crazy about sun and the old passion for shade trees—for elm- and oak-lined streets—languished. With air conditioners humming away at every window, who needed trees to cool the air and shade the roof? We all spoke feelingly of openness and light and the joys of having the sun shine in our windows.

There were holdouts, of course, and my mother, Muv, was of them. When everybody else in her little town took down their fences on the ground that there was no longer any wandering livestock in the streets, Muv painted hers and trained a wisteria along its top runner. When her neighbors, lately come from yards hard swept with gallberry brush brooms, went in for wide and treeless lawns, Muv cut swatches out of hers to allot to a magnolia tree, a new water oak, a mimosa, a jacaranda, a tea olive, and assorted beds and borders of azaleas, camellias, and roses. Further offending the eyes of her neighbors, she planted a screen of vines and bridal wreath stage center so she would have a hiding place to sit unseen and sip her coffee in the early morning.

Newcomers to her street made the mistake of thinking Muv lived in this jungle because she was getting along in years and lacked the strength to prune. So when she went to the hospital for a few days once they generously got together and trimmed up her trees and leveled her bushy tangle of coral vines and bridal wreath to the ground.

155

It suited me very well not to be present when they came for their thanks.

By the time I got there she had replanted. The result is not one to gladden the eye of a landscape architect and draw photographers from *House & Garden* magazine, but it is right for Muv and her birds and her cats.

When she wanders forth with her coffee in the mornings she has, even on her smallish lot, some place to *go*, something to see. There are crooks and turns, little paths to follow, minute views to surprise the eye. You don't take it all in at once. There's a small patch of open lawn big enough for a bird bath and a feeder but not so big it taxes the strength of the man who comes twice a month to cut the grass for her. There are caverns of coolness beneath the bushes for her cats and a bench here or a chair there for Muv to rest upon.

Oddly enough, the crowding doesn't seem an impediment to most of Muv's plants. The pomegranate tree by the kitchen wall puts out blazing flowers all summer and an occasional harvest of fruit. Her tea olive by the screened porch sweetens the late winter and early spring air with its fragrance and a magnolia between her and her neighbor's fence perfumes the late spring and summer. Defying all the rules for growing roses as to spacing and pruning, Muv still manages to have something blooming all the time. Her camellias are a wonder and when all else peters out quantities of lilies lift pristine, gold-filled cups above an untidy green snarl of foliage, their own and other plants'.

156

Weeds

They are not content to creep along the earth but must reach for the sky and I guess they have more dominant personalities than effete, citified, cultivated grass blades. Anyhow, with a resignation born of desperation, I began to look, really look, at those weeds and they began to strike me as more interesting than grass.

For one thing, most weeds are herbs and are good for something. You can't make a poultice or a tea with grass. At least, I never heard that you could. But weeds...ah, country lore is full of stories about their magical healing properties. Cocklebur, for instance, can be steeped in a tea, sweetened with honey, and served up for sore and husky throats. (One ounce of dried leaves to one pint of boiling water, honey to taste, an old herbal says.)

Ground ivy, the tenacious little plant with the sharp, aromatic odor, filled me with despair when it got in flower beds and spilled over and snuffed out grass, until I read that the scent of its crushed foliage inhaled deeply will cure headaches when all other efforts have failed. It is also good for poultices for "abcesses, gatherings and tumours" and valued by gypsies for making ointments for cuts or sprains. Now I leave it where it grows and enjoy the scent it gives off when I walk or push the lawn mower over it.

Plantain, which took a stand in my yard, sending big turnipy roots down to China, didn't look at all ornamental to me until I learned its other name is "Englishman's foot." This is said to have been given to it by the Indians because seemed to spring up everywhere the white man went. Romeo in *Romeo and Juliet* recommended it "for your broken shin" and all sorts of authorities have found use for it in poultices to draw out poison, in infusions for diarrhea, and ointments for sore eyes.

But you really can't turn your front yard into a weed patch without offending the taste of all your neighbors and any random passerby. Which brings me back to the need of privacy. A woman's log cabin should be her castle and she should feel free, even comfortable, to have a lawn, mown or unmown, a weed patch, or a jungle, if it suits her. I wouldn't go so far as to say she could have a fence made of old tires painted silver or a gate of old bedsteads. But on the other hand, if she wanted such in her yard and kept it hidden from the general view...?

Fertilizers

From time to time when my daughters or other visitors help with the cleaning up after a meal bits of bread and an occasional meaty bone will find its way into my counter compost trove. (I used to use a bowl covered with a plate but at a wayside teahouse in Devonshire I bought a tin Devon cream bucket with a bail and a lid and it's perfect by the sink.) When it happens that tidbits of food get in the garden there's always danger the dogs will scent it and start digging. For a while I patiently picked out anything, however small, that might attract them, but then my friend Julia Fitch, Roswell librarian and a good gardener, gave me a priceless tip. Pluck a few toadstools and toss them on the heap and the dogs won't go near it.

"It seems a dirty trick," said Julia, who likes dogs. "But it's quick and it works. They evidently know a poison mushroom, even if we don't, and they steer clear of them."

Natural fertilizers have always appealed to me. Not that they smell any better—neither is Chanel No. 5. But you can *see* that they improve the texture of the earth. The soil in my garden and most of the gardens in this area has a substantial base of that famed Georgia clay. It looks beautiful when it's plowed in the spring, running the gamut from pale yellow to peach to burnt orange and finally that deep plum red. But for a hundred years or more most of it was planted to cotton and when a horticulturist speaks of land as being "cottoned out" you know what he means. It looks naked and exposed and gets that tired and drained look that you've seen on the faces of sharecroppers' wives. Nothing was put back into the soil except guano in the spring. It baked and cracked under the summer sun and washed and ran red into gullies and creeks under heavy rains.

My little patch, once part of a big cotton farm, was no better except that the last people who lived in my cabin back in the 1930s kept a few chickens out there and in all the years it has been vacant, weeds

158

grew up and died and returned to the soil. So there was a layer of top-soil containing some organic matter. I determined that it should have more and every time I heard of somebody who had cow manure or chicken litter free for the hauling I organized work parties. Once my son brought his girl out for the weekend and I awakened her early Sunday morning with a clarion call.

"Come on!" I cried. "Jack has brought his truck and we're all going to Alpharetta!"

She didn't ask what was going on in Alpharetta, a little town six or eight miles to the east of us, and it must not have occurred to me to tell her. I don't *think* I was so unsporting as to deliberately conceal the nature of our mission. Anyhow, when I handed her the shovel in a dairyman's cow barn and commanded her to start loading the truck I noticed for the first time that she was wearing superbly tailored slacks, hand-sewn loafers, and a cashmere sweater. She didn't whimper or try to beg off. She shoveled. (I always did like that girl.)

Out of every batch of cow manure I try to save some for what my mother calls "tea"—a dark brown liquid made from putting a sack of fertilizer in a barrel or drum of water and allowing it to steep. When Muv called, "Tea time!" in the late afternoon in Creola, Alabama, she didn't mean for us. She meant for her ferns and coleus and her tomato plants. She filled a bucket at the "tea barrel" and carefully and judiciously ladled it out, a dipperful at a time, to anything that looked the least bit "peaked."

159

The trouble with me and the natural fertilizers, of course, was that after hauling them and spreading them I expected to jump back and watch them do the rest. If I didn't step lively, I thought, I would be inundated by a lush green tide. I was. A lush green tide of weeds. Everything those cows and chickens had ever even looked at, much less eaten, came up in my garden and reached for the sky.

Arrangements

It was an old blue granite teakettle filled with Joe Pye weed. The soft mauve plumes of the roadside-creek bank wildling and its rough pointed leaves looked absolutely stunning in the battered tea kettle. Joe Pye is called "Queen of the Meadow" in the Southern mountains and many of my neighbors regard it affectionately because in the old days before paved roads and easy access to doctors and drugstores they found it useful for teas and poultices. And here it was in a flower show in the homely old kettle looking beautiful and regal and special—and far more interesting than three gladioli and seven carnations or even five orchids climbing a pole, which I saw in a show once.

For some reason that teakettle of Joe Pye weed took the hex off flower arranging for me. Why shouldn't flowers be homemade and handy too? Why shouldn't you use what you have—flowers if you have them, weeds if they interest you, leaves and boughs of pine and magnolia where you can get them? When I decided that I started having fun with flowers.

A big part of the joy of flower fixing is trying to suit the container to what the arrangers call "the material." Now I think everybody, even the florists, has deserted the on-purpose vase and let his imagination have free rein. I saw an old boot with cactus growing out of a hole in the toe in Dingle, Ireland. A neighbor of mine sticks Wandering Jew and geraniums in a wooden stirrup she found in the barn. I used to keep fresh bouquets in an old ironstone chamber pot in the bathroom but I sometimes had the feeling that it was awfully darned whimsical and cute and, besides, the chamber pot leaked a little so I gave it up.

But there are containers that manage to be interesting and fun without being notional and affected. I have a few that I cherish not only because of the way they enhance whatever they hold but because of their association. Before he closed up shop to enter retirement and make way for urban renewal, Walter Bailey, who had run a hardware store on Atlanta's Decatur Street that went back to the days of wagon yards, gave me a half a peck tin measure that he used to measure out seed corn. It's a dark almost brown red and all manner of things look pretty in it but especially the first bronze chrysanthemum of the season. I couldn't be separated from a jugware vase with a broken lip that Jack picked up at a roadside junk stand once. It is uneven, obviously homemade, but its grainy brown surface has a handsome glaze and when I put sunflowers in it I feel sorry for Van Gogh, poor thing.

Bottles are fine for a single bloom and a leaf and each year I find that I am growing more partial to the lone flower or the small bouquet. They accomplish that rite known as "bringing the outdoors indoors" without taking much away from the flower beds or robbing the woods. I was charmed to read somewhere that two or three violets, dug up roots and all and put in a shallow container of water with moss and rocks to anchor them, would last a lot longer than the picked bouquet and would look prettier and more natural. It's true. Every spring I get giddy at the sight of the old-fashioned gray Confederate violets which come up all over the yard, the bird's-foot violets which show their pansylike faces on dry banks along the roadside and the little white violets down by the creek bank. The children and I have brought home handfuls of them. It's hard to find something to hold them, although if you tie them together with one those little wired tapes and put them in a small cream pitcher or a toothpick or match holder, if such survives in your household, they look pretty. Even so they wilt fast.

Now we seldom pick. We take a trowel and dig up one or two plants, preferably those with some open flowers and some buds, gently wash the dirt from their roots and arrange them in water on the pewter plate, which is one of my favorite containers. A small fern or a foam flower plant makes a congenial companion and when the children have finished adding moss and rocks from that vast collection

161

they bring back from every walk (causing our washing machine to send out a horrendous clunking sound if you aren't careful to search blue jean pockets), the effect is woodland natural.

Pesticides

When one of my red rosebuds, whose unfolding I await with great excitement, doesn't unfold at all but looks like it was scorched with a hot iron I'm not exactly serene and accepting. I stomp around looking for the culprit and swearing vengeance. And when great ripening tomatoes, just hours from the table, come down with cancerous sores, the sound of my weeping, wailing, and gnashing of teeth rends the country quiet.

Nevertheless, before I launch chemical warfare I feel compelled to know more about what I am doing. The experts, although saving us from plagues of locusts and boll weevil and potato famines in the past, have had their moments of doubt and error. Remember how jubilant we all were about the way DDT disposed of flies and other household pests? (In South Alabama I know old-timers who still sing hosannas to it for giving us a generation or two of freedom from bedbugs alone.) The trouble was that the few pests that escaped the spray fled to bosky dells somewhere where they regrouped and promptly produced DDT-resistant offspring. So it looks like the only recourse is bigger and more deadly sprays. To be followed by bigger and more resistant pests? It's a grim prospect.

There must be a better way and I believe it begins with studying insects well enough to be able to identify them. The handiest book I have for this is Ralph B. Swain's *The Insect Guide: Orders and Major Families of North American Insects*. The pictures really look like the insects I encounter in life and the text is easy, concise, and oddly enjoyable. In addition to telling you which of your crops the chewer or sucker is likely to attack, it adds nice little gossipy notes about the minute monster's home life. For instance, Bessybugs. They are members of the prominent *Passálidae* family and, it occurred to me, probably in the South called Betsybug, which your relatives frequently say, "You haven't any more sense than." These citizens live under rotten logs and "bestow great care upon the young," even chewing the wood before their babies eat it. And the larvae of carpet beetles, officially *Derméstes maculàtus*, are sometimes used by museum workers "to clear the dried flesh from the delicate skeletons of small animals."

In fact, if this book has a fault it's that when you tear into the house sweating and breathing fire to look up some strange bug you might get so absorbed in reading about why the scarab was sacred in Egypt or how fireflies use their lights as a signal for mating that you forget entirely about the critter waiting in the jelly glass for identification.

Once you have identified the bug—and a magnifying glass is good for this—and know what to expect of it, if it prefers cabbage to carrots, for instance (and most insects eat one kind of plant, ignoring other kinds), then you can decide for yourself how far you want to go in poisoning him and his relatives and, incidentally, some of the air and the earth.

To me there are other routes that are appealing because they seem less drastic, more imaginative and just plain interesting.

My neighbors Jerry and Polly Eaves, notable for building the settlement's first swimming pool, are also impressive because they leave insect control to a family of potracking guineas.

Guineas never touch a vegetable or a flower, they tell me, because they sate themselves on juicy bugs. Even better, they make such an infernal racket that the young Eaveses practically never see a snake. Snakes, being lovers of peace and quiet, take to the tall timber to avoid the clatter of guineas.

For some time I've thought of installing a few guineas at Sweet Apple, but recently bantam chickens have taken my eye. They are peerless when it comes to insect pests, my neighbors tell me, amazingly prolific and hardly ever touch garden truck unless a low-growing and flamboyant tomato takes their eye. The care needed by domestic fowls has deterred me so far, but my neighbor Olivia Johnson says she will give me a start of banties—a rooster and two hens—out of her very next setting of eggs. And I'll take them, I think, because my mother says a country place doesn't seem furnished if you don't have at least one rooster to crow and a few hens to supply eggs for the table and fertilizer for the garden.

Somewhere I read that turkeys are highly recommended as garden police and if they eat their weight in bugs, as birds are said to do, it would be an orgy to end all orgies. Ducks and geese have been used in some places to eat the insects and weed strawberry beds and cotton fields. Generally they have a reputation for sticking to business and leaving garden crops alone, but I've heard that ducks have a secret yen for young onions, especially in the spring, and since I only plant one row of onions, one row of shallots, and a small bed of chives it wouldn't take a duck on a spree long to decimate my entire crop. Funny, while ducks relish young onions, rabbits, they tell me, abhor them and won't even darken the garden that is surrounded with onions.

Enlisting the aid of fowls to handle weed and pest control appeals as a simple and direct approach. So is hand-picking the bugs from the plant and dropping them in a bucket of kerosene but ah, how I hate that job, particularly those big soft green horned cutworms. It seems easier to make paper-cup or foil collars for the tomato plants when they are young and it works. I've noticed that if you can get a young tomato plant up some size it doesn't seem attractive to cutworms. Other things move in, of course, but there's a saying among organic gardeners that if the soil is good and the plant is strong and healthy it will probably survive, and I believe it. The idea is maximum biological efficiency in your department to throw off the effect of insect attackers, as human beings in the pink frustrate disease germs.

Gardening lore is full of all kinds of safe home remedies for pest control, some of them time tested and some of them, I suspect, old wives' tales. Since I am in the midst of trying some of them for the first time I can't vouch for their effectiveness. I can say they add a new element of excitement to gardening.

There are hideous brews, of course, which I won't try except as a desperate, last-ditch measure—urine to repel grasshoppers, for instance, and an evil potion made by picking off the most troublesome bugs, putting them in a bottle containing a little water and letting them decompose. The resulting juice is said to be very efficacious as a spray because most insects have a superstitious way of avoiding the dead bodies of their own kind. You try it if you like, but I lost my license to practice witchcraft.

My sage, which Olivia planted for me back of the woodpile one spring day when I thought it was too hot for the young plants to survive, flourishes on neglect. But watch it, warns another neighbor, there are certain people whose very touch will kill sage. These include menstruating women.

The nicest and most interesting garden health measures are plant repellants or the practice of companionate planting. Janet Gillespie advanced the cause of marigolds in her book, *Peacock Manure and Marigolds*. This smelly little beauty affects some insects as it does some people. They turn up their sensitive noses and move out of its range. Its roots are also said to excrete something which kills soil nematodes. So I edge my garden with dwarf marigolds and plant the tall beauties anywhere I can find a spot to stick them. They have blossoms almost as big as football-season chrysanthemums and one package of seed, started early in a flat in the house, goes further than practically anything you can buy.

Garlic is also said to be as effective in holding some insects at arm's length as it does some people. I planted a bulb beside each rosebush, and next year I'm hoping to have enough to stick them around every peach tree to see if they will turn back the borers.

Up at Chadwick's, the old-time general store which has served the people of this area for more than a hundred years, when you buy your turnip and mustard seeds loose from the big seed bins, instead of in the more expensive packages with pictures on them, they will throw in a scoop of radish seed. It's the custom of the country to sow them all together, counting on the radishes to save the mustard and turnips from lice. So far I have a good stand of young greens without a sign of trouble anywhere. Radishes are also said to protect squashes from squash bugs.

The stinging nettle school interested me. This powerful plant (advocated as an aphrodisiac in old herbals) is said by old gardeners to repel aphids and to enrich the soil. So I left a few plants in my salad-green bed expecting great results. Olivia is so kindhearted she hated to tell me that those stalwart nettles I was counting on weren't stinging nettles at all but another kind of scratchy weed which was not only of no value but could become a pest itself.

Anything that is strong smelling seems to excite or disgust bugs. Even a fragrant hand lotion will draw so many bees, yellow jackets, and gnats on a summer morning that you have to come in the house and wash with yellow soap. The herb fragrances which are a delight to people—mint, rosemary, and sage—are said to disgust the cabbage butterfly. Corn borers, according to some observers, can't work within range of geranium or marigold smell. Santolina and southernwood, which I have planted on the rock wall near the porch, should by all accounts be in the garden to keep away moths. And let's see, there are moth balls which will keep away rabbits if scattered around the lettuce patch and black pepper which, if sprinkled around squash vines, will repel squash borers. (An old recipe for keeping houseflies, blowflies, and those nasty green bottle flies away from the gardener is to wash your clothes in soap suds to which oil of anise has been added.)

166

Just as there are plants that jog along together happily neighboring, there are many others that seem to offend each other. Tomatoes are good neighbors to asparagus, they say, repelling the asparagus beetle, but poor neighbors to peppers and corn, drawing the same kind of pests.

Wood ashes, which I have in abundant supply in fireplace weather, go on my garden automatically and I don't have any way of knowing if they turn back hordes of maggot flies and scab, as they are supposed to do. I put them there because somewhat vague assurance of most of my gardening friends that they are "good for the soil." Since I haven't seen any maggot flies or beet scab I like to believe it's true. It may be that maggot flies and scab didn't see anything that interested them in my small patch and passed on to better pickings.

Bees

"Yet not without some soul does one eat the honey of his own hives. One cannot assist his bees in all their sweet work without learning many a lovely thing among the meadows, without hearing many a sweet wild note within the woods."

—Dallas Lore Sharp

L arry Chadwick, scion of the old storekeeping family up on Arnold Mill Road, is a young man of many interests and enthusiasms, all of which appear to be infectious. At least, when he told me that what I needed at Sweet Apple was a hive of bees—a hive of *his* bees—I capitulated at once.

"Where are they? Can I have them now?" I asked right away.

Busy as he was waiting on customers, Larry paused to give me a quick lesson in beekeeping. You don't just grab up a hive of bees in the middle of the day and stick them in the back seat of your car and haul them home with you, he said. For one thing, workers of the hive are likely to be away at their far-flung places of employment. And there was the additional matter of getting stung. Had I ever been bee stung, he asked.

Well, I've been stung by a great many members of the flying fraternity but I don't remember any bees. The reason, I told him smugly, is that I'm a very calm and tranquil person. I don't exude fear or nervousness, both of which excite bees. In fact, I suggested modestly, I am probably a natural-born beekeeper.

All the beekeepers I ever knew were quiet people. I might say, *admirable* people. They have been peaceable, contemplative types—farmers, philosophers, poets—eternally caught up in the mystery and beauty of life.

"Really?" said Larry distractedly, ringing up the price of a sack of fertilizer and a tractor part for another customer. "Well, my wife, Sandra, is caught up in honey. That's why I've got to get rid of some of my bees. It's all over the place in tubs and dishpans and on the kitchen floor and in the baby's hair. Sandra says it's those bees...or her."

It wasn't exactly the approach of Pliny or Vergil, a couple of other well-known beekeepers, but it was all right. Larry was going to give me some bees and I couldn't wait to get them.

It took several months for the bees to be delivered. That was summer and not a good time for disturbing them, Larry said. Early autumn came and the evenings should have been cool enough to drive them in to bed early so we could take the pickup truck and move them about first dark. But it was a pretty hot fall. And every time I'd call up and ask Larry if the propitious hour for bee moving had come he would say no. Like small-town people before air conditioning, all the bees seem to gather on the front porch of the hive and fan themselves on a hot evening.

Sometime in the winter I finally got my bees. My neighbor Quinton Johnson, who used to carpenter for me occasionally, said he would take his truck and go get them first chance. And one morning before good daylight I heard Quinton's truck in the driveway and then the sound of the wheelbarrow—and then the sound of Quinton running!

Despite Larry's efforts to tape up the entrance to the hive for the trip, something had joggled loose and the bees were pretty mad at finding themselves in a mobile home. They took their wrath out on Quinton.

He's not allergic to bee sting, and after he had brushed off a few stingers and applied a little tobacco juice to the wounds he came back and we edged the hive into position in the woods beyond the garden.

There began the love affair that no gardener should be denied— the cultivation of bees.

Bees are more company than beans or tomatoes and their product is without compare. At least, to the doting beekeeper. I used to be choosy about getting light honey, giving myself connoisseur airs about that which is made from the blossoms of the sourwood tree. But now whatever comes out of that hive back behind the garden is Our Own Honey and richer and prettier, more fragrant, and more delicious than that which the sacred bees on Mount Dicte fed to the infant god Zeus. (You know, of course, that's why bees have so much shining gold on their bodies and in their wings? Zeus, when he finally made it to Mount Olympus, rewarded the bees for feeding him honey by clothing them with gold. The goat Amalthaea, who supplied him with his milk, was placed in the sky as the star Capella, which shows you what the rewards for social service were in those days.)

Ever since I read of a man who grew cucumbers in glasshouses in New England and had to pollinate the blossoms by hand until he hired some bees for the job, I have been certain that my garden needed bees. Then I read of California fruitgrowers who rent bees to make sure their orchards are well pollinated and I knew at once that my two apple trees and halfdozen peach trees were crying for bees.

The bumblebees and butterflies and sundry pollen gatherers and spreaders were all right in their places, but how could you be sure they were really working? With bees, there's no question. Every day the sun shines those bees beat me out of bed and if there is a flower blooming anywhere they are there, dipping into it for nectar, coming out dusted with pollen. The least impressive flowers in the yard get their loving and diligent attention. When the wild persimmon blooms I scarcely notice its flowers but the bees cover it. They fill the wild cherries with their humming and make a lyre of the pear tree.

Clearly every garden needs bees. More than the garden maybe, the gardener needs bees. Their life style is so interesting, their place in literature so entrancing, the lore and superstition surrounding them so hair-raising. All this and honey, too.

Since I read Maurice Maeterlinck's classic, *The Life of the Bee*, many years ago I have been a potential beekeeper. He made their golden cities of wax, their flower-filled world seem far too fascinating to miss.

"To him who has known them and loved them," Maeterlinck wrote, "a summer where there are no bees becomes as sad and as empty as one without flowers or birds."

Of course, I can't really see what goes on in that hive. I hope someday to invest in one of those glass-sided hives that dealers in beekeeping equipment sometimes have so I can observe their highly organized home life in operation. Meanwhile, I go out daily to check their goings and comings and to be sure they are still there.

When the weather gets very hot they are prone to congregate outside the hive and the first time I saw that happen I was sure they were swarming. I rushed to the telephone and called Larry Chadwick, who interrupted some transaction in seeds or fertilizer or farm machinery, to soothe and reassure me. That's just par for hot weather, he said.

The next time we yelled for Larry it was a bona-fide swarm. I walked out to the car on my way to work one morning and the air was full of bees, gold-winged little bodies dipping and swirling in some kind of gala holiday dance.

By midafternoon my neighbor Olivia had found them clotted in a sort of heart-shaped wedge on a pine branch at the edge of the woods. I had a spare hive, bought for two dollars at an old farmhouse auction, and Larry suggested that we put it as close as possible to the hanging cluster of bees. To make sure that it was really close, Jack and Jimmy constructed a platform out of two-by-fours right under the pine branch and set the hive on it.

We held hourly consultations with Larry. No matter how busy he was, this was urgent. Suppose the bees went away? Something I had read gave me the feeling it was terrible luck to be deserted by one's bees.

As long as we could see we sat on the back steps and watched that clot of living bodies on the pine tree. When it got too dark to see we gave up and went indoors and worried.

The next morning the cluster on the tree limb was gone. There was no activity around the spare hive. I went fearfully to the old hive, expecting to mourn an empty house, and there were the workers coming and going as if nothing had happened. They had apparently enjoyed one day off from their labors and then slipped back into the old routine. Now we are waiting out the time when a new queen is crowned and the drones take to the air with her.

But you can't say bees are capricious, notional creatures. Whatever they do is part of some super plan. If they kick up their heels on a cool and shining day in June you can bet your boots they'll work overtime to make up for it.

The trouble may have been, Larry suggested, that they had filled their house with honey and were looking for new worlds to conquer. Anyway, a few days later he and another neighbor, Jim Holland, were robbing their bees and they offered to come and rob mine. I had to be in town at the time and I thought they might decide to skip my hive in their rounds of their own, but the next morning when I walked out on the screened porch there were four little television tables set up with dozens of plates they put meat in at the grocery store holding wedge after wedge of creamy comb oozing dark amber.

—from *The Sweet Apple Gardening Book*

A PROCLAMATION
IN HONOR OF
CELESTINE SIBLEY

WHEREAS, Columnist Celestine Sibley remembered old teachers whose contributions to Georgia education have been considerable, and

WHEREAS, She investigated the plight these faithful teachers are enduring due to meager pensions, and

WHEREAS, She wrote an article, published January 8, 1984 in the Sunday edition of THE ATLANTA JOURNAL and THE ATLANTA CONSTITUTION calling attention of the public to the need for assistance to these teachers, indicating her own willingness to lend support, and

WHEREAS, She requested in the article that public support for House Bill 169 be forthcoming, including letter writing to Governor Joe Frank Harris; be it

RESOLVED, That Miss Sibley be thanked by the Georgia Association of Retired Teachers and presented a copy of this Resolution; and be it further

RESOLVED, That Miss Sibley be made an honorary member of the Georgia Association of Retired Teachers.

Date: June 12, 1984

To Celestine, my Favorite
Figure Skater
(Inspired by Holiday on Ice)

ATLANTA. GA.
es
N ELEPHANT
AL FARM
AMPSHIRE
"NASHUA"

To the
SCHOOL CHILDREN of
ATLANTA, GA.
for your Pet
COCA 2"
From the
SCHOOL CHILDREN of
NASHUA, NEW HAMPSHIRE

Everyday Friends

Chapter 7

FRIENDS

Celestine Sibley knows that God and literature are in the detail and that they are congenial there. She reaches into all of the corners of life and describes the specifics so precisely that she is forever breaking through the particular to the universal. She tells you about a little girl that lives off a country road somewhere in Florida who hasn't even heard of Christmas. She makes you cry and breaks your heart, but her heart is not broken. She can get by with her good work because she is the reporter, the storyteller. There is a dry, acerb quality to her perception that keeps her clear-eyed. What she sees is awesome.

In some odd way, Celestine's writing depends on friendship and contributes to it. Her books and columns reach a vast confederacy of readers. A huge number of them become her friends. They pop up all over the place: waitresses, parking-lot attendants, dog trainers, governors, presidents, bootleggers, safecrackers, and if this weren't a serious introduction I would add chicken-catchers, earth-stoppers, and human cannonballs. Wherever she finds them, they identify themselves with great confidence and do whatever they can for her in that moment.

Celestine's masterly talent for friendship seems to involve no art at all. Oh, she is an artist in the true sense in her work. But the remarkable thing to me is that she does not set out to dazzle, overwhelm, or befriend anybody. No grandstanding, no social climbing or odious toadying of any sort. Her genius for friendship seems to depend on the fact that she is never looking for advantage. Celestine is not acquisitive. She is constantly being enthralled by people who have absolutely nothing to offer her except the pleasure of their company.

Who pleases her? How is the landscape of Celestine Sibley's life peopled? Extravagantly. She has a Dickensian gift for enjoying the whole zoo of life around her. If you read Celestine, you are acquainted with:

- Mrs. Arizona Bell, who wore a football helmet when she sold newspapers at Broad and Walton Streets in Atlanta. She had ridden a horse in Buffalo Bill's Circus and was unintimidated when Celestine dressed her up and took her to the Metropolitan Opera.

- Miss Anna May Smith, who drank water out of a rain barrel and lived on Bass Street in a house pulled down by kudzu. The police picked her up on some charge and gave her a bath. They called Celestine to report: "We found $10,000 sewed into her clothes and underclothes."

- "Pee Wee, the safecracker, who was a sweet person. I got him out of jail."

But, of course, sometimes Celestine is a high flier. In 1996, the Georgia House passed a Resolution of Special Praise for Celestine. She was proclaimed the best-known and most beloved journalist in Georgia, and it was noted that the state's politicians generally regarded her as the finest reporter they had ever known.

It is not necessary to say that they were her friends.

Celestine writes about the connectedness of all human beings. Sometimes this becomes a covenant that brings people into accord. Readers find redemption and hope in her work. It is almost as if she had the power to make all people friends.

William A. Emerson, Jr.

—William A. Emerson, Jr.

Photographs on page 174:

top left: From the Ralph McGill Award for Lifetime Achievement in Journalism to this proclamation from the Georgia Association of Retired Teachers, Celestine's many awards
could fill a vault.
top right: Parker Lowell, a friend of Celestine who worked at the copy desk at the *Atlanta
Constitution,* drew this cartoon upon Celestine's receipt of the Christopher Award
bottom left: Coca the Elephant (Photograph by Associated Press)
bottom right: Celestine at Larry Ashmead's house on the Hudson River

Photographs on page 175:

top: Ralph McGill, famed editor of the *Atlanta Constitution* (Photograph by Kenneth Rogers)
middle: Mayor Hartsfield at the Atlanta Driving Club congratulating Celestine on her
Woman of the Year Award
bottom: art project made by Celestine's daughter Mary Little at Sunday School

Ralph McGill

Once somebody said I wrote what McGill told me to write. He laughed aloud: "I never *told* her what to write—and if I did make a suggestion she ignored it."

That's not exactly true but it's close. He didn't tell us what to write. He took pride in saying that the *Constitution* hired writers and let them write.

A young newcomer to the staff came to my desk not long ago.

"Who is that man in the picture out there in the hall?" she asked.

"Why, Ralph McGill," I said, surprised.

"And who was he?" she asked.

She was polite lest she offend me by her failure to recognize some local hero, but she was also a determined seeker after knowledge.

It was a question I found unsettling. How could any newspaper person, however young, not know? Could any American who knew of George Washington and John F. Kennedy not know of Ralph McGill?

"Did you know him?" she asked, and I told her that I did. And then I sat there for ten minutes wishing I had known him better, had paid more attention and learned more from him in all the years that he had wandered, distracted or amused or curious, about in the *Constitution* newsroom.

He was often there, leaning over to read telegraph copy as it flowed in a paper tide from the Associated Press printers. He questioned reporters and editors about local and state stories. He often sneaked into his old bailiwick, the sports department, to hide out and knock out a column while visitors waited and the telephone shrilled in his office.

I have a favorite example of how he handled words—oddly enough at a time when he was supposedly handicapped by strong drink. You will find people even today, bitter, hate-harboring individuals, who like to say that McGill was a drunkard. It is not so. In all the years that I knew him I never knew him to drink excessively—at most a glass or two of wine.

But I have a friend who did see him drunk once. She lived next door to Mr. McGill and his first wife, Mary Elizabeth, and she adored them. One night she saw them arrive in their driveway but before she could speak to them, Mrs. McGill, who was driving, got out of the car and stalked angrily toward the house. Mr. McGill appeared to be drunk.

She said Mrs. McGill called, "Come on in, Ralph," but he was weaving somewhat and kept bumping into the only tree in the yard. "Ralph, come on in the house!" Mary Elizabeth repeated.

"I'm trying to," our boss said piteously. "I just can't get through this impenetrable forest."

Even under adverse circumstances he had a grip on the language. Members of the staff were always welcome in his office. In fact, *everybody* was welcome there, business and civic leaders perhaps less so than colorful politicians, a black waitress looking for a job for her son, the retired farmer who sold flowers down at the corner.

The ubiquitous *meeting,* which is so essential to today's newspaper operation, was then unheard of. Communication between the editor and the staff was personal, one on one.

Once I witnessed what amounted to an editorial meeting. Mr. McGill walked out into the newsroom and inquired about a brilliant, alcoholic, old-time reporter who was in Savannah on assignment.

When had he been heard from?

It had been quite some time.

The editor sighed heavily.

"When you hear from him," he said, "for God's sake, somebody read his copy. He can call everybody in Chatham County an S.O.B. so subtly it'll take them three days to know it."

He walked away. End of meeting.

More often, reporters went in his office to borrow rent money, to get him to co-sign notes at the bank, to tell him their troubles, or to just prop up their feet on his desk and talk.

On one occasion that I know of he dealt with a cuckolded husband even more adroitly than his friend Ann Landers could have done. We had a staffer who came back from the war to find that his wife had been having an affair with a *Journal* reporter. The husband, a veteran Marine, got drunk and got a gun and went to see Mr. McGill. He was on his way to shoot the scoundrel at the *Journal*, he said.

He was absolutely justified, Mr. McGill told him. There was clearly only one thing to do and that was to kill the rascal. But—and Mr. McGill appealed to that strong sense of loyalty in all *Constitution* staffers— "Don't do it on *Journal* time. No use giving them the story. Wait till their deadline has passed."

The angry husband saw the logic in that. He laid his pistol aside and waited for *Constitution* time—and incidentally sobered up. The urge to kill passed, and he ultimately divorced that faithless woman and married another, nicer girl.

McGill's celebrated predecessor, Henry W. Grady, is said in the school books to have "loved a nation back to peace" after the Civil War. Love of region may have had much to do with McGill's stubborn, persistent, sometimes wrathful fight to get the South ready for integration. There's no doubt that he loved the land of which he wrote so movingly, but I think it was love of humankind that propelled him into the long, patient fight for civil rights.

McGill flayed the South and the nation about the inequities of integration, about the Ku Klux Klan, and about the demagogic politicians as represented by Eugene Talmadge. Like the alcoholic reporter on the Savannah assignment, he did it so skillfully that his subjects sometimes didn't know they had been harpooned until they saw blood.

Talmadge didn't take McGill's assaults on his brand of politics lying down. He incited his followers to near riots at political rallies

181

throughout the state when he lit into McGill. "Tell 'em about Rastus McGill, Gene!" the group called "the tree-climbing Haggards" would shout. And ol' Gene would reply, "I'm a-comin' to that!"

It introduced a litany that enlivened barbecues and campaign stops, but back at the shop we worried about our boss. He and his family had been bomb-threatened and marched against by robed, masked Klansmen. He was the target of nasty phone calls. Sometimes at the office we were able to field them for him, particularly if he was away.

He handled those that came to his house with typical imagination. He had a little dog he named Rastus and trained to bark into the telephone. So when in the middle of the night he was jangled awake by the telephone and a voice said, "Is that you, Rastus?" he could say calmly, "You want to speak to Rastus? Just a minute."

He would hold the receiver out to the dog, who would leap into action, barking vociferously until the caller, eardrums aching, hung up.

When a political battle was over it was not Mr. McGill's nature to gloat or engage in recriminations. He became a personal friend of both John and Robert Kennedy, bringing them through the newsroom for the staff to meet when they visited Atlanta and accepting an invitation for himself and his family to dine with them in Palm Beach.

He was boyishly pleased that the *Constitution* was one of the papers President Kennedy read each day. When Jack Tarver, as publisher, pointed out that getting our newspaper on the White House breakfast table every morning was horrendously expensive, McGill sulked.

"I'll pay for it myself," he mumbled. "Out of my own pocket."

Tarver told of the high cost of getting the paper specially delivered to the airport, paying its air fare, and then getting it specially delivered to the White House. It was a tidy sum but not too much, McGill insisted heatedly. In the end, he realized Tarver was baiting him and he subsided, grinning, knowing that he wouldn't have to foot the bill personally.

Even as he sent off a telegram congratulating John Kennedy on his election, McGill dispatched condolences to Richard Nixon, a man he seemed to like personally after participating in his "kitchen cabinet" meeting in Russia. But he had privately suggested that election of Nixon might be punishment from God, a "scourge" comparable to visitation from Attila the Hun.

And he did not live to see Watergate.

"The only way McGill could have supported Nixon was for him to have been running against Count Dracula," wrote Harold Martin.

He did, however, cover Nixon's first inauguration—a performance notable to the staff because he suffered miserably having his copy cut, even as we did.

Turned loose on a story, McGill was prone to overwrite, and copy came pouring in from him in a flood, a deluge. At the inauguration he covered everything, including how Atlanta's police chief Herbert Jenkins looked in white tie and tails.

And like that of any other reporter caught by a space shortage, his prose was amputated. He set up a howl heard 'round the newsroom, dashing off a memo humorous but with undertones of anger. He delineated the deletions one by one, ending with, "At any rate—as I learned forty years ago—it is hell to be cut."

183

—from a speech given at the ceremony for the
Thirteenth Annual Ralph McGill Award
for Lifetime Achievement in Journalism

Sister Henrietta Keel

It must have been November when I first met Sister Keel. I always associate getting ready for Christmas with her. Somebody told me about a plain, aging angel in commonsense shoes who gathered children around her for games and stories on a vacant lot in Cabbage Town every afternoon, and I went to see her.

The wind blew hard and cold across the hard-packed earth of the corner lot. Two dozen youngsters from toddlers to teenagers raced across the scraggly grass, yelled shrilly from seesaws and slides, pummelled one another, and engaged in a one-sided football game more spirited than it was skillful. In the midst of them stood a sturdy, vigorous-looking woman wearing a bright wool dress, a scarf on her graying head, and an expression of sunny serenity on her wind-reddened face.

Seven years before, Henrietta Hollis Keel had gone to work in the nursery at the nearby textile mill, telling Bible stories to the children of millworkers and illustrating them with pictures on a big board. She noticed—as she talked one day in the fence-enclosed nursery play yard—that an even bigger crowd of children had started gathering outside the fence to hear her. They came every day, ragged, barefoot, often dirty, and clustered against the fence listening.

"I asked myself, 'What am I doing in here with them out *there?*'" she related. "They need my stories worse than the children whose parents are working and who are eating regular!"

So Mrs. Keel resigned and set up shop on a vacant lot a few blocks away on Savannah Street and Pickett's Alley, in a grime-and-poverty-darkened neighborhood that was called "Cabbage Town" because cabbages kept its citizens alive during the depression.

The grief and the need Henrietta Keel saw around her astonished her. She had lived a comfortable life, rearing her own four children in a pleasant house on a tree-lined street, with food and clothing sufficient to their needs. She hadn't really known that there were children in the same city who couldn't go to school or to Sunday school because they didn't have shoes to wear. She was appalled and heartsick when she found that little babies—who she loved with all her heart—were born every day into misery and want, with hardly a diaper to cover defenseless bottoms.

"I was ashamed of myself for what I had taken for granted," she remembered.

But Henrietta Keel, unlike most of us who are shamed by our complacency, did something her four grown-up children must have regarded as rather drastic. She took literally her Lord's admonition to sell all her goods and give to the poor and to take up her cross and follow Him. She sold her house, disposed of most of her furniture, and moved into a tiny basement apartment which she wangled rent free.

From mill officials she begged the vacant lot and persuaded them to put a sturdy fence around it to keep the children safe from traffic. She got a farm bell to summon the children to play and she set out on foot in the neighborhood to get acquainted with the people.

The way she became known as "Sister" Keel in her nondenominational, unorganized church work was typical of her intuitive feeling about her new friends.

"This neighborhood is visited by a lot of social workers," she said. "Policemen, policewomen and truant officers are always coming and going. And they are all 'Miss' or 'Mister' or 'Mrs.' I wanted to be closer to these folks than that. I asked them to call me 'Sister Keel.'"

It was as if she had become blood kin to the residents of Cabbage Town. They took her to their hearts and she and the old farm bell became symbols of comfort and safety in a troubled world. She was there when the sheriff pitched their furniture onto the street, when the doctor wouldn't come, when a man went to jail and there was no grits or fatback for supper.

Living frugally herself, she begged from old friends and church groups so she could feed the hungry and clothe the naked.

Gradually, with the passage of time, help came. Young people's groups from churches pitched in to help her run the playground after school, to teach and direct. Churchwomen came and helped her run a vacation Bible school in the summertime, sending teachers and, as she told me with a grin, "best of all—refreshments!"

First, she got a shed as a shelter from the winter wind and the blazing summer sun, grandly naming it the Haygood Memorial Methodist Shed for the church contributing the posts. Then the churchwomen began a campaign for funds for a little mission house.

With help, trouble inevitably came. Churchwomen made tours of the neighborhood to assess the need, and with them went newspaper reporters who saw the situation with ruthless objectivity, calling Savannah Street and Pickett's Alley a "slum" and reporting vividly its squalor.

Sister Keel's distress reflected the distress of some of the people up and down the street. They had pride and they loathed being objects of cool-eyed, bloodless charity. Some of them blamed Sister Keel and threatened to boycott the little mission house and to keep their children away from the playground.

"They are right," said Sister Keel sadly. "I am one of them and I hurt when they hurt, but I brought in outsiders who didn't understand. I should have handled it differently."

To try to make amends, Sister Keel asked me to talk to some of the long-time residents of Cabbage Town and to publicize their points of view.

She introduced me to a slim young mother of four children, who was one of her helpers at the mission and who was angered by newspaper references to Cabbage Town as a slum.

"I tell them it's not the street that's a slum," Sister Keel said, smiling at the girl, her strong, gentle old face looking humorous and affectionate all at once. "The street is just earth like the good Lord put everywhere. We ourselves make a slum with the way we live."

The girl, Sylvia, nodded.

"I love this neighborhood," she said simply. "I know it don't look like much, but I was born here and my husband was born here and it's home to us. We moved away twice. We tried it in the project and the project apartments are nice and convenient. But I'm a hard person to get acquainted. Seems like I missed Savannah Street so much I could hardly stand it...so we came back."

Things were improving, Sylvia pointed out. Sister Keel had worked with the city and landlords to get minimal plumbing in the houses—not tubs or showers, of course, but water spigots and toilets. And the vacant lot where the children were playing bloomed now with the children themselves and the flowers which they and Sister Keel planted every spring. Sylvia remembered when it was just a catch-all for trash and junk "and all the men that got drunk would lie out here under a tree, cutting up and raising sand."

Sylvia was but one of the neighborhood women who worked with Sister Keel to change things and I was there in their moment of triumph. For weeks, Sister Keel had been collecting old clothes for a sale which Sylvia and some of her neighbors conducted. Good dresses and coats and little trousers were sold up and down the street for a few cents a garment. When the sale was completed, Sylvia came in just as the churchwomen were canvassing the returns from their drive.

Sylvia held up her hand. "Cabbage Town," she cried, "gives seventy-five dollars!"

It was a triumph for Sister Keel, too.

"We have good people here," she said. "They'll make it."

The little mission was eventually finished and named Keel House over Sister Keel's protests.

"Ugliest name I ever heard of," she objected. "It doesn't mean

187

anything. Name it Hope or Faith House—something that means something."

"Keel is another word for hope and faith," Sylvia said firmly, closing the matter.

Sister Keel loved Christmas and wherever she was, was somehow the Christmasiest place on earth. She started early every year with her sewing classes for young mothers and once I found her happily distributing materials for basketmaking.

"I want them to have something pretty in their homes that they made with their own hands," she said. "To make something yourself and to be able to look at it and see its beauty and see its flaws and think how you would improve on it the next time...that's a growing thing."

She had a warming, unabashed way of talking about poverty and happiness and God. She could report a conversation with the Lord as if He were the comfortable, understanding corner grocer and I always believed every word of it.

There was the time when she decided she was too old to climb around the roof of the shed on the play yard, to put up the manger scene which the men at the Union Mission made for her.

"When it's up there in the yard, oh, it brings a brightness to the whole street!" she said. "I didn't see how I was going to get it up and finally I told the Lord about it. I said, 'Lord, I want that manger scene out there but You know I'm too old to put it up. Lord, is it one of the things I ought to fold away and not worry about?'"

The Lord, Sister Keel assured me, gave her an almost immediate answer. The phone rang and an Emory University theology student said he and a group of his friends wanted to offer their services to the mission for some Christmas chore. They were able-bodied young men who, he said, could "do anything."

"Can you put up a manger?" demanded Sister Keel quickly.

Sure, said the young man, and they'd give the mission a window

188

washing and cleaning for good measure.

The students cleaned and the J.O.Y. Girls (Jesus-Others-and-You) were busy sewing away on Christmas surprises for their mothers. Another group of youngsters—who had been getting Saturday piano lessons from a volunteer music teacher—were rehearsing like mad for the community's first piano recital. All the other children practiced Christmas carols for the Cabbage Town Christmas party and Sister Keel stayed in a state of happiness very close to tears when she heard the little three-to-five-year-olds piping, "Away in de manger, No crib for He bed."

Eventually, Sister Keel moved on from Cabbage Town to Kelly Street to launch a new mission and that was the one she wanted to talk to me about at the hospital. She wasn't going to be able to stay with it long, her own strength wasn't what it had been, she said, but some of the churchwomen who had helped her on Savannah Street had transferred to the new Fellowship Mission and she spoke of them.

"Pretty soon now, they'll be making that Maytime check to see how many children will be starting to school next fall and helping them get ready. There's lots to do. New babies coming..."

Sister Keel's face softened and her eyes showed the first flicker of sadness. Death did not dismay her. She believed wholeheartedly in that "better place," but she hated to miss the arrival of one single new baby.

189

The day she left the hospital she summoned me and all her "girls" at the mission to meet her there at eleven o'clock. She was going to the home of a relative in the country to rest a while and she wanted to commit the little mission and its charges to all of us—the women who had helped her so faithfully and to me as a sort of professional kibitzer.

"You don't have to write about it," she said, giving me a sharp warning glance. "God doesn't need any press agents for His work. But if my girls should need you, be there, won't you?"

Leaning on some of us, she walked around and looked at everything, pausing at an easel to pick up some cutout figures of Bible characters.

Her face glowed as she picked them up and lovingly smoothed and sorted the figures.

"When you tell this story to little children, keep it simple," she said.

And slowly, a little breathlessly, she began telling it, peopling it with the figures set on a felt-backed easel very like the one she had started out with in the mill yard.

There was a poor man who fell among thieves and was robbed and beaten and left by the roadside to die. A priest ("a preacher") and a Levite ("that's us...church members") came by and looked at the poor fellow and "passed on the other side."

Sister Keel paused when she came to that part of the story and her eyes moved over the faces around her.

"We have to be careful," she said gently, "that we don't do the same."

—*from* Especially at Christmas

Mayor Bill Hartsfield

For as long as he lived, of course, Hartsfield was "Mister Mayor" to many Atlantans. He held the nation's record for service as a mayor—more than a quarter of a century—and he has been named in many polls as one of the country's top municipal chieftains from the standpoint of achievement.

Caustic, witty, full of fight, it was characteristic of Mayor Bill that when he retired in 1961 he didn't sag down in a rocking chair or on a park bench somewhere and settle for being the city's elder statesman. He got himself a new wife, a new job, a new home—and he joined the PTA!

Some Atlantans tut-tutted when he filed suit for divorce from the first Mrs. Hartsfield, a shy, retiring woman who had been practically invisible to the public the thirty-two years of their marriage. Some of his contemporaries chuckled appreciatively that at the age of seventy-one he was eligible for the PTA. (The second Mrs. Hartsfield was a widow with a little boy.)

I interviewed Mayor Hartsfield a couple of weeks before he went out of office and found him unable to keep his mind on reminiscences. Looking back did not interest him half as much as looking ahead. Besides, some of his recollections caused his adrenalin to flow so freely that he would be caught midway in a story and leap nimbly from his chair and give a blistering, devastatingly funny imitation of a detractor, a footdragger, or an all-out opponent to some of his civic innovations.

Once Hartsfield was defeated—by a real estate/insurance man named Roy LeCraw and a margin of 111 votes in 1940. LeCraw had served but fourteen months when the United States entered World War II and he was recalled to active duty with the National Guard, in which he was a major. Hartsfield reclaimed the office with a sweeping victory over a field of seven other candidates.

191

But he learned something from that 1940 defeat. "I thought I did such a helluva good job I didn't need to campaign," he said. "But that's not right. You've got to fight every time! You could pave the streets with gold, reduce taxes to a nickel a year and scent the sewers with Chanel No. 5 and they wouldn't remember you unless you reminded them."

Although Hartsfield valued the voter, as only the successful politician can, he never let the desire for votes obscure his vision or dull the edge of his tongue when he felt the occasion warranted it.

There's a now-famous story of the time some movie press agents brought a trick horse into his office to receive the official welcome. The mayor hadn't known the welcome involved anything but a photograph and perhaps a pat on the nose for the horse, but when the press agent asked him to say a few words, he was by no means speechless.

"This is an historic occasion," he began with a fine roll of rhetoric. "It is the first time I've had the pleasure of receiving in my office a *whole horse!*"

Coca the Elephant

They say the wife is always the last to know, and I never understood better how she, poor wretch, must feel than I did in the spring of 1950. I was practically the last to know about the merger of the two big Atlanta newspapers.

Just as the deceived wife, who finds that her husband is involved with another, must start mentally retracing the path, trying to remember where her attention was when he started these shenanigans, I think back to the merger as somehow coming about because I was bogged down in that elephant idiocy.

It doesn't matter now, of course. The thing is past. The morning *Atlanta Constitution*, founded in 1868 and published by the Howell family since 1876, and the evening *Atlanta Journal*, founded in 1883 and published by the Cox family of Ohio since 1939, are under one roof and one ownership now. If it was not a love match but a marriage of convenience with, editorially speaking, separate beds and separate rooms for the partners, it's still a lot different from the way things were the winter an old elephant named Alice died at the Atlanta City Zoo.

The two newspapers lived apart and were as hotly competitive as is possible with different deadlines and different press times. We of the *Constitution* staff had only recently moved into a new building at the corner of Forsyth and Alabama Streets (later acquired by the Georgia Power company but vacant and boarded up in 1986) and were feeling smug, albeit a little homesick for the dingy, cupolated old Victorian home across the street where Henry Grady, Joel Chandler Harris, and Frank L. Stanton had worked. The *Journal* also had new digs—a whole refurbished office building and, going up cheek by jowl, a new structure to house its mechanical departments.

There was outwardly nothing to indicate we were about to be blended.

And then, as I said, that old elephant named Alice died. I was out of town covering a murder trial at the time and paid scant attention to the emotional stories in both papers about this cataclysmic tragedy at the zoo and the widespread mourning among kiddies. The jury brought in an acquittal for the defendant in my murder trial (a state senator) and I came home to pick up a new assignment.

"This is right down your alley," said Luke Greene, our then city editor—and I winced, recognizing the preface to a clinker of a chore.

It was.

"I want you to get us an elephant for the zoo," said Mr. Greene. "You may have noticed the *Journal* has started a campaign for one. So you'll have to get us a bigger and better elephant—and get it faster."

I had indeed noticed that the *Journal* had a campaign going to buy a replacement for Alice. How could I miss with my own children, sharper than a serpent's tooth, demanding dimes to contribute to it through their school? The *Journal's* elephant drive was surging ahead, no school child left unturned.

For a day or two I followed the same tack, working children's hospitals and orphanages and coming up with a grand total of $7.82. After about a week I knew I had to find an angle for our elephant campaign, and I started casting about for some public-spirited citizen in whose heart there burned—or could be kindled—philanthropy and a tender regard for elephants.

It came to me in the middle of the night: Asa Griggs Candler, Jr.

Mr. Candler, son of the founder of the Coca-Cola Company, was a man who thought so highly of elephants he once maintained a stable of them in the front yard of his home on Briarcliff Road. In fact, he may have been the only man on the continent of North America to plow his kitchen garden with elephants. He had a whole zoo on his grounds, established after his first wife had, on a trip west, expressed a desire to have an antelope for a pet. She found one waiting for her when she got home, the nucleus of a full-scale zoo.

The neighbors complained about every aspect of that zoo, smells, sounds, and escapes. Some people had even gone to court about it, among them one badly shaken woman who went out to get in her car one morning and found a fugitive monkey behind the steering wheel. Mr. Candler had reluctantly given up his menagerie, presenting the whole works to the city, including four elephants—the forerunners of the late lamented Alice. Their names: Coca, Cola, Pause, and Refreshes.

I didn't know Mr. Candler, but I was desperate. I put in a call to his public relations expert, a nice young man named Harold Brown. Would Mr. Candler, proven friend of the zoo, care to go for another elephant?

Harold wasn't sure that Mr. Candler would feel like further philanthropy in this direction. Atlanta's zoo was then terribly run down and seedy-looking. His other pachyderm gifts there had not flourished.

Pause, Refreshes, and Coca had preceded Alice in death. Even multimillionaires aren't eager to throw good elephants after bad.

However, Harold promised to talk to Mr. Candler and call me back. I moped around the office, scrounging a few elephant fund coins where I could—and thinking about Mr. Candler. His public relations, even to my untutored eye, looked a bit frayed and in need of mending. The zoo suits had been followed by a fire in his dry-cleaning establishment, in which hundreds of Atlanta citizens had literally lost the shirts off their backs. And before that could be adjusted, Mr. Candler had embarked on a program to take the tombstones out of old Westview cemetery, which he owned, and make it a modern, park-like burying place with vast sweeps of green lawn, all perpetually cuttable by power mower. The howls of outraged citizens were even then reverberating throughout the Fulton County courthouse.

Harold Brown called me back. Mr. Candler would see me—in his office in a vast, windowless building in the middle of Westview Cemetery.

Well, the result of our meeting was, from my point of view, fantastically successful. Mr. Candler, who in his youth had been an African big game hunter in the best Hemingway tradition, would on the following Saturday give a wild animal party for children in his trophy room in the cemetery. At the height of the party he would unveil a check made payable "To the Children of Atlanta" in the amount of whatever sum would be needed to supplement the lagging *Constitution* elephant fund. In exchange we were to conduct an essay contest, "Why I Would Like to Help Select Coca II," with six school children winners to fly with Mr. Candler in his private plane into the wilds of darkest New Hampshire to Benson's Wild Animal Farm.

There were minor disparagements. On the very Sunday the *Constitution* triumphantly bannered this story with a picture of Mr. Candler, children and check on the front page, columnist Doris Lockerman,

195

who had not been apprised of the coup, wrote on an inside page that there were plenty of rich men in Atlanta who could buy an elephant for the zoo but that we didn't want that—"We want the elephant to be bought with the pennies of children." And at Sunday School one of my dearest friends remarked churlishly that *that* Asa Candler had committed the crowning outrage of his career—"wild animal party on the hallowed ground of old Westview."

But I weathered them and the most wholesale-entered essay contest I ever saw, and early one spring day photographer Marion Johnson and I met Mr. Candler, his press agent Harold Brown, his son-in-law Tom Callaway, City Parks Director George Simon, and six essay winners at the airport to take off for New Hampshire.

Our departure was only slightly clouded by a brief story in the morning paper to the effect that during the night the *Journal* had attended the going-out-of-business sale of a defunct circus in Athens and brought home, under cover of darkness, a moth-eaten little old elephant, to be named "Penny"—for guess whose pennies?

Beating them to their own announcement had taken the zing out of their story, we felt, even if the razzle-dazzle of our elephant hunt had not. And it was a razzle-dazzle hunt, for sure. Mr. Candler was an aviation enthusiast. His harness racetrack was the site of the Atlanta Airport and he was one of the first businessmen in America to acquire a private plane. So he had a luxury, twenty-passenger plane with two pilots to take us first to Washington, where we were received by his old college roommate, the Veep, Vice President Alben Barkley. We had a day of sight-seeing by chartered bus and then on to Boston, where another chartered bus picked us up for the trip to New Hampshire and the wild-animal farm.

The essay winners picked an elephant, with only a little prompting from Mr. Candler and me. (He knew quality and I was interested in size.) We flew back to Atlanta and the elephant, dispatched with bands playing and flags flying and a ceremony attended by the mayor of the town, was to follow us in a heated van with a vet in attendance.

He was due on Saturday, and on Thursday our then managing editor, Lee Rogers (now assistant to the president at Lockheed) flung another journalistic hand grenade in my direction.

"We should have a parade to welcome our elephant," he said. "Get one up."

It would have been a little silly to protest that I was a reporter and not a promoter since I had already promoted an elephant. So numbly, not knowing the first thing about it, I set to work and by Friday night I had conned every acquaintance, every new source at my command into putting something—bands, clowns, tumblers, *anything*—into the parade. As an afterthought I looked around for a parade marshall, and Mike Benton, longtime Southeastern Fair impresario and a veteran of many parades, came to my rescue. It was he who mentioned the matter of the police permit.

Police Chief Herbert Jenkins, normally a brave man, blanched in horror.

"Do you realize it's Easter Saturday?" he whispered. "We can't add a parade to that traffic!"

Eventually, of course, the chief relented. And after a bad night, during which I alternately tossed fitfully and phoned the State Patrol to be sure the *Journal* had not hijacked our elephant, we were ready for the arrival of Coca II.

Governor Herman Talmadge was not available for official welcoming but Mayor Hartsfield was, and the First Lady and the little Talmadge sons, Bobby and Gene, were going to meet Coca II in front of the *Constitution* building and give him his "first taste of Georgia peanuts."

The *Journal*'s then city editor Bob Collins declined our telegraphed invitation to cover the festivities, but everybody else was there, radio, television, wire services, and newsreel.

Our chief, Ralph McGill, emceed the show from the *Constitution* lobby—in front of the gold seal which reads, "Wisdom, Justice, Moderation." At the crucial moment, when we hoped the eyes of the world were riveted on our triumph, the little Talmadge boys, their hands loaded with Georgia peanuts, took one look at Coca II and turned tail and ran, howling in terror.

Editor McGill snatched up Gene, the eldest—named for his grandfather, the old governor—spanked him soundly and thrust him back to his duty.

Beautiful Betty Talmadge was mighty gracious about it when Mr. McGill apologized to her afterward. He didn't know what possessed him to start spanking the child, he confessed ruefully, unless it was reflex action—the old irresistible urge to hit a Talmadge.

I slunk home for a week's vacation. And the very next Saturday our political editor at the time, the late M.L. St. John, telephoned me to tell me that the Sunday papers were to announce the merger of the *Constitution* with the *Journal*.

"We might not need you any more," he warned me. "We've decided to put all our elephants in one basket."

Time magazine recorded the event another way: "Atlanta now has two newspapers, two elephants and one publisher."

198

—*from* Peachtree Street, U.S.A.

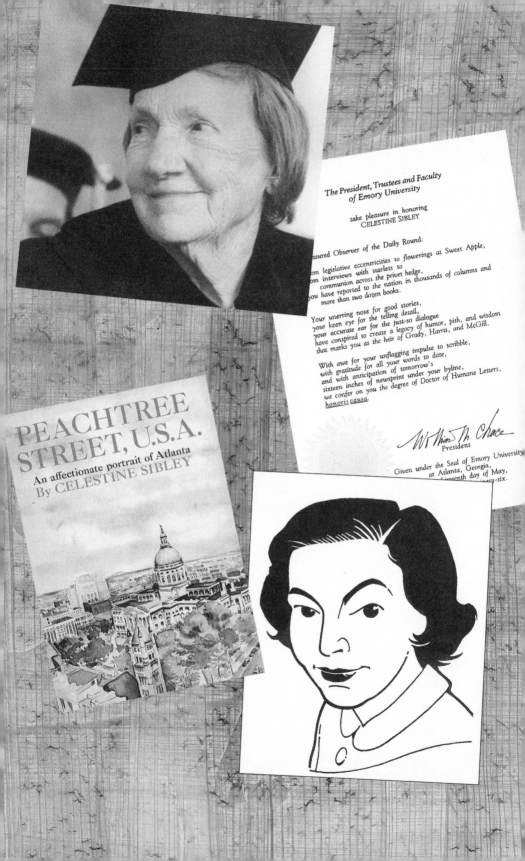

The President, Trustees and Faculty
of Emory University

take pleasure in honoring
CELESTINE SIBLEY

...sured Observer of the Daily Round:

...om legislative eccentricities to flowerings at Sweet Apple,
...om interviews with starlets to
communion across the privet hedge,
...ou have reported to the nation in thousands of columns and
more than two dozen books.

Your unerring nose for good stories,
your keen eye for the telling detail,
your accurate ear for the just-so dialogue
have conspired to create a legacy of humor, pith, and wisdom
that marks you as the heir of Grady, Harris, and McGill.

With awe for your unflagging impulse to scribble,
with gratitude for all your words to date,
and with anticipation of tomorrow's
sixteen inches of newsprint under your byline,
we confer on you the degree of Doctor of Humane Letters,
honoris causa.

William M. Chace
President

Given under the Seal of Emory University
at Atlanta, Georgia,
...teenth day of May,
...nety-six.

PEACHTREE
STREET, U.S.A.
An affectionate portrait of Atlanta
By CELESTINE SIBLEY

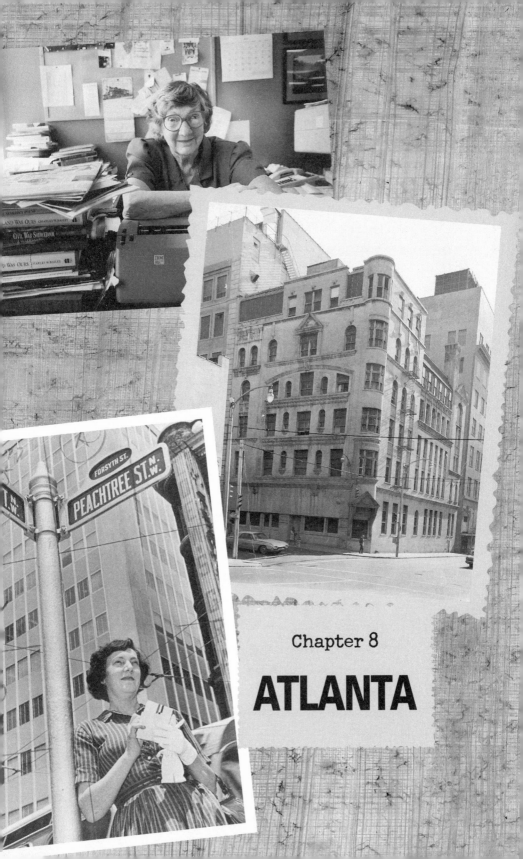

Chapter 8

ATLANTA

It was at a bar in Underground Atlanta in the early 1970s that I made an important discovery about Celestine Sibley. She knew stuff! Callow cub reporter that I was, I had taken Celestine for a "ladies page" columnist, strong on flowers and gardens and not much else. I soon discovered that she knew more about the Georgia General Assembly than the rest of us in the press gallery combined. Best of all, she was happy to share.

She knew all the great characters in Georgia's political pantheon, rogues and boneheads alike, from Gene Talmadge to Lester Maddox, and she could sip a toddy and spin glorious tales about them for hours on end. I took Georgia Politics 101 from Celestine and I've never had a better education.

Were she job-seeking today, Celestine might have trouble meeting the requisite levels of detachment and cynicism. She actually *liked* most of the politicians she covered, and admired many of them for their public service. But she was nobody's fool. One of her favorite stories concerned a rural Georgia legislator, a pillar of fundamentalist rectitude, who was caught one night in an upstairs corridor of the Henry Grady Hotel embracing a young woman. "Sins of the flesh!" he explained cheerfully, confessing with barely a hint of contrition. If there is a more concise fable about hypocrisy, I've yet to hear it.

As a chronicler of Atlanta and its institutions, notably Rich's department store, Celestine has always been guilty of letting her sentiments show. Both of her histories, *Dear Store* and *Peachtree Street, U.S.A.*, are subtitled "An Affectionate Portrait," an open admission of her bias. It may be fashionable these days to twit Atlanta for ambition and excessive grasp, but Celestine belongs to the school that remembers and appreciates the contributions of a remarkable group of leaders—Ralph McGill, Bill Hartsfield, Grace Hamilton, Robert Woodruff, to name a few—who shepherded the city through an intensely demanding time with uncommon good sense. Since I share her outlook, I've been pleased to steal from her books for my own.

Part of Celestine's gift is her eye for detail. I was always curious about why the prominent black developer Walter Aiken named his landmark luxury apartment complex the Waluhaje. I assumed it must be some fanciful Indian title, until I learned from Celestine that it was taken from the first two letters of his family's first names—Walter, Lucy, Hazel, and Jefferson. These are the sorts of intimate details people ought to know about their city.

Above all else, Celestine's great strength is in telling stories. In the finest Southern tradition, she is a spinner of glorious tales, full of humor and human foible. The heart of any place is its people, and Celestine has spent a lifetime collecting their moments of comedy and tragedy for the rest of us to savor and share. In the following pages, you will get to know some of her favorite characters. Like me, you'll be glad that she knew them—and that you know her.

—Frederick Allen

Photographs on page 200:

top left and right: Celestine and her Honorary Doctorate from Emory University
bottom left: original cover of *Peachtree Street, U.S.A.*
bottom right: line drawing portrait of Celestine for the Women's News Service

Photographs on page 201:

top: Celestine in her old *Atlanta Journal-Constitution* office
middle: the old *Atlanta Constitution* office building (Photograph by Henry P. McCoy)
bottom: Celestine in a publicity photo from the original *Peachtree Street, U.S.A. (Photograph by Ken Patterson)*

Indian Trails and Cowpaths

D idn't you know," a friend of mine inquired somberly, "that the only fixed and immutable fact about Atlanta is that the Yankees won the war?"

That's not quite true. The fact of change, growth, continuing surprises, and excitement prevails. Atlanta is not a boring, stodgy, set-in-its-ways city. That you can count on. And besides, who can be sure the Yankees really did win that war? Victorious in battle, perhaps, but won over and assimilated in peace.

Although we're crazy about planning, spending many hours in committee meetings, zoning sessions, and traffic engineering conferences, we have some of the most flagrantly unplanned streets in the world. The downtown thoroughfares were once old Indian trails or cowpaths, winding leisurely along ridges, dipping down at springs, and coming together at a swift-flowing artesian well which was drilled in the 1880s to supplement the town's water supply. The artesian well has since been plugged up; the flagpole which was erected in its place has been removed. A wide area in the middle is Five Points, where skeins of traffic are perpetually knotted and snarled, where most parades are reviewed, many civic campaigns are launched, and where Atlanta children used to go on New Year's Eve to hear firecrackers explode.

It is the nominal, although not the actual, center of our city and, of course, part of the language. A loudmouth is somebody who would "tell it at Five Points." A politician who has nothing to hide or, in the phrase given national coinage by President Eisenhower, a record "as clean as a hound's tooth," is one whose career has been as accessible to the public as Five Points. People have paid off their bets by trundling their opponents in a wheelbarrow through Five Points. The ultimate in public embarrassment, in raw exposure, is summed up in the phrase, "like being caught buck nekkid at Five Points."

Actually, Five Points is a sedate looking junction, as befits a financial section with banks and office buildings presenting a dignified facade. But a little of the old town pump atmosphere was restored to it when Atlanta's richest man and number one philanthropist, Robert W. Woodruff, enabled the city to buy up and raze a couple of shabby business blocks and substitute a real people's park where something lively—and often loud—is usually going on, where birds sing and flowers bloom and there is a greensward and benches for resting and sunbathing. There's little tangible evidence, however, that this was the site of the first rude huddle of country stores in 1836, that where the tall William-Oliver Building now stands, Thomas Kile, grocer, had the honor of housing the first municipal election in 1848; that the First National Bank occupies the site of the old Jacob's Pharmacy where in 1887 a citizen with a headache turned Coca-Cola from a tonic to a beverage.

Only old-timers remember that here the horse cars loaded and unloaded, that a young lawyer named Woodrow Wilson passed here on his way to his first law office two blocks away, that Presidents have paraded here and such returning heroes as Bobby Jones, the grand slammer, have been welcomed here.

Sometimes somebody writes a letter to the editor bemoaning the passing of such Five Points institutions as Pitts' Cigar Store and Sweet Shop, which once faced Peachtree Street between Decatur Street and Edgewood Avenue. Pitts' closed in 1926, but the chocolate sodas he dispensed over his big square marble counter from 1894 to 1926 live on in memory.

Atlantans are prone to refer to the corners that jut out from Five Points as the points of a star—a figure which has been modified and carried on by city planners with Atlanta's expressway system depicted as a starfish, reaching out into a trade area of eighteen counties and drawing workers from a radius of a hundred miles.

But that is a planned star—or starfish—a product of traffic engineering with landscaped parkways and on-purpose greenswards and limited access. This other one, the one that chance and the moccasined feet of the Creek and the Cherokee laid off, is the one at heartbeat level, the one of teeming foot traffic, of intimate sounds and sights that are distinctly Atlanta.

Nobody agrees where Peachtree ends. Some mileage-minded people say it turns north a distance of seventeen miles, becoming in due course Peachtree Road and then Peachtree Industrial Boulevard, but I know Atlanta men who give smiling credence to the story which was told to them as little boys—that Peachtree Street runs to New York City.

Sired by an Iron Horse

You think we're crazy on the subject of Peachtree?" The old settler asked the question of a visitor. "Sir, I'll tell you something. This town was sired by an iron horse but its dam was a *peach tree!* Remarkable union, remarkable offspring."

The speaker picked up his cane and limped off the bus at the Capitol City Club, chortling appreciatively at his own joke and leaving the baffled tourist just where he was, leafing dispiritedly through Mr. Gilmore's Street Guide.

He didn't explain, but history does.

Even before a New Hampshire Army engineer drove that stake in the ground in 1837, marking the beginning of a new kind of American city—a lusty, brawling little railroad town—there was a peach tree here. It was a tough and brave peach tree which by some magic found its way inland from the cultivated orchards of the coast and came to bloom and bear fruit on a strange high mound on the edge of the Cherokee Nation.

So phenomenal was the presence of a peach tree in the wilds along the Chattahoochee River that from time to time skeptics have tried to explain it away by saying that what the Indians called "Standing

207

Peachtree" was really just another big old resinous pine or "pitch tree."

If that's right, the soldiers who built and manned the fort there during the War of 1812 were even worse spellers than the War Department archives indicate, because they called it Fort Peachtree *at* Standing Peachtree and the road connecting it with Fort Daniel in Gwinnett County thirty miles away was named—what else?—Peachtree Road!

Because Atlanta is such a young town, a lot of its history has the freshness of word-of-mouth telling. Until 1903 George Washington Collier, who was here when the Indians were and long before the railroad men, could give eyewitness account of the early days. He was a plain-spoken old farmer who lived in the woods north of Atlanta for eighty years, long enough to see his fields and vast woodland acres become high-priced urban real estate. He died a rich man, leaving a large family of descendants to enjoy positions of wealth and leadership in the upstart town which had followed him to the woods, yapping at his heels and shattering his solitude.

A *Constitution* reporter who went out to interview him in 1894 quoted the old man as saying, probably irascibly: "Towns? Towns? Why, there were no towns here when I came. There was nothing except land lots and trails and corn patches. There was no money. There were no railroads, no papers. We didn't get the mail but once a week. There wasn't any business to do, much. The farmers just made their own corn and ate it for bread, that was all."

208

Wash Collier didn't try to substitute the unbelievable peach tree with the mundane "pitch" tree. He said he saw the peach. "Standing Peachtree was right where Peachtree Creek runs into the Chattahoochee—right where the pumping station is now...There was a huge mound of earth heaped up there, big as this house, maybe bigger, and right on top of it grew a big peach tree. It bore fruit and was a useful and beautiful tree. But it was strange that it should grow on top of that mound, wasn't it?"

Maybe the seed was brought in by some Indian trader circulating between the Cherokee and Creek nations. Maybe that stern-visaged old Indian fighter, Andrew Jackson, refreshing himself with a lunch from his saddlebag, dropped the seed there. Perhaps an Indian squaw had it in her small pouch of kernels and planted it along with the corn one spring.

Whatever the explanation, Atlanta was identified by a beautiful, fruitful tree long before Georgia caught the national railroad fever and sent right-of-way crews forth in 1837 to find the spot at which a state-authorized railroad, to be built south from Tennessee, could pass around the mountains and head for the rich cotton country and the seaports to the south.

The railroads came in, bringing a new kind of life to Wash Collier's woods and the isolated country where a farmer named Hardy Ivy had erected a log cabin and started breaking the land. Crews of Irishmen felled trees and cut through the hillsides and built fills to make way for the Western and Atlantic first and then the Monroe Railroad and, by the start of the Civil War, three other railroads, the forerunners of the fifteen main lines of eight systems which made Atlanta the largest railroad center in the South.

They threw up their crude shacks, their saloons, and their rough country stores. All kinds of people followed the railroads, and it's no wonder that some of the citizens of Decatur and Marietta looked askance at what was happening at the settlement the railroads had spawned.

There were prophecies of every stripe, but two cherished ones are recorded in Franklin Garrett's *Atlanta and Environs* in his chapter on the 1830s. Alexander Hamilton Stephens, who was to become Georgia's beloved "Little Aleck," U.S. senator, vice president of the Confederacy and later governor, visited the southeastern terminus of the W&A [Western & Atlantic] Railroad as a young man of twenty-seven. He is said to have looked on the near-wilderness and cried, "What a magnificent inland city will at no distant date be built here!"

The other prophecy is attributed to a Decatur citizen, Dr. Chapman Powell, who, unlike many of his neighbors, thought the railroad might be an advantage to a community instead of a noisy, dirty nuisance. To a colleague in the legislature who predicted that the terminus of the railroad would "never be any more than an eating house," Dr. Powell retorted, "You will see the time when it will eat up Decatur!"

Decatur hasn't exactly been consumed, but it has grown accustomed to finding itself referred to as a part of Greater Atlanta. By 1851 Atlanta was four times the size of Decatur and had taken a chunk of Decatur's DeKalb County to make itself a brand-new county. With typical frontier thoughtlessness, nobody remembered to make note of why the name Fulton was picked for the new county, and historians are probably destined to remain in eternal disagreement. Franklin Garrett was inclined to favor Hamilton Fulton, the chief state engineer who was a member of the first railroad survey party, but after weighing the contemporary evidence he reluctantly concluded that the honor belonged to Robert Fulton, inventor of the steamboat. Dr. N. L. Angier, a native of New Hampshire, is credited with having chosen the name for the new county, and historian Garrett thinks it likely that Dr. Angier was more impressed by the man whose invention made the *Savannah* the first steamship to cross the Atlantic than by an obscure railroad surveyor.

But there's no doubt where Atlanta got its name—from the railroads, of course.

Called first "the terminus" and then "Terminus" and finally incorporated under the name of Marthasville (for the daughter of Wilson Lumpkin, one of the railroad builders and an ex-governor of Georgia), the little town was rechristened Atlanta in 1845 in a high-handed gesture from a railroad man.

Richard Peters, superintendent and resident engineer of the finished portion of the W&A Railroad from Augusta to Covington, had the job of announcing the opening of the road from Covington to Marthasville and for some reason the name Marthasville didn't suit him. Martha's father later said it was "the low voice of envy," but whatever prompted the change, it was no trouble for the railroad to make it.

Mr. Peters asked the chief engineer, J. Edgar Thompson, who was later to become president of the Pennsylvania Railroad, to suggest a better name.

"Western and Atlantic," mulled Mr. Thompson. "Atlantic masculine, Atlanta feminine. Eureka...Atlanta!"

The railroad adopted it, the town followed suit, and the legislature promptly ratified it. Then everybody spent the next few years explaining to literary-minded newspaper editors elsewhere that it was Atlanta and not a typographical error. They naturally thought the rambunctious little town must have been named for Atalanta, goddess of fleetness and strength.

Henry Grady

Henry Woodfin Grady, the ardent young editor of the *Atlanta Constitution* who first wrote and then, blossoming into an orator of renown, spoke of a New South—a region where old enmities were forgotten, where resources in men and land would be expended on something besides those one-crop despots, cotton and tobacco. He preached that economic betterment was the key to all the South's problems and that "waving the bloody shirt" and nursing old hostilities were profitless gestures. He visualized for that New South "her cities vast hives of industry, her countryside the treasures from which their resources are drawn, her streams vocal with whirring spindles."

211

Mr. Grady came to the *Constitution* by way of the University of Georgia in his native Athens, the University of Virginia, and work on two or three other newspapers, including the *New York Herald*. He was but twenty-six years old when he joined the staff of the *Constitution* and in thirteen years he was to become one of the most persuasive writers and speakers in the whole nation. His friend and associate on the paper, Joel Chandler Harris, author of the Uncle Remus stories, was to write of him after his death: "His gift of expression was something marvelous...Above any man I have ever known Mr. Grady possessed the faculty of imparting his personal magnetism to cold type."

Mr. Grady used these talents to plead constantly for a healing of the breach between the North and the South and to work to bring the three "I's"—investors, industries, immigrants—to the depleted land of his Confederate father, who was killed at Petersburg. Atlanta's four railroads were overtaxed by 1879 and Mr. Grady became fascinated by the prospect of bringing in new railroads. He visited all the railroad centers, made friends with the railroad barons of the day and spent the winter of 1880–81 in New York writing and trying to interest northern capital in the South.

"I am firmly convinced that as soon as the South is firmly planted on her platform of liberation and progressive development and her position is well understood," he wrote back to the *Constitution*, "we shall see northern capital seeking southern investment with eagerness and the stream of immigration turned toward Georgia."

Mr. Grady's first major and most famous out-of-state speech was delivered in December 1886 at the banquet of the New England Club in New York. He began with an alleged quote from Senator Ben Hill, some lines which Grady's biographer, Raymond Nixon, later tried to track down and found had been spoken by Hill but were improved immeasurably by Grady himself: "There was a South of slavery and secession—that South is dead. There is a South of union and freedom—

that South, thank God, is living, breathing, growing every hour."

That speech, later called the New South speech, established Grady as an orator and as a "great pacificator," although he was not alone in these endeavors. He was invited back again and again, and in 1889 he stood before the Bay State Club of Boston and told the story of the poignant little "one gallus" fellow's funeral in Pickens County.

But only for contrast. For by that time Mr. Grady thought his Southland was well on the way to the new era he had worked for.

"Now we have improved on that," he said, referring to the necessity of importing all the "made" accouterments of the funeral. "We have got the biggest marble-cutting establishment on earth within a hundred yards of that grave. We have got a half-dozen woolen mills right around it, and iron mines and iron furnaces and iron factories. We are coming to meet you. We are going to take a noble revenge, as my friend Mr. Carnegie said last night, by invading every inch of your territory with iron, as you invaded ours twenty-nine years ago."

A few days later Henry W. Grady, not quite thirty-nine years old, was dead. He died at home on Peachtree Street December 23, 1889, from pneumonia. His death rocked Georgia and the nation. His friend Andrew Carnegie wired Captain E. P. Howell, publisher of the *Constitution*: "Only those who stood at Mr. Grady's side as we did and heard him at Boston can estimate the extent of the nation's loss in his death."

213

Coca-Cola

The South as a whole might have needed the spur of Grady's vision and energy, but Atlanta, although missing him, already had the bit in her teeth. She was building, building fast and big.

Already a druggist named John S. Pemberton, who had led cavalry troops under General Joe Wheeler and moved to Atlanta after the war, was puttering around in the backyard with a mixture in a three-legged black iron pot which was to do more for the economy of the nation than Mr. Grady ever dreamed of in his visions of "vast hives of industry." Dr. Pemberton, as he was known, had been calling the stuff "French Wine Cola, the Ideal Nerve and Tonic Stimulant," and more or less dividing his attention between it and a couple of other homemade nostrums, Triplex Liver Pills and Globe Flower Cough Syrup.

The year Mr. Grady was making his New South speech, Dr. Pemberton fiddled around some more with his brew, taking out the wine and substituting a pinch of caffeine with the extract of cola.

While he was about it he also changed the name to one which may now be more familiar in some parts of the world than the name of the United Nations or even the United States: Coca-Cola.

Whether Dr. Pemberton's tonic did anything for the nerves is not known, but a favorite story in Atlanta is that it was very efficacious as a hangover cure and a queasy-stomach soother.

Asa Griggs Candler, who had come to town with $1.75 in his pocket and taken a job at another drugstore, was too good a Methodist and too frugal to have hangovers. But he did have an uneasy stomach and he found Dr. Pemberton's brew so helpful that he bought the formula for two thousand dollars in 1891. Meanwhile, somebody had discovered by happy accident that a teaspoonful of the syrup mixed with charged water, instead of plain water, was a zippy drink, and Mr. Candler decided to take it out of the medicinal class and start peddling it as a drink for pleasure.

Local lore is full of accounts of how the Candler boys enraged the tenants beneath them in a building on Decatur Street by forgetting to watch the source of the family fortune—the Coca-Cola syrup kettle—and letting the sticky brown liquid boil over and run downstairs. Whether this is true or not, the boys watched their papa's $2,000 recipe boil into an asset which in 1919, while the old man was busy serving as mayor of Atlanta, they and other relatives sold for

$25 million. (Mr. Asa Candler, Sr., did retain for himself one percent of his Coca-Cola stock.)

One of the three banks handling the transaction was local, the small Trust Company of Georgia, now known the world over as "the Coca-Cola bank." Ernest Woodruff was president of the Trust Company, and that is how his son, Robert, happened to give up the trucking business and become immersed in the soft drink business. The dominant figure in Coca-Cola management for six decades, Woodruff died in 1985 at the age of ninety-five years, having given an estimated $350 million to benefit medicine, education, social services, and the arts. His was called one of the greatest success stories in American business, but little more than a month after Mr. Woodruff's death Coke management announced a change in the formula. Few stories beyond the declaration of war have set off a greater worldwide hullabaloo. So incensed were traditional Coca-Cola fans, so heated were their protests that after battling the opposition for three months, the soft drink tycoons called a press conference and threw in the towel. They would retain the new, sweeter Coke, all right, but they were returning to coolers and grocery shelves the old well-loved brew under the name Classic Coke.

Margaret Mitchell

I f Atlantans were to speak of "The Good Book," they would, in all probability, mean the Bible. When they speak of "The Book," there's no question. They mean *Gone With the Wind.* A cozy, more local name still in fairly common usage is "Peggy's book."

The querulous suggestion, sometimes voiced, that we make a good deal out of *Gone With the Wind* in this neck of the woods is no more true than the suggestion, for instance, that Carl Sandburg got hold of a molehill and turned it into a mountain of Lincolniana.

For the evidence is indisputable that *Gone With the Wind* was and is a phenomenon. It has been translated into twenty-seven languages,

215

including the Arabic, copped most major literary prizes, including the Pulitzer, sold more than twenty-five million copies, and was made into a movie which even now, fifty years after its release, is always playing somewhere in the world.

All these tangible evidences that *Gone With the Wind* was a very special book are a source of pride to Atlantans. But even dearer to the home folks is recurring evidence that Peggy's book established a peculiar rapport between Georgians and people in all parts of the world. Wherever people have suffered war and subjugation, Margaret Mitchell's story of survival in the South has intensely personal meaning. It dramatized for citizens of sacked cities the world over that Atlanta was also a city—the only American city—totally destroyed by war and rebuilt.

Peggy did not want to offer *Gone With the Wind* for publication. She wrote it between 1926 and 1929, let it lie untouched for six years, and even denied that she had a book when Harold S. Latham, Macmillan trade editor and vice-president, came to Atlanta looking for manuscripts in 1935. Medora Field Perkerson, an author who had been a colleague on the *Sunday Magazine* before she married their boss, Angus Perkerson, introduced Mr. Latham to Peggy with a cautious suggestion that he might ask about her manuscript. He did and she very "pleasantly but with firmness" got him off the subject, Mr. Latham related.

When she mentioned Mr. Latham's inquiry to her husband later in the day, he pointed out that she had nothing to lose by letting such a pro as a publisher have a look at her work. A few hours later, just before Mr. Latham was to depart for San Francisco, he received a call in his hotel room from Peggy. The sight she made, waiting for him in the lobby, must have been wonderful. She sat there, a little woman, overshadowed by a mountainous heap of smudgy, dog-eared typescript. Mr. Latham rushed out and bought a suitcase to pack the manuscript in and boarded the train.

Gone With the Wind was on its way.

The book came out June 30, 1936. The casting of the movie kept the nation in a state of argumentative suspense for a couple of years, and on December 13, 1939—one of Atlanta's more memorable dates— the world premiere was held at Loew's Grand Theater. Slightly more than two thousand people got in the theater that night, but thousands jammed the streets to pay tribute to the little author, to Vivien Leigh and Clark Gable, the cinema Scarlett and Rhett, and half a dozen other Hollywood luminaries who came to town for the event.

Amazing fame and fortune had arrived for Margaret Mitchell, and Atlanta basked in it. To Peggy herself it made little appreciable difference. She and John continued to live in the second-floor apartment at 1268 Piedmont Avenue, where Margaret Baugh was already installed to help handle correspondence. Peggy, as a friend noted, seemed to buy nothing for herself except a fur coat and a secondhand automobile. But her gifts to others, given quietly, were generous and far-reaching. She dispatched hundreds of food packages to Europe during the war. As her devoted maid, Bessie Jordon, wrote of her after her death:

She Fed the Hungry

She gave drink to the Thirsty.

She clothed the Naked.

Sheltered the out of doors.

Ministered to the Sick and in Prison.

Personal charity, a concern for the ill and needy, had been a habit of life with Margaret Mitchell, even before the book brought her affluence. And although she was reared in comfort, the only daughter of a prominent lawyer, she had known lean days. She and John were married on the Fourth of July 1925, not quite a year after her unhappy, short-lived marriage (1922 to 1925) to Berrien K. Upshaw ended in divorce. John was in heavy debt as the result of a long illness and their combined salaries weren't impressive, but Peggy told her family and friends, "John and I are going to live poor as hell and get out of this jam."

Their first home was what Bill Howland called "a physically dark but intellectually bright" small apartment at 979 Crescent Avenue, just back of the Tenth Street shopping center, which they accurately referred to as "The Dump." It was here that she started writing on her book.

It was four blocks from "The Dump"—on Peachtree Street at Thirteenth—that she was to be fatally injured the night of August 11, 1949. An automobile driven by an off-duty taxi driver struck Peggy as she and John started across Peachtree Street to see a movie at the Peachtree Art Theater. She died in Grady Hospital five days later. She suffered massive head injuries and never regained consciousness. The taxi driver, Hugh D. Gravitt, twenty-nine at the time, was convicted of involuntary manslaughter and sentenced to from twelve to eighteen months' imprisonment.

Two things helped to convict Gravitt of an accident which may not have been entirely his fault. After all, Peggy had apparently panicked while crossing the street and run into Gravitt's path because John, who stood still and waited, was not grazed by the car. But because Gravitt was photographed smiling when he was docketed at the jail and because he had a record of twenty-five violations, a public outcry which reached around the world sounded against him. The smile was wrongly interpreted to reflect the callous, unrepentant attitude of a killer.

Later, when he was serving time in the Bellwood Public Works camp, I talked to him and found him a desperately unhappy man who had been the victim of his own reflexes.

"A photographer said, 'Smile,'" he told me, "and I did it without thinking. I didn't feel like smiling. If I could I would have been the one in front of that car instead of the one driving it."

Integration

O n August 29, 1961, the Atlanta Police Department's bulletin, a mimeographed newssheet issued daily to more than seven hundred officers, carried this announcement:

"In accordance with Federal and State regulations and under orders from the Federal Courts the Atlanta schools will be desegregated when schools open on August 30, 1961.

"If there are any objections to the manner and method of operation of the Atlanta Public Schools those objections must be made to the superintendent of schools office at City Hall and under no circumstances will objections, discussion or disturbance be permitted at any of the individual schools."

Very matter-of-factly the bulletin noted that "hate" literature would probably be distributed and that representatives of "hate" organizations might be on the scene. It listed the names and addresses of these individuals.

Toward the bottom of the page there was another list—the names and addresses of the Negro students and the schools each planned to attend.

A score card, a cop remarked later, "so we'll know the players."

But that wasn't all. The bulletin reminded the officers of their duty:

"The highest value of the law is the keeping of the peace. The Atlanta Police Department has full responsibility and authority to maintain the peace and good order over the entire city and especially at and around the schools."

The bulletin concluded by citing chapter and verse of that authority from local and state laws. It was signed by Herbert Jenkins, chief of police.

What happened in Atlanta on August 30, 1961, is now known throughout the world. The public schools were integrated peacefully. The next day newspapers all over the nation editorially hailed this

Deep South city's "display of sanity and good sense."

The Police Department had planned and performed as their bulletin indicated they would—calmly, watchfully, meticulously "keeping the peace."

That bulletin, of course, was by no means the cause of Atlanta's peaceful school integration. It was, instead, the effect of a community attitude, of cumulative forces a long time abuilding.

There were times in the days leading up to August 30, 1961, when it appeared that Atlanta might have gone either way. To many old-guard Southerners, breaking the traditional patterns of segregation was unthinkable. To some the very word "integration" was a dirty word connoting all kinds of hideous social evils, ranging from syphilis to consorting with Communists. Many people believed sincerely that if by any chance the South had not yet provided "separate but equal" schools, housing, health, and recreation facilities for the races, it could and would, if let alone.

Two men knew better. One was an idealist, the late Ralph Emerson McGill, editor of the *Atlanta Constitution* from 1940 to 1960. The other was a practical politician, William Berry Hartsfield, who ended twenty-three years as mayor of Atlanta the first of January 1962.

McGill, long before the 1954 decision of the Supreme Court, had been attacking the inequities from the side of conscience.

"I wish those among us who are always so ardent in defense of their own interpretation of Southern traditions would be ardent in the defense of the Southern tradition which says that we always treat the Negro fairly," he wrote back in 1947 when the city spent fifty thousand dollars on a saddle ring for white citizens at Chastain Park and there was no park at all for Negroes.

"We don't and we never have given him a square rattle in education, before the bar of justice or in housing or in public parks. We have laws which separate the races but the same laws call for equal

220

accommodations in facilities and transportation and we have cheated on that too. Yet if you begin to discuss such things, the clamor arises about 'social equality' and 'nigger loving' and the fearful run for cover."

Mayor Hartsfield wasn't so vocal about the rights and wrongs of the question, but he felt very strongly about what was good for Atlanta. From the time Negroes first began to push for small gains—members on the police force, the right to use city golf courses—when the mayor acted in their behalf, his political enemies might call him "nigger loving" and the NAACP candidate, but the Negroes themselves knew better.

"Make no mistake," a Negro leader once said. "Mr. Hartsfield is by no means our Great White Father. He is simply a very practical man."

The mayor had no apology for that.

"When you stop to hate," he said again and again, "you stop all constructive work."

The golf course issue came up in 1957 with a U.S. Supreme Court decision. Mayor Hartsfield knew it would be invoked in Atlanta at any time and he got ready. He observed in cities where the golf courses were already integrated that relatively few Negroes played anyhow because it was a leisurely, time-consuming game. So he called a meeting of city parks employees to discuss the ruling and pointed out two simple home truths:

(1) If the court order was not complied with the golf courses would close.

(2) If they closed, one hundred white employees would lose their jobs and seventy thousand white users of the public links would lose a place to play.

Then in the courts he fought a delaying action aimed at one little-known thing—to get the compliance date moved to the Christmas season.

"It's not easy for people to hate each other at Christmas time," he pointed out. "It's the time of year of universal goodwill. I couldn't believe we'd have any unpleasant incident then—and then we didn't."

Being both a practical and an imaginative man, Mayor Hartsfield took another little precaution. He called the Negro leader who had filed the suit and asked him not to begin his golf game at the time and the place announced where cameras and television crews would be assembled. It would avert a possible demonstration, he pointed out. The Negro doctor and his golfing companions agreed, and two days before Christmas they teed off on the city-owned Bobby Jones Golf Course without fanfare and without incident.

The desegregation of the city's trolleys went almost as smoothly, although in recognition of state Jim Crow laws the police had to arrest the hymn-singing Negroes who boarded the trolleys, Bibles in hand, and sat down on the front seats. Both sides understood what was going to happen, however, and a police lieutenant tells the story of one Negro would-be rider who got to the scene too late to demonstrate. He came panting into headquarters after the paddy wagon had arrived with the Rev. Williams Holmes Borders and his band of demonstrators and was so embarrassed to be left out that police obligingly locked him up with the others.

After the courts ruled, trolley integration went off without a hitch. But there were plenty of hitches elsewhere. Lunchrooms and restaurants in the department, variety and drug stores, normally the refuge of the downtown worker and shopper, closed right and left before the arrival of sit-in-throngs from the Negro youth movement. These were frequently joined by sympathetic students from the white high schools and colleges, which added even more to the ire of White Citizens Council members and similar white supremacy groups. Students picketed the stores, and on occasion the Ku Klux Klan, in full regalia but sans masks, which are prohibited by state law, picketed the pickets.

Through the intercession of the mayor and the Chamber of

Commerce, this phase of the conflict ended with the integration of public eating places in the spring of 1962.

Through it all, however, the schools were at the heart of the conflict—all the schools of Georgia eventually, but the schools of Atlanta almost immediately.

U.S. District Judge Frank Hooper had already ordered the city Board of Education to submit a desegregation plan, and when that came back—a stair-step plan to begin with the twelfth grade—he ordered it to take effect in September 1960. Later he added the eleventh grade to that order. State law stood in the way and the legislature's answer was the appointment of a study commission headed by John Sibley, seventy-one, a prominent Atlanta lawyer-banker.

The commission collected opinions for many weeks, meeting in the cities and small towns of the state—and the majority of that opinion was that it was better to close the schools than to desegregate. Nevertheless, the commission's majority report recommended local option on the question.

Local option, as far as one group of Atlanta mothers was concerned, had to be swung to open schools at all costs. These were the women who were to later gain renown as the founders of HOPE (Help Our Public Education). They were a group of mothers who began by being horrified at having their broods at home on their hands all day long *if* the schools closed and went on from there to contemplate the long-range results of no schools.

Like Mayor Hartsfield, Mrs. Hamilton Lokey and Mrs. William Breeden, founders of HOPE, didn't waste any time hashing over the ideological aspects of segregation versus integration. They didn't even consider raising the question of how parents felt about sending their children to school with Negroes. All they wanted to do was to combine forces with parents who were determined to send their children to school, period.

223

Up until the organization of HOPE, the only people who were making themselves heard with any volume were the Negroes speaking through their court suits and such arch-segregationist groups as the Ku Klux Klan, the White Citizens Council, and the newly organized GUTS (Georgians Unwilling To Surrender) and Separate Schools, Inc.

Now other groups began to be heard from. Ministers issued manifestos. There were three in all, signed by a total of several hundred ministers, white and black, of all faiths.

On Christmas Day 1960, in a special Christmas message, the ministers of the city said in part:

"We cannot ignore the differences which exist among us. It is not likely that we shall soon be fully agreed as to the specific steps which should be taken for the solution of our problems. We are convinced, however, that the only pathway to progress lies in the direction of friendship, of respect for the convictions of others and of determination to maintain communications between the leaders of all racial and religious groups within our community."

State leaders maintained their adamant stand against integration, however, until the event which shocked and horrified people in all 159 of the counties of the state: rioting at the University of Georgia.

Two Negro students, Hamilton Holmes and Charlayne Hunter of Atlanta, presented themselves to the registrar at the university in Athens on January 9 and were admitted as freshmen. Things were apparently going smoothly. They were assigned dormitory rooms and had started their classes and then darkness fell and the mobs gathered.

Local segregationists were joined by imported racists and rabble-rousers. Athens police and sheriff's officers were summoned by the university officials. The State Patrol was called out, rocks sailed through the air, tear gas bombs exploded. Inside the dormitories, girls from all over Georgia cowered in their darkened rooms, uncertain and fearful. The Negro students were sent home for a few days in the interest of peace while state officials pondered what to do.

It was a bitter cold night on Capitol Hill in Atlanta when the legislature convened in "unusual and emergency session" to hear what Governor Ernest Vandiver had to say. He had been elected on a firm campaign promise that "no Negro...no not one...will ever attend a white school in Georgia."

If he adhered to that promise now the university would close, to be followed perhaps in weeks by the closing of schools in Atlanta and then elsewhere in the state.

The governor's wife and their three school-age children accompanied him down the aisle of the House chamber to the rostrum. They listened attentively to what he had to say.

"These past few days have been trying ones for all of us," he said. "Days of shock, frayed tempers, anger, shouts and even violence, but, over in the distance, through it all shone a steady light—the light of Georgia character, the innate, inbred integrity of our people."

A bit later he continued: "Having seen what can happen in the University System, we must move to protect the public schools and Georgia schoolchildren within the legal framework left to us. There is no—NO—sentiment in this state for a blind destruction of public education without offering an effective alternative. There never has been.

"Every legal means and resource to circumvent the effects of the decision, yes. Defiance, no. Private schools offered as a last resort, yes. Destruction of education, no. That has been the policy. That is the policy today. Our course is lawful resistance—not defiance—not violence."

Mandatory school-closing statutes were repealed, and a package of open-school bills was passed in their place.

The crisis was by no means over, but Charlayne Hunter (now Hunter-Galt, a public television anchorperson) and Hamilton Holmes returned to the University of Georgia where they proceeded in peace with their education.

In Atlanta the women in HOPE began promoting public acceptance of the change in tone from the state government. Out of this
grew OASIS (Organizations Assisting Schools In September). It embraced fifty-three groups, ranging from civic clubs, labor unions, religious and business and professional organizations to Boy Scouts.

All over town OASIS affiliates held meetings to plan for desegregation. Community discussions were organized. Speakers and literature
were provided, community leaders were encouraged to speak out and
the campaign reached a climax the weekend before schools opened with
"law and order" observances in churches. There were neighborhood
coffees and PTA and garden club programs. The Society of Friends
(Quakers) even arranged get-togethers for the white and Negro students
who would be attending school together "to cushion the transition."

So on August 30, 1961, Atlanta became the first Deep South city
to peacefully desegregate its public schools.

The scores of newspaper, magazine, and wire service reporters and
radio and television representatives who flocked into town, anticipat-
ing another Little Rock or New Orleans, might have been personally
relieved but professionally let down at the outcome of the story.

Characteristically, Mayor Hartsfield, the old showman, turned it
into an occasion to sell the charms and wonders of Atlanta to outland-
ers. Journalists from as far away as London might have trouble in years
to come remembering the details of ten young Negro boys and girls
starting to school with their white contemporaries in Atlanta. But they
probably will never forget the fantastic handling of that story by the
then mayor.

It was an era, remember, when newspaper photographers were
having their cameras smashed by mobs. Reporters had their cars over-
turned, sometimes burned. Members of the press were often hurt. Later
one was to lose his life in Mississippi. And nearly everywhere when all
else failed, people blamed the strife on the presence of the press.

226

Contrast that to the Hartsfield reception in Atlanta.

The council chamber at City Hall was turned into a gigantic press room with tables, typewriters, and telephones for all. Teletype machines were installed for those who needed them. A radio system was installed for instant communication with the principals of each of the five schools and the officers on duty outside. Mayor Hartsfield, who manned the City Hall microphone most of the day, spelled from time to time by School Superintendent John Letson and Assistant Superintendent Rural Stephens, had but to flip a switch and the press was in communication with the people on the scene—able to ask questions and hear the answers. There was nothing to be gained by going out to the schools and constituting a crowd on a sidewalk, although most of us had a try at it. When there was a ripple in the smooth operation and there was a little one—the arrest of four teenage boys who refused to move on when told to at one of the schools—the people in the council chamber were instantly alerted and taken to police headquarters to see the boys and to hear their stories in court.

Meanwhile in an anteroom to the council chamber, the Chamber of Commerce helped the visiting press to stave off starvation by setting forth snacks of Smithfield ham, hot biscuits, coffee and fruit juices, and, of course, the ubiquitous Atlanta beverage, Coca-Cola.

Publisher McGill dropped by and Mayor Hartsfield introduced him as the South's "great man" and the architect of Atlanta's peaceable approach to its problems. McGill took a bow, remarking wryly that such fulsome praise was "what you get when you vote for Bill Hartsfield every time."

When school was out and the last piece of copy had been moved, buses provided by the transit company whirled up to take the guests on a tour of the city, with the mayor himself acting as guide. And they came back to a cocktail party whomped up in their honor by the merchants at the Biltmore Hotel.

227

H. W. Kelly, principal of Northside High School, inadvertently found words to describe the day so long prepared for. Asked at the radio-telephone press conference how things had gone at his school, Mr. Kelly remarked solemnly that as opening days went, that one was "a bit more normal than usual."

—from *Peachtree Street, U.S.A.*

some children would want
a balloon to float, and maybe
you want a motor boat. but I would
be the happiest girl in town if
I had that coat of brown.

Little Brown Coat
Dear Mr. Sibley I'm writing
this note, asking you to please
buy me a coat. now the coat
which I have in view comes
in ether brown or blue. and
the price is only 2 98. and if you
dont hurry it will be to late
another little girl will buy
the coat and leave. and I will have
to wear my old one on christmas
eve. I can do without a dress and a
new hat to, but I do want that brown
coat and so would you. the coat I am
wearing is faded and green and when
I put it on I'm shame to be seen.
when I was younger I wanted a white
coat, but now I rather have that
little brown coat.

Mobile, Ala., Dec 19 19 74 No. 1

MERCHANTS BANK
MOBILE, ALA.

61-29

Pay to the order of *That Little Little old ugly Freckled Face Gal* $ 1 Switch

1 Extra Heavy Switch — DOLLARS

Her Old Buddy

Chapter 9
CHRISTMAS

I cannot write well of Christmas.

Too expansive, it is. Far too grand for the simple stitching of words.

The words I write always seem to tear loose from the story and the story spills out all over the place, like the springs and nuts and bolts from one of those simple-to-assemble-battery-not-included toys that must be made ready in the late hours of Christmas Eve.

The humbling fact is this: Some people can write of Christmas and others can't.

Celestine Sibley can. Better than almost anyone.

When Celestine offers us a Christmas story, it is one of those absolute experiences, one that humanizes the occasion, brings it to focus, follows us off the pages and stays with us.

Over time, every writer realizes that the best way to travel into a story is to have been there already. Find a familiar landmark and go to it.

Celestine's Christmas stories have always had the clear sense of having been lived, not invented. She *has* been there. She knows the setting, the sensations of sight and sound and scent. Her characters are flesh and bone, not watercolor renderings on a lovely card.

I do not think I have ever read one of Celestine's Christmas stories without thinking, "Ah, that's a novel."

My favorite is the story of the tramp who appeared at her parents' home on Christmas morning during the Depression.

A less accomplished writer would have made the whole

thing a too-sweet sermonette about the kindness of poor people sharing their skimpy dinner with someone down on his luck.

Not Celestine.

Celestine told us about the tramp.

An aviator from "...Up North somewhere." A man who had barnstormed with Charles Lindbergh had built his own plane and crashed in it, leaving him "...crippled and scarred and losing the sight of one eye." He is invited to share Christmas dinner by Muv, and as they are seated at the table, Celestine confesses a look at their guest: "I thought he must be the ugliest person in the world, gnomelike and twisted in body, the face beneath that repulsive blank eye stretched and puckered in a hideous scar. And he still smelled."

If the tramp had been simply a tramp, it would have been just another story—an old one, in fact, for taking in strangers is about as theme central as one can get with a Christmas tale. Celestine gave us the tramp as someone with history and with dreams, a quaintly heroic man braving tragic circumstances with a croker sack slung over his shoulder. We know his appearance, his smell, his voice. We know him.

And that is Celestine Sibley's gift.

Having been there, she understands.

And from her fingertips on the word-keys of machines, she makes Christmas a special reality.

And I envy her.

Terry Kay

—Terry Kay

Photographs on page 230:

top: Celestine's angel ornament from her Christmas tree
middle: a letter from a very young Celestine to her stepfather, "Pap," requesting a brown
coat for Christmas
bottom: Celestine with copies of *Especially at Christmas.* Faith Brunson, the legendary book
buyer for Rich's Department Stores and head of the American Booksellers Association, staged this photo shoot as the books arrived in Atlanta via train.

Photographs on page 231:

top: Celestine's stepfather Pap affectionately called her his "little old ugly freckled face gal."
This banknote was an early Christmas present in 1924.
middle: Celestine as an honorary angel in an early production of the African-American spiritual "Heaven Bound" at Big Bethel AME Church in Atlanta (Photograph by Arroyo)
bottom: another of Celestine's tree ornaments

There's No Such Thing as a Poor Christmas

My mother, Muv, once made dumplings to go with three cans of Vienna sausage for Thanksgiving dinner.

If you've ever bought Vienna sausage for seven cents a can at a sawmill–turpentine still commissary, you will understand the significance of that.

It bespeaks a woman of imagination. Who else would think the union of Vienna sausage and dumplings possible, much less feasible?

More important, it indicates an unquenchable zest for celebration.

Muv believes that you should put everything you have and everything you can get into an important occasion. We *had* the Vienna sausage—and very little else in those Depression years of the 1930s. She made the dumplings.

When I think of that Thanksgiving dinner, served out of the Sunday dishes, on the very best tablecloth, with a fire burning brightly on the hearth and a bowlful of apples our cousin sent from Virginia polished to a high sheen for a centerpiece, I wouldn't dare question Muv's convictions about Christmas.

For if Thanksgiving is important—and oh, it is!—how much more important is Christmas. Anybody who would po' mouth Christmas, contends my mother, is guilty of sinning against both heaven and his fellowman. He's a hangdog, mean-spirited character who is unworthy of receiving the greatest Gift of all time.

My father, reared a Scotch Presbyterian with a more moderate (Muv would say tepid) approach to most things, may have once regarded Muv's feelings about Christmas as a bit extravagant. But early in their marriage she beat him into line with weapons he normally handled best—ethical and spiritual arguments.

He made the mistake one grayish December morning of observing bleakly that the lumber business was going badly and "it looks like a poor Christmas this year."

235

"A *poor* Christmas!" cried Muv. "Shame on you! There's no such thing as a poor Christmas!"

Poor people and hard times, yes. They were not new in Christ's time and they were certainly not new in rural Alabama. But no matter what you had or didn't have in a material way, Christmas stood by itself—glorious and unmatched by anything else that had happened in the history of the world. Jesus himself had come to dwell among men, and with a richness like that to celebrate, who could be so meaching and self-centered as to speak of a "poor" Christmas?

"Make a joyful noise unto the Lord!" directed Muv gustily, and if my father found he couldn't do that, he at least didn't grouse. He was to learn later that he didn't dare to even *look* unjoyful about the approach of Christmas, or Muv would do something wild and unprecedented to cheer him up, like the year she took tailoring lessons and made him a new suit and topped it off by buying him a pearl stickpin at a dollar-down-and-charge jewelry store.

The suit was beautifully made and a perfect fit and Muv had even worked out the cost of the goods by helping the tailor, but I think it made my father a little uneasy to be so splendidly arrayed at a time when he had come to accept, even to take pride in, the image of himself as a "poor man." And the idea of *owing* for something as frivolous as a piece of jewelry was so repugnant to him that he finished paying for the stickpin himself. But he loved having it, wore it with pleasure, and thereafter looked at Muv and the ardor which she poured into preparations for Christmas with a touch of awe.

Things aren't important, People are, Muv preached, and it sounded so fine it was years before I realized what she meant *to us*. Things weren't important to us, so as fast as gift packages came in from distant kin, Muv unwrapped them, admired them and with a gleam in her eye that I came to dread said happily, "Now *who* can we give this to?"

It's funny that with the passage of the years only one or two of the

Things stand out in memory. There were some lavender garters a boy in the sixth grade gave me. ("Beautiful!" said Muv. "You can give them to Aunt Sister!") And there was a green crepe de chine dress I think I still mourn for a little bit. ("Oh, it's so pretty! Don't you want to give it to Julia Belle?")

Julia Belle was a skinny little Negro girl in the quarters who had lost her baby in a fire and kept wandering up and down the road wringing her hands and crying. My green dress was such a dazzling gift, it did divert her from her grief a little, and it may have helped her along the road to recovery.

At the time, I remember protesting that I loved the dress and wanted it myself and Muv said blithely, "Of course you do. It's no gift if it's something you don't care about!"

It must be true because the other Things are lost to memory, but the People remain. Through the years there have been a lot of them, disreputable, distinguished, outrageous, inspiring, and at Christmastime I remember them and the gifts they gave to me—the gifts, in fact, that they *were*.

—from *Especially at Christmas*

237

The Aviator

My mother Muv was bad about not practicing what she preached. She admonished me never to speak to strangers and to be careful about the caliber of my friends, for you are judged, she contended, by the company you keep. To hear her tell it, nobody in the great outside world was safe for me to talk to except "men in brass buttoms"—policemen and firemen, of course— and, if you were desperate and had to ask for directions or help, a man who wore the insignia of the Masonic order.

As a child I heard all that and heeded it. My mother did not.

She regularly picked up strangers on street corners, or trains, and on buses. Once she fell into conversation with an old lady on the Dauphin Street trolley and brought her home. The old lady, a gentle, myopic soul who couldn't remember where she lived, stayed three weeks.

Not many months before she died, my mother became so thick with a soldier she met on an airplane that she was invited to attend his wedding. I think she would have gone but for the prohibitive price of airfare to Wichita. (She thought it was a town in France.)

Once when she was hostess to her beloved WSCS (Women's Society for Christian Service, the old name for the Methodist women's group), she invited the town's only known prostitute to join them for lunch.

"But Muv, she's..." I sputtered, aghast. "What did the others...?"

"She's my friend," my mother said firmly. "She's always treated me well. And if you were going to ask, what did the others say, what could they say? She was my guest and this is my house."

But it was not just her house or just her guest that Christmas day during the Depression when she invited a tramp to have Christmas dinner with us. We were accustomed to feeding what my father called Weary Willies, the great fraternity of jobless, often homeless men who beat their way across the country on freight trains, looking, looking—

for jobs, for a bed, for a meal. Many of them came to our door, offering to cut wood or hoe the garden or do any work at all for a meal. Muv never turned one away empty-handed. Sometimes our larder offered slim pickings, but if there were anything at all in the house—a few cold biscuits, some baked sweet potatoes, apples, or eggs—my mother handed it out the back door.

We knew she would do that, and because it seemed important to her, we accepted it. A friend who suggested that she was motivated by superstition, fearing that if we didn't help we, too, would fall upon hard times and hunger, got no argument from Muv.

"Sure," she said, "As ye sow..."

Then on Christmas morning, a particularly unattractive tramp showed up at the front gate.

The smell of a baking hen and cornbread dressing, rich with homegrown onions and sage, perfumed the frosty air. There was a big fire in the living room fireplace, and the wood heater in the dining room glowed rosily, sending out warmth from its corner. Muv had set the table with the best cloth and dishes the night before, lamenting that having only three places didn't make it a festive board. Apples from a cousin in Virginia, polished to a satiny sheen, blazed like mammoth rubies in the center of the table. I knew that on a cold shelf in the pantry that best-of-all Christmas desserts, ambrosia, waited in Grandma's cut glass bowl to be served with Muv's nut cake. (We had plenty of pecans that year, but the high cost of citron and candied cherries and pineapple made real fruitcake a casualty of the Depression.)

My Santa Claus presents had engrossed me all morning, but you can stretch your delight in a game and a book and some beads and a bracelet just so far, so I was beginning to anticipate the next major attraction on the day's program—Christmas dinner. That's when our hound dog Bertha began barking languidly (Bertha was not a very

239

spirited watchdog) and we heard a gruff "Hello!" from the front gate. My father and I went to the door.

A scruffy little man in filthy khaki pants, recognizing Bertha's lackadaisical attitude toward watchdogging, was coming up the walk. He carried the tramp's inevitable croker sack over his shoulder.

"Howdy, neighbor," he said, drawing close enough for me to get a whiff of the stench of unwashed body and clothes, old grease, the acrid smell of train smoke, and something worse that I was too young to identify.

"Neighbor?" I thought with the scorn of the young. "We don't have any filthy neighbors like that."

He had mentioned food, and my father was directing him to the back door in automatic concern for Muv's clean floors when Muv came up behind us.

"Merry Christmas!" she called. "Come in, come in!"

We looked at her in amazement. Tramps always came to the back door and ate what she had to offer on the back steps.

The tramp himself was apparently startled to be welcomed at the front of the house. He looked at his broken shoes, one of them bound around with a dirty rag to hold the sole in place.

"Oh, ma'am," he said, "I wouldn't want to track up your floors."

"That's perfectly all right," Muv said cordially. "I can have clean floors any time. This is Christmas, and we want you to have Christmas dinner with us."

The man stared at her in surprise, and I saw for the first time that one of his eyes, half hidden by the slouch brim of his battered, black felt hat, was as white and blank as a porcelain doorknob. My father turned to look at her and then he rallied.

"Yes, yes," he said. "Come right in to the fire."

They must have exchanged names. I know that my father took the visitor to the little room we called the washroom, which antedated

240

a real bathroom, and carried a kettle of hot water to him. Muv hurried to set another place at the table. Presently we were seated, had bowed our heads for the blessing, and were waiting expectantly for that lovely ritual of carving the fowl. I looked at the man across from me and thought he must be the ugliest person in the world, gnomelike and twisted in body, the face beneath that repulsive blank eye stretched and puckered in a hideous scar. And he still smelled.

Muv appeared not to notice, although, if it had been me, she would have sent me in search of more hot water and lye soap. She asked the usual bright and sociable questions. Where was he from? Where was he going? Did he have family?

At first he said little, applying himself to chicken and dressing and sweet potatoes and the beans and squash Muv had put up in the summer with this meal in mind. He ate rapidly but neatly, and after a time he leaned back from the table and told Muv the things she was dying to know. He was from Up North somewhere. (That was usually enough for us. What did we know or care about place-names in that distant and foreign land?) He was job hunting, of course, and had spent the night before "with friends" (this with a wry glance at my father) under the railroad trestle. As for family, he had a wife and a child, but they had left him because he had a crazy sickness: He flew airplanes!

"You're an aviator?" my father said, pushing back his chair, the better to inspect our visitor.

I sat up straight. Although I was beginning to admire boys at school and at church, my real heroes, the males I worshipped from afar, beyond even Eagle Scouts and cowboy movie stars, were flyers. I read all the newspaper stories about speed and endurance flyers. I drew books out of the library about Admiral Richard Byrd, Wiley Post, and, of course, the wondrous "Lone Eagle."

"Do you know Charles *Lindbergh*?" I blurted out the question.

241

"Slim?" he said. "Oh, sure. We've barnstormed together."

Of course, I knew that magic term, "barnstorm." We had been out to Bates Field in Mobile to see rakish, devil-may-care men in helmets and puttees set those marvelous birds down on the muddy ground and offer people rides over Mobile Bay for five dollars a head. I knew somebody who had spent a wild and profligate five dollars that way and reported that you could see the boats and even big fish in the bay, *just as plain*. I neglected my ambrosia and pecan cake to drink in our visitor's stories.

He had even built a plane once—the one he crashed, leaving himself crippled and scarred and losing the sight of that eye. He had been a long time recovering, he said, and his friends who might know of jobs had migrated to the placid clime of Florida for the winter. He knew if he could find them, they'd have work for him.

"You can still fly, you think?" my father asked.

"Yes, sir," he said, lifting his scarred face proudly. "When this Depression is over, there's going to be a golden age of aviation. We'll all be flying everywhere—most freight and certainly all mail. I will be up there with 'em. I don't look like much of a aviator." He threw a shame-faced look at my mother. "I must smell pretty awful. I got sick on some local shinny last night. But I *am* a flyer."

242

Naturally, my father didn't believe that talk about freight and mail being carried by airplanes. What did we have railroads for? But I believed, and I thought his words, "golden age of aviation," the prettiest I ever heard.

He sat by the fire and talked a little while after dinner, and then my mother packed him a lunch for the road. We walked to the gate with him, hating to see him go. When we had waved him out of sight, my father put an arm over Muv's shoulder and said teasingly, "You're not going to tell us that we entertained an 'angel unawares' in him, now are you?"

Muv could have been complacent but she wasn't.

"How do you ever know?" she said thoughtfully. "We just did what we're supposed to do, especially at Christmas." And she quoted: "I was a stranger and ye took me in, a-hungered and ye fed me."

—from *For All Seasons*

The Lost Christmas

Sandra Dunstan looked around to make sure nobody was watching her, then she carefully poured her milk into the guppy tank. The milk mushroomed slowly downward, leaving a widening cloudy trail that blotted out the tiny fish, the feathery water plants, and the little stone castle in the sand on the bottom of the tank.

Sandra, who was ten and should have known better, shook her soft blond hair out of her face and giggled softly.

She heard a noise behind her and spun around guiltily. Her older brother, Michael, who was twelve, had come into the breakfast room and was looking at the aquarium with interest.

"Save the women and children first!" he called out suddenly. He picked up a piece of toast and threw it into the tank.

"Oh, Mike, what fun!" cried Sandra. "Let's give them some oars. How about bacon?" She grabbed two pieces of bacon off a plate on the table and crisscrossed it on the toast.

"They need provisions, too," said Mike. "A shipwreck kit. Put in a little cereal."

Sandra threw him a delighted smile and picked up a bowl of oatmeal. "A spoonful for each guppy," she said, ladling it generously onto the soggy toast, which promptly sank from the weight.

"Too bad," sympathized Michael. "We'll have to launch another life raft. Here." He set another piece of toast afloat on the surface of the water.

"How about a grapefruit boat?" inquired Sandra. "Rub-a-dub-dub, three men in a tub!"

"Swell," cried Michael, throwing half a grapefruit into the tank with such vigor the cloudy, fish-smelling water splashed all over the floor.

"Quick, we need oil to pour on troubled waters," Sandra said and turned from the table to the sideboard where the cruet holding the vinegar and oil customarily sat.

At that moment Mrs. Hoyt, their father's housekeeper, walked into the breakfast room.

"Children!" she cried. "What are you doing to the poor fish? Quick, get them out of that slop!"

Michael looked from the plump gray-haired woman, whose always pink face was now red from annoyance and distress, to the puddles on the waxed floor. He smiled.

"Show us, Mrs. Hoyt," he invited. And then so softly only Sandra could hear it, he added, "Show us, as Hansel said to the old witch."

The words were no sooner out of his mouth than Mrs. Hoyt walked toward the guppy tank, her feet met the puddle on the floor, and she lurched and slid and sprawled flat on her back on the breakfast room floor.

Both children doubled up with laughter.

"Mrs. Hoyt, you're so funny!" cried Sandra. "You look positively cute!"

And Michael, who had anticipated the housekeeper's accident, was speechless with merriment.

That was the scene which met Mr. Daniel Dunstan's eyes on a December morning a few days before Christmas when he came down to breakfast in his home on Peachtree Road.

His housekeeper floundered awkwardly on the floor, the guppies rose to the top of the tide of garbage in their aquarium and gasped their last. And his beloved son and daughter, who were, as he well knew, responsible for the whole mess, clutched their sides and laughed uproariously.

Dan Dunstan was a patient man, lonely since the death of his wife five years before, and normally soft-spoken. But that morning he let out a roar that caused his comfortable, handsome home to rock on its foundations.

"Shut up, you little monsters!" he yelled at his children as he hurried to help Mrs. Hoyt to her feet. "Shut up and get the mop!"

Now nobody had ever told Sandra or Michael Dunstan to get a mop before—and, odd as it may seem, that was really the beginning of the most remarkable Christmas they ever spent. That was the first step in the strange Christmas adventure of two of the most spoiled children who ever lived in Atlanta, Georgia, or elsewhere.

I f ever two children needed Christmas it was Sandra and Michael Dunstan. They needed it worse than Mrs. Hoyt thought they needed a spanking. They needed it worse than their exhausted and exasperated teachers thought they needed to be taken out of their elegant private school and committed to the state training schools for delinquents. Even their psychiatrist didn't really know how much Sandra and Michael had lived without really knowing about Christmas.

Only their father, tired and rich and sometimes awfully lonely, suspected the sad little secret about his children. Because their mother was dead he had tried to give them everything he could think of that children needed, including the most lavish Christmases money could buy.

Yet that December morning when they wasted their food and killed the guppies and stood by laughing while Mrs. Hoyt skidded and fell on the floor in the mess they made, Mr. Dunstan realized that Sandra and Michael were ignorant, underprivileged little children.

"Did you realize that Mrs. Hoyt might have hurt herself?" he asked them after the housekeeper had limped out and they had sat down once more to a fresh breakfast.

Michael looked bland and innocent.

"Oh, no, sir," he lied.

"How about your fish," the father asked. "Did you intend to kill them?"

Sandra and Michael exchanged pained looks and Sandra rolled her eyes heavenward with a show of great boredom. Michael sighed heavily and pushed his untouched food away. They hated lectures and they planned not to listen if they could help it.

"I'm really surprised that you should behave so badly so close to Christmas," Mr. Dunstan went on.

Sandra laughed scornfully.

"You mean we won't get any presents?" she said. "Well, okay, don't give us any presents."

"There's nothing I want particularly anyhow," said Michael indifferently. "I've got a lot of junk you can have back if you want it."

Mr. Dunstan sat quietly a moment looking at his children—Sandra, a delicate little blond girl so like her beautiful mother, and Michael, strong and sturdy with bright close-cropped brown hair and fine blue eyes. They were handsome children and he loved them but they weren't any comfort or pleasure to him and he couldn't understand why.

He sighed heavily.

"I wasn't thinking of presents," he said. "There's something more to Christmas than that. I guess it's my fault you don't know. I tell you what..." His eyes brightened and he looked at them hopefully. "How would you all like to go away with me for a few days—just the three of us?"

"Where?" said Sandra. "California? I'd love to see the movie stars."

"Oh, California," sneered Michael. "Let's go some place decent for a change. I'd like a little excitement."

Mr. Dunstan looked at them sadly.

"I think we'll try the north Georgia mountains," he said. "One of the men at the office has a shack up there I think I can borrow. It's primitive. We'll have to do our own cooking and probably cut wood and haul water but it's very quiet and we'll have wonderful walks and talks."

"Oh, great," commented Sandra bitterly.

"*Some* Christmas," muttered Michael. "Of all the corny things to do!"

Sandra didn't have any idea how long she had been riding when the headlights of the car picked up a little side road and her father slowed down and stopped. She was on the back seat with the boxes of groceries and covers and Michael was slumped down on the front seat, pretending to sleep because he had run out of sulky answers to his father's conversation.

"This must be the place," said Mr. Dunstan cheerfully. "There's the big white pine tree with the lightning blaze on its face and there's the little creek. We've come about eight miles since we left the pavement— and that's where Sam said we'd turn off."

He maneuvered the car into the little side road and started moving slowly down a bank toward a creek.

"And there's the house," he said triumphantly. "This is the place."

"Where's the house?" asked Michael, peering into the woods.

"There," said Mr. Dunstan. "Two rooms and a screened porch. That's what Sam said."

"Call that a house?" said Sandra petulantly from the back seat. "Looks like a little shack to me."

"Dump," said Michael briefly.

Mr. Dunstan said nothing but concentrated on fording the creek and getting up the small hill beside the house. He parked the car and got out with his flashlight and keys to try the door. The door swung open and he turned to the car and called, "This is it, kids. Hop out and let's get unpacked."

"I don't feel so good," said Michael. "My side hurts again."

"Have we got to stay here?" inquired Sandra. "I'm so co-old and it looks so dark and scary. Can't we go back to a motel, Daddy?"

Mr. Dunstan opened the door and began pulling boxes and bundles out. "Let's give it a try, children," he said. "Come on. We'll build a fire and have the cabin warm in no time at all. I know you're hungry. Mrs. Hoyt packed us a nice lunch and there's a bottle of cocoa back here somewhere. Give me a hand."

Michael and Sandra climbed reluctantly out of the car and stood looking about them. The December moon was big and it threw a frosty light on the little cabin and the stiff winter grass. Somewhere behind them in the shadows they heard the icy tinkle of the creek. It sounded cold and lonesome and they hurried after their father into the cabin.

The beam of his flashlight showed a long, plain room with bunk beds in the corners and a big stone fireplace in the center. He found a kerosene lamp and lit it and then knelt by the hearth and began building a fire from the dry wood he found in the box by the chimney.

The flames leaped up and he hoisted a big gray log in place. Turning from the hearth he rubbed his hands together and faced his son and daughter, smiling.

"Poor babies," he said, reaching out a hand to draw each of them close to him. "You're tired and cold and sleepy. Sit here and warm up and I'll bring in the rest of our things and we'll eat something and go to bed. Tomorrow we're going to have a fine time. First thing in the morning I'm going to show you how to make the best flapjacks you ever put in your mouth."

"Ugh!" said Sandra, shrugging off her father's arm.

But Michael waited until their father had gone back out to the car again before he said anything. Then he said softly but determinedly, "Tomorrow, Sandy, we're going to run away."

The morning was bright blue and silver-blue sky and frost-silvered earth with the bare branches of the trees making a delicate tracery of charcoal shadows against both earth and sky. But Sandra and Michael were too busy running away to notice that.

They left the little cabin before breakfast, when the ring of an axe on the wooded slope back of the cabin told them their father was where he would not see them.

Now it was midmorning and the air in the North Georgia mountains was sharp and sparkling as a cut-glass goblet—and Sandra and Michael were hopelessly lost.

"My side hurts," said Michael, stumbling up a rocky slope.

"Oh, your side!" scoffed Sandra. "You're all the time using your side since you had your appendix out. Use it on Daddy and Mrs. Hoyt but don't tell me it hurts. I know better. You got us lost and a hurting side's not going to find us."

"Aw shut up," said Michael but without much heat.

He was hungry and worried. Somehow his sense of direction was off. It had been his plan to take a shortcut through the woods to the highway, where he knew he and his sister could hitchhike back to their home in Atlanta. That, he felt, would show their father that they did not intend to be pushed into spending Christmas in an isolated mountain cabin and listen to his lectures.

He smirked a little, thinking how even now Daddy would be searching for them and worrying, maybe even cursing himself, Michael thought hopefully, for bringing his children to such a place.

He stepped on a loose rock and his feet slipped out from under him, sending him sprawling among the rocks and briars.

Sandra began giggling, but a long thorny branch snapped back and hit her in the face, scratching her nose and drawing blood from her cheek. She cried instead.

Michael sat up and caressed his bruised ankle with his hand. There was a time when he would have laughed at Sandra's tears but something—maybe his hurting leg or being hungry and lost—made him feel sorry for her.

"I tell you what, Sandy," he said gruffly. "Let's go back to the cabin where Daddy is. We probably got him worried enough. And we could get something to eat."

"Yes," said Sandra, gulping a little and wiping her eyes. "He was going to make flapjacks. But are you sure you know the way back?"

"Sure," said Michael, getting to his feet. "We'll get back on that little creek and just follow it."

Sandra wiped her cheek where the salt of a tear caused the briar scratch to smart and smiled at her brother in real admiration.

"Let's go," she said.

They did go, slowly and painfully, with more briar scratches on their faces and arms and occasional falls where footing was tricky. They found a creek and began following it. A dun-colored cloud floated lazily off the top of a mountain and hung itself over the sun, turning the day from blue and silver to dull gray. They got their shoes wet in the marshy places along the creek and their feet grew stiff and ached with cold. Michael lost his cap and Sandra lost one of her bright red mittens.

The creek bank was a tangle of vines and dark green clumps of mountain laurel and rhododendron, so dim and jungle-like in places the children didn't realize for a time that it was growing dark.

When they came to a clearing and saw the light had gone from the sky, Sandra began to cry.

"Hush, Sandy," said Michael desperately. "Hush. I think I hear something."

And miraculously enough, when Sandra stopped crying he did hear something. He heard a whistled tune and the tune was the sweetest of all Christmas melodies—"Silent Night, Holy Night."

Just then as he and Sandra stared into the gathering darkness, they saw the tune came with a boy—a boy who was driving a cow along a path at the edge of the clearing.

Sandra and Michael thought they had never seen a prettier sight in their lives than the house to which Pete Mills and his cow, Fancy, led them that cold December evening.

It was a humpbacked little house nudged up against a

mountainside for warmth. It had no paint on its walls but a tendril of blue smoke from the chimney was busy skywriting a welcome over its roof. And its doorway, standing open, was a bright square of firelight.

They stood by the fireplace and felt the warmth of the flames steal achingly over their numb hands and feet while the voice of Pete's mother, who sat in a chair in the corner, warmed them with its welcome.

Her face was thin and pale but her voice was strong and hearty.

"Young'uns, git to stirring," she called out to the four little girls, all younger than Pete, who made a circle about Sandra and Michael and stood smiling shyly.

"We got company—Christmas company! You know how that banty rooster has been crowing all day. I told you company was coming and here it is! Ivy, set places at the table. Maybeth, warm up the leather britches and the crackling bread. Pete, hurry with the milking. Warm milk will taste good on a night like this!"

The children scattered as she spoke, throwing Michael and Sandra radiant smiles.

"Now!" said the mother. "Give the least ones your jackets to hang up and pull up chairs. We're the Millses. Them least ones is our twins, Katie and Laurie. They're little but the most he'p to me. Hand 'em your coats."

252

Shyly Sandra and Michael complied. Then Michael, because he was the oldest, gravely took upon himself the responsibility of an explanation.

"We're the Dunstans," he said. "I'm Michael, she's Sandra. We live in Atlanta but we were up at Mr. Sam Jackson's cabin with our father and we...we got lost."

"Lost?" said Mrs. Mills. "Mercy! Is your father lost too?"

"We don't know," faltered Sandra, suddenly thinking of her father, who might be wandering through the dark woods, looking for them. "We left him at the cabin." She looked anxiously at Michael. She didn't want to tell this nice, welcoming woman they had run away.

"Then you'uns is all right," said Mrs. Mills, relieved. "He'll find you. I don't know where that there cabin you're talking about is. We seldom git over yon mountain. But you'uns stay put and your folks'll find you."

She laughed. "Like I tell my chaps, a lost bairn is a heap easier to find than a lost calf. Bairns rare back in a clearing and stay still but calves git the go-yonders."

Her tone was so merry Michael and Sandra laughed in spite of their weariness and their hunger.

"We'll make like a barn," offered Michael sturdily.

"Yes, do that," said Mrs. Mills. And then in a more serious tone she beckoned them closer to her chair. "I been sitting here praying the Lord would send the young'uns something fine and special for Christmas," she whispered. "I think you'uns come a-purpose to answer that prayer. I couldn't be prouder to see anybody."

Sandra and Michael looked at each other uncomfortably.

"We haven't got any presents," Sandra said apologetically.

"Presents!" cried Mrs. Mills, "Lord love you, we don't want presents. You brought yourselves. And hit's Christmas Eve. After you've et and rested we'll have ourselves a Christmas party!"

The leather britches—tender green beans which were snapped and threaded on strings and hung in the rafters to dry until they were pale gold—had been boiled with bacon rinds and a pod of red pepper and they tasted of sun and summertime. The crackling bread had been cooked in a pone so it was crisp outside but rich and moist with bits of lean pork inside. The milk, foaming and warm from the cow, Fancy, tasted so good Michael and Sandra could scarcely believe it was the same stuff they had poured in the guppy tank.

They ate and as they ate the young Millses stood watching them happily.

253

"When you'uns done eating," said Pete, "reckon you'll feel like coming out to the barn and he'p us with our surprise?"

Michael and Sandra answered the question in one breath.

"Sure!" they said.

The twins, Katie and Laurie, stayed by the fireside with their mother, but Ivy and Maybeth and Pete led the Dunstan children to the barn, shepherding them along in the light of the kerosene lantern.

"Hit's a Christmas tree we got," little dark-eyed Maybeth confided to Sandra in a whisper. "Have you'uns got a Christmas tree at your home?"

"Yes," said Sandra, thinking of the tall blue spruce which stood in the living room at home, decked with its strings of electric lights and glittering ornaments and scarcely noticed by Sandra and Mike in their boredom with Christmas.

"Oh, I know hit's a pretty one," said Maybeth politely. And Ivy, who was ten, smiled over her younger sister's head at Sandra.

"Wait till you see our'n," she said. "Maybeth's put the prettiest decorations of all on it."

Pete swung the barn door open and Michael and Sandra looked at the tree and swallowed miserably.

It was a little tree, straight and symmetrical, with its roots carefully packed in earth in a wooden bucket, but not a light did it have on it, not a glittering ornament, not a piece of tinsel, not a candy cane.

Paper chains cut out of the colored pages of the mail-order catalogue were draped over its branches. But the other things on it certainly were not colorful. In fact, they were almost indistinguishable in the lantern light.

"It's pretty," offered Sandra at last.

"Oh, hit ain't much to look at," said Pete offhandedly. "Hit's a smell and taste and feel tree. For Ma."

"For your mother?" said Michael, surprised.

"Ma's blind," said Pete quietly.

"Blind!" The Dunstans said the word together and then stared at Pete in horror and disbelief.

He smiled serenely. "Ma can see things a lot of folks can't see, but she can't see a Christmas tree. And she loves Christmas better than any time. We put the tree in a bucket so it would live and stay green and smell good and then we gathered up the presents she could smell and taste and feel. See?"

He drew Michael and Sandra closer to examine the little bunches of dried, sweet-smelling herbs Maybeth had tied to the branches, the bright chain of hot peppers from Ivy, and the little bird's nest Pete himself had found last summer and saved.

There were packets of flower seeds from the twins and a bag of black walnuts they had picked up on the mountainside. Pete had put two arrowheads on a branch next to the base of the tree.

"Watch Ma when her fingers touch 'em," he exulted. "She'll know right off they're arryheads and she'll hold them in the palm of her hand and tell stories about the Cherokee Indians that used to live in these mountains and hunt with them things instead of bullets. Ma knows a heap of stories."

"What about the children?" asked Sandra anxiously. "Don't children get presents too?"

255

"Sure," said Pete sturdily. "Ma's got dolls hid away for the twins. Ivy and Maybeth had boughten dolls when our daddy was a-living and they give 'em to Ma to dress up all new for the least ones."

"Oh, I wish I could give your mother a present!" Sandra said suddenly. And she didn't realize it was the first time in her life she had ever wanted to give anybody a present.

"Me, too," said Michael unexpectedly.

Pete and Ivy and Maybeth looked at them attentively. Finally Pete said to Michael, "Can you read?"

"Of course," said Michael, mystified.

"Good?" put in Ivy.

"Why, yes, I think so," said Michael.

The three Mills children exchanged delighted looks.

"Then you can read to Ma," said Pete. "We'll take the tree to the fire and have the party. And you can read Ma the Christmas story out of the Bible. She purely loves to hear it."

Michael grabbed hold of the bucket bearing the little tree and marched ahead, holding it triumphantly aloft. Sandra had to run to catch up with them but she grabbed Pete's sleeve at the steps.

"I...I could sing," she offered breathlessly. "I could sing your mother a song."

Pete's eyes on her were bright with approval and gratitude.

"Why, that'll be a fine present," he said. "Fine as silk."

All the rest of the Christmases they lived Sandra and Michael were to remember that Christmas Eve in a little house in the North Georgia hills.

When they had helped the Mills children haul their "smell-taste-feel" tree in to the fireside they placed it before the chair of the bright-faced blind woman who sat there. Then they all gathered at Mrs. Mills's feet on the floor for the presents.

Michael gave his present first—the Bible reading. Proudly little Maybeth brought him the worn family Bible and all their faces turned toward him, waiting expectantly. He had trouble finding the place in the Bible and his hands trembled and his voice quavered a little as he started, but as he read his voice gathered strength.

And the radiance on the face of the blind woman and the eager hush in the little room made the words seem to sing as he read them out:

"And, lo, the angel of the Lord came upon them, and the glory of the Lord shone round about them: and they were sore afraid. And the angel said unto them, 'Fear not: for, behold, I bring you good tidings of great joy, which shall be to all people.'"

"You see, children," said Mrs. Mills reverently, "that's the way it was. Oh, it was a wondrous thing the way we come to have Christmas! How could a body ever feel any way but happy knowing how He come into the world, the pore little mite of a thing!"

The children listened, and she talked over the details of the Baby's birth, making it seem as real to them as the firelight about them. It was to her a most loved story and she savored the words as she spoke them, pausing now and then to shake her head and smile at the wonder of it all.

Then she reached out her hands, the sensitive, seeking, work-worn hands of a poor blind woman, and Sandra watched them move over the plain little, grand little tree. They touched every gift upon it with so much love Sandra looked quickly at Michael to see if he noticed too.

Love, she thought, that's what Daddy was trying to tell us about Christmas. It's the loving and the giving that count. Not the presents, either poor ones or rich ones.

Pete brought a bottle of sweet apple cider out of the fruit house and Ivy fetched gingerbread from the kitchen. Sandra, who could tell from the solemn face on Michael that he was thinking of Daddy and wanted to see him too, put an arm around each of the twins and started singing. She sang all the Christmas carols she knew—the ones she had scorned in school and the ones she pretended not to know in church.

And then patiently she went back over the words and taught them to the Mills children.

The firelight hardly showed at all outside the house when the door was closed, so it must have been the sound of their voices lifted joyfully in the song "Angels, from the Realms of Glory" that guided Mr. Dunstan and his search party to the door.

257

And the welcome he got when Sandra and Michael heard his loud "Hello!" outside! They went tumbling out the door to meet him and drag him to the fire, hugging him and laughing and crying in a way the poor bewildered man hardly understood at all. If he had intended to punish them for running away he changed his mind. But that may have been because he saw something different in them.

When they rode down the mountain together in the back of the forest ranger's jeep, they leaned against their father and looked at the big bright star in the east. It seemed very close and bright and Sandra thought she knew what Mrs. Mills would say about it.

"That star," she murmured to her father, "has the most important story to tell."

Mr. Dunstan smiled and held them close. He knew all along the Christmas story is a love story.

—from *Especially at Christmas*

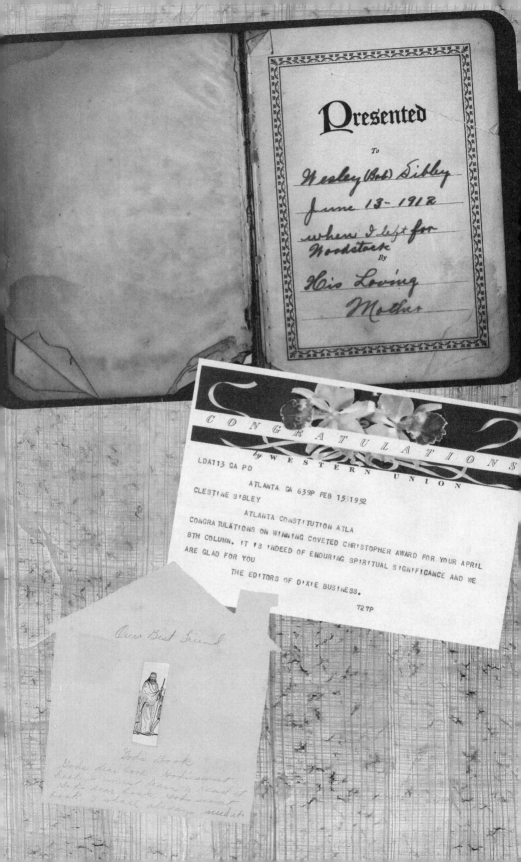

Presented

To

Wesley (Bob) Sibley

June 13 - 1912

when I left for

Woodstock

By

His Loving

Mother

Our Best Friend

God's Book

Loretta Young accepts from Father Keller $2,000 prize and medallion for Newspaperwoman Celestine Sibley of Atlanta, Ga.

Presented
to Celestine
May 28th
by her School
teacher for
attending
Sunday
School on a
rainy
day.
Mobile
Ala..

5-28-22

Chapter 10

FAITH

Faith is not blind, when seen through the eyes of Celestine Sibley. Faith involves something more than reading the Bible and going to church—in fact, God and church don't come into it much, nor do mysteries of the great unknown. If some highly religious person spray paints "Repent or burn in hell!" in bright yellow letters on a rock, the author learns "the art of instant repentance" and drives off to cover a murder trial.

Although she has an almost mystical ability to remember everything meaningful that has ever happened to her, and to render it in prose so clear and evocative that it seems to happen to us as well, Celestine Sibley is completely human. She is a seeker after hard evidence, pursuing visible traces of the divine as manifested in the tiny miracles of our daily lives.

Faith comes from learning to believe in things you can see with your eyes sensibly wide open: your family and friends, the natural world, the possibilities of joy inherent in every day. "Small, quiet, often fleeting blessings," she calls them.

Witness the joy she feels, after half a lifetime spent watching other people ride bicycles, when she finally masters one herself. The supporting hand falls away and she pedals furiously: "I felt absolutely airborne—just for a second before I realized that I was in truth balancing and pedaling and riding my bicycle by myself. Then I fell."

The moment of faith that keeps her "airborne" is the mirror-image of the faith a writer must have in her own voice, if she is to sustain a lifetime of work that shines as brightly as this.

The fall is the moment of doubt, from which she will recover. She will get on that bicycle and ride it again, even after the fall. This is how she keeps the faith.

"The subject of knowledge," an old friend tells her impatiently, "is to know—to know. To see, to feel, to understand, to know!" Seeing, feeling, understanding—with these tools, Celestine sets about her task, which is not just to know a thing for herself, but to transfer this knowledge, intact, to her readers. Her technique is often incremental, the accretion of one precise detail upon the next, her essays built like coral reefs from carefully chosen bits of memory and sensation.

Although she is always present in her work, a sharp, amiable, tart-tongued, and generally sympathetic observer, Celestine Sibley is not the sort of writer to engage in deep tortures of the soul. Always she is triumphantly outward-looking, finding wisdom and beauty in the people around her, in her beloved landscapes of piney-woods Alabama, north Georgia, and the Florida Gulf Coast. She comes closest to religious rhapsody in her garden, among the things that grow and bloom. A remarkable catalog of "good smells" does for the reader what the aroma of gingerbread does for the author—a whole lost world is invoked with one whiff.

"Grown-ups see the shape and color of the day, the hulk of that gray rock, the pattern of that stand of young pines against the sky," she tells us. "Children drop to their knees with sounds of excitement and discovery and pick mirrorlike fragments of mica out of the earth." It is our great gift that Celestine Sibley is able to approach life from the point of view of that little girl, dropping to her knees, in awe of the small mirrorlike thing she has brought to light, in perfect faith that the thing, uncovered and examined, will reveal its meaning.

Mark Childress

—Mark Childress

Photographs on page 260:

top: Pap's Bible, given to him by his mother in 1912
middle: one of many telegrams congratulating Celestine on winning the Christopher
   Award
bottom: Celestine's daughter Mary Little's Vacation Bible School artwork

Photographs on page 261:

top: Celestine couldn't take time off from work to receive the Christopher Award in person. Here, Loretta Young accepts it for Celestine from Father Keller .
middle: Hat Pin Church where "Muv" was married to Henry Colley
bottom: Celestine's "umbrella" award for attending Sunday school on a rainy day in 1922

Knowing

A few years ago when many counties still had what they frankly and unabashedly called "almshouses," instead of places now euphemistically known as Happy Hearts Haven and Sunset Manor, I became friends with an old man who may have been the richest person ever to inhabit a poorhouse.

He had absolutely no possessions, except the rusty old suit, the grayish food, and the grayish dormitory bed the county gave him, and yet he glowed with happiness. He wasn't as you might suppose, a mental case, unaware of his surroundings and his situation in life. On the contrary, he was the *most aware* person I ever saw.

In his younger days he had been a successful lawyer, but his wife had died, he took to drink, and a series of miserable circumstances had resulted in his being disbarred. He lost his profession and his home, he had no money, and by the time a county welfare worker found him he was weakened by starvation and near death from pneumonia. Although he was seventy years old and apparently had no reason to make the effort to live, he rallied and recovered.

When I knew him he was a jaunty little fellow who walked miles in the nearby park every day, spent hours watching birds, and had not missed a sunrise for ten years.

I used to visit him for sheer pleasure in his company and the luxury of being cheered up when things were not going well with me. He never failed me. He had the florid speech of one who in his youth had been nurtured on the classics, and sometimes when we sat on a bench under a tree he would pull his stately courtroom manner on me.

"If it please your Honor," he would sometimes begin, and he often prefaced a statement with "I submit to you." Sometimes he left me puzzled and unsure of his exact meaning, but I usually had a feeling about what he was telling me and frequently it would come clear later.

There was the day he interrupted a story he was telling me about some intramural skirmish among the inmates of the almshouse to stare out across the field and cry, "To know...to *know!* That is the sum total of discovery! Read your Plato, madam."

Being abysmally literal-minded I asked, "What? To know what?"

"The subject of knowledge," he said impatiently, "is to know—to *know*. To see, to feel, to understand, to *know!*"

Another day he came down the almshouse steps to greet me, swinging his cane as if he didn't need it to lean on. When he reached me he searched my face intently and said, "Are you happy?"

"We-ell," I began, playing for time.

He stalked ahead of me to the bench under the tree. "Sit down," he directed, "and think. What do you have to be happy about?"

For some time I had been thinking what I had to be *unhappy* about and I was not so facile with the exercise in reverse. But quickly I went over in my mind the things that I automatically considered sources of happiness, although at times they were a plague and a pestilence—my children, if only they would behave themselves, my parents, our old house, which nagged me with its need for paint and repairs, my job.

When I had enumerated them to myself I started to tick them off to him.

"Never mind!" he said impatiently. "I don't need to know. *You* need to know."

And then he told me why. The greatest waste in life, he said, is not to know when you are happy, not to store up good fortune and rejoice in it when you have it but to wait until the end of life and look back in surprise and say, "I was happy then. Why didn't I know it? If only..."

"Know!" he directed. "*Know!* Otherwise it is all a waste."

Presently we talked of other things, and when I left he was checking a crape myrtle tree at the edge of the yard to measure the progress of a couple of nest-building brown thrashers.

A week later he died while taking one of his long walks through the park. He had insisted on going out in the midst of a thunderstorm, although the superintendent had tried to keep him in. I couldn't feel sorry for that, even as the aggrieved superintendent told me about it, because it did seem to me that in his way he had taken friend Plato's advice. He had emulated the swans, which have sung all their lives, when they come to die "do then sing more lustily than ever."

Flying

The person who said Christmas is too good for children wasn't necessarily a cynic. Some things which are normally associated with childhood are better if they come to you later in life. I'm thinking of bicycles.

As a country child living in the piney-woods country of south Alabama, where the roads were deep rutted sand, I never thought to want a bicycle. I'm sure children in the city had them but, as I recall, they were always older boys and I don't remember ever knowing anybody who got one for Christmas.

But when my own children came along a bicycle became Santa Claus's number-one priority. My son Jimmy was in the first grade and we were living in a fishing camp out from Orlando when he got his first bicycle. It was a major item for Santa Claus that year and for a time it altered the way of life for all of us. We couldn't do anything else until Jimmy learned to ride, and I spent many an afternoon trotting along beside the new Christmas bicycle, holding it steady while its owner pedaled desperately.

The day he sailed off on his own, riding straight and true down the side of the road, I felt like a mother eagle who had just seen her baby eaglet soar from the aerie. I watched the leggy little redhead toil up the slight inclines they have in orange-grove country and zip down them—at first tense and a little fearful and then with increasing confidence and finally no-hands, feet-on-the-handlebars, and I was caught up in the bicycle fever.

Everybody should have one, I knew. But we had many bicycles to go before I ever got my own. Susan turned ten and had to have one for Christmas. For her ninth birthday Mary got a pretty good secondhand one. At twelve Jimmy had a new Schwinn, and when he was fourteen English bicycles with gears were the thing. We awakened one Christmas morning to find both Jimmy and bicycle missing. He had checked out Santa Claus's loot at 4 A.M., found the bicycle, boarded it, and toured the sleeping city in the predawn darkness.

Later he and a friend, who had been similarly endowed by Santa Claus, took off with sandwiches for a day at Stone Mountain, eight miles away. It seemed to me that a bicycle was the most liberating machine I had ever heard of. You needed nothing but it and your own arms and legs to carry you like the wind anywhere you wanted to go. I used to stand on the porch and watch my children and their friends ride up from the park, where they had been to swim, or the library with a basketful of books, and I admired and envied both their skill on their brightly painted steeds and their freedom to move around our town swiftly and at will. My own movements were either by foot—not very fast—or by bus, which placed me at the mercy of transit-company schedules and routes and involved some little money. (Later, when we got a car, it involved more money, of course.)

Looking back it seems that my children had hardly stopped riding their bicycles before they were learning to drive and then owning old cars, then better cars, then getting married and having children who were suddenly ready for bicycles. And we had come full circle, so fast I don't remember when or how the grandchildren learned to ride. It seems to me that they sprang into their bicycle saddles, competent, even showy riders, from the beginning.

At one time my son-in-law Edward managed to outfit four of the children, himself, and his wife, Susan, with bicycles from parts of old ones people gave him or they picked up from trash piles in front of suburban doorways. Their small living room was a mess while Edward was in this bicycle phase with chains and fenders and wheels and a litter of greasy tools spread over everything. But their two little boys, John and Ted, and their cousins Byrd and Tib still talk of the summer evenings when the six of them went for long bicycle rides together. They all remember with pride that they had *good* bikes which hardly cost anything besides the paint, which they themselves helped Edward apply.

All this time I was an interested, admiring, and somewhat envious spectator. I knew better than to dream of riding a bicycle because I had already found out to my astonishment that I couldn't water-ski, which I figured would be a snap if I ever got around to it, and I had spent some traumatic hours on icy ski slopes in the north Georgia mountains finding out that I couldn't do that either. (It had looked so easy, too.) I had even been thrown by horses, so I knew better than to think I'd know how to handle a bicycle.

Then one Easter Sunday my friend Jack showed up with a brand-new five-speed bicycle for me.

"You're always talking about how much fun a bicycle tour of England would be," he said. "I got you this on sale so you can learn to ride."

It was the prettiest thing I had ever seen in a lifetime of looking at other people's bicycles. I walked around it and stroked it and propped it against the stone coping of the well and sat on its neat little saddle, but I didn't have any more idea than a goose how to ride it.

Jack had worked that out. There was the perfect slope at the edge of the yard, he said, fast at the top but tapering off to a long, flat, grassy plain. All I had to do was to mount my glittering contraption and hang fast to the handlebars while somebody steadied me and gave me a slight shove over the bank. Moving, the bicycle would stay upright and so, perforce, would I. At the bottom of the bank it wobbled and fell and so did I. But it was a slow, cushioned fall and did me no harm.

My grandchildren delightedly got into the act, holding me up and launching me and shouting words of encouragement as I sailed with increasing steadiness down the bank, slowing to a stop and even braking at the bottom. But I had not tried pedaling and the day I was to check into the hospital for a minor throat operation Byrd and Tib came to the country to "wish me off," as they put it, with a lesson in pedaling down a level stretch of road.

We took off down the firm dirt and gravel road with one on either side of me, holding the bicycle up, pushing to give it momentum and yelling, "Pedal, 'Tine, pedal!" I pedaled wildly, my bike broke from their grasp and was off down the road under its and my power alone! I felt absolutely airborne—just for a second before I realized that I was in truth balancing and pedaling and riding my bicycle by myself. Then I fell.

With a mighty wham bike and I went down in an ignominious heap on the dirt road. Later, in the hospital when they prepared me for my throat operation, the nurses were to wonder at the vast areas of purple and black epidermis covering me.

But I was hooked on bike-riding and I still am. It seems to me to be the most sensible mode of transportation in this mechanized age—quiet and inexpensive and as fast as it need be. Most of the year I get in several bike rides a week, daily if possible. When I am in my mother's little town I try to take my bicycle along for the convenience of quick trips to post office and store and for the pleasure of late-afternoon junkets down a long, smooth dirt road which crosses the creek and winds through a forest of magnolia, bay, swamp myrtle, and live oak trees to the lake. There's a small waterfall where I get off and sit a moment, enjoying the sound of the water and the scents of fern and sweet bay.

Walking

It's funny how after you grow up and get busy you forget the pure delight of taking a walk, looking at the sky, wading a creek, lying on your belly in the grass making a clover chain with someone you love.

In her younger days my mother was a woman of tremendous energy and almost limitless ways of using it, and she didn't often knock off work and wander in the woods with me. But when she did it was a marvelous treat for me. Looking back, I remember all the walks we took together more vividly and with more happiness than I remember all the useful, practical, necessary things she did in the house when she was too busy to take a walk.

The scrubbed pots have long since been forgotten. The mended clothes, the let-down hems were probably of more importance then, as were the meals she cooked, the walls she painted, the garden she tended. But the times she spent just with me "getting some use out of the world" are the times I remember best.

Sometimes when we walked, plants engrossed her and we went home laden with flowers or bright-colored leaves. Sometimes she marked special little bushes, a sweet shrub or a laurel, and made plans to come back and move them to our yard. Sometimes we sat on an old wooden bridge used by the logging teams and dangled our bare feet in the water or watched entranced as a scarlet maple leaf made its way downstream through the shoals of pickerelweed and white hatpins. Sometimes she climbed fences like the tomboy she had been in her girlhood and raced me to the next bend in the road.

Because of the memory of my own delight in a walk with my mother I have seldom felt guilty over dropping any household chore and sallying forth with children and grandchildren. And great is the reward.

As Rachel Carson wrote in her lovely posthumously published book, *The Sense Wonder*, children, probably because they are small themselves,

271

are more likely see the "world of little things," the parts instead of just the whole. Grown-ups see the shape and color of the day, the hulk of that gray rock, the pattern of that stand of young pines against the sky. Children drop to their knees with sounds of excitement and discovery and pick mirrorlike fragments of mica out of the earth. They see stones shaped like wondrous birds and beasts, they note that the gray rock is starred with tiny lichens in designs very like green snowflakes. A single sassafras leaf, shaped like a mitten and colored Christmas red, pleases them as much as a forest full of brilliant leaves.

A snail on a rosebush in the yard is a great nuisance to me, and I have plotted to trap the slimy slugs which infest baby seedlings in the greenhouse. But a child watching the damp trail of silver one of these creatures makes across a leaf or a stone is caught up in the wonder of his life.

The white-veined leaf of a diminutive pipsissewa in the pine woods attracts the child, the stand of bracken on the hill is a rain forest to him. The day sky in all its changeable moods engrosses him and if, forgetting bathtime and bedtime, you go out with him and look at the night sky you have seats to an extravaganza. As Miss Carson pointed out, if the "misty river of the milky way, the patterns of the constellations standing out bright and clear, a blazing planet low on the horizon" were to be seen only once in a century we would throng out in great crowds to look at them. But because we can see them almost any night we end up not looking at them at all.

Maybe the best thing about these small voyages of discovery with the children is what the sharing builds between us. Our boy Charles, called Bird, was seven or eight and had been out exploring by himself many times, but after one of our walks together he invited me, with an air of mystery, to come and see his "Place." His own, his special place, was a secret enclosure of green so close to the house and our road that I should have seen it. But I hadn't and I was overwhelmed when he

272

pushed back a curtain of muscadine vines and made me welcome to a mossy hillock by a sandy ditch, where a little rain water stood and ferns and bluets grew.

There was a tree for climbing and a thick wild grape vine for swinging. He waved me to the loop the vine made for a seat and placed himself on the lowest branch of the tree, convenient for talking.

"Do you like it?" he asked.

"Like it?" I said chokily. "I love it. It's the finest 'Place' I ever saw."

It still is because of the memory of the day and the little blond boy perched on the bough over my head like a goldfinch and the honor he had bestowed on me.

Giving

Where I grew up in Mobile, Alabama, we learned many things from our French and Creole neighbors—the proper appreciation of garlic, for example, and the joy of the lagniappe. Every child who went to the grocery store to make a sizable purchase for his mother or to pay a grocery bill of standing did so with the exciting knowledge that the grocer would give him a "'nappe."

Bold boys would sometimes demand their 'nappes. I remember my early embarrassment at hearing an older cousin demand imperiously of the grocer, "What about our 'nappes? Whatcha gon' give us for a 'nappe?"

Being a girl and shy I preserved the fiction that the "little something extra" which constitutes a lagniappe was always a surprise, totally unexpected and altogether delightful. Sometimes it was a bitter disappointment to me—when the grocer gave you licorice, for instance, and you hated licorice.

But mostly the lagniappe was what it was meant to be—a little gift, an unsought treat, a spirit-lifter, a day-brightener.

Grocers no longer give you lagniappes, I'm afraid, but that doesn't mean that they have vanished from our civilization. They come in other ways when you least expect them, the little something extra, an unexpected note in the mail, the basket of vegetables a neighbor leaves by the back door, the little goodie you neither ordered nor earned.

There was the day I came home and found an earthenware soup pot on the back porch, for instance. I had admired one in my neighbor Duke Wolff's kitchen when I saw her boiling corn on the cob in it one night. She told me where she bought hers, but when I went to get one they were out.

"Mrs. Wolff just bought our last one," the clerk said.

So when I found it on my back porch I thought she had merely shopped for me, and I tried to reimburse her.

"It's my gift to you," she said lightly. "You can't pay. After all, it's just a soup pot, not a Jaguar or a Rolls."

Without meaning any disrespect to those fine automobiles, I'd rather have the soup pot. It's a lovely brown pot, made in Italy with the proper glaze for using on the stove and then storing in the refrigerator—plump and capacious and a fine catchall for that leftover roast and gravy, the half cup of green beans, two or three tablespoons of cold turnip greens. (I tried this and it's almost as good as the Portuguese kale soup they serve on Cape Cod at Provincetown.) It will inspire me to try those French soup recipes which run heavily—but more glamorously—to the staple fare of my childhood, dried peas and beans. I'll even try what one French soup-maker suggested, boiling onions whole and unpeeled in my soup. The skins give the broth a nice color and, best of all, you don't have to chop 'em and weep, say the French.

Anne McFarland, who lives up the road from Atlanta in the old town of Marietta, is an inveterate clipper and mailer and the donor of what may be the best lagniappe you can have: response. To have somebody listen to what you say or read what you write and respond is somehow always a surprise to me—an enchanting, bolstering surprise.

A letter from Anne is a collection, an accumulation—clippings and notes with penciled comments all through the text and along the margins. Sometimes she jeers, sometimes she applauds, often she adds an experience or a recollection of her own. Now and then to keep me up to snuff she throws in a religious tract she has picked up somewhere like the magpie she is.

Although I am nearly always alarmed by handbill and signpost scriptural warnings, I read them faithfully, sooner or later. Those signs the zealous put along the roadside were meant for the likes of me, I'm sure, because when I career around the rocky precipice in the north Georgia mountains at night and my headlights pick up the warning in yellow paint on a boulder, "Repent or burn in hell!" my adrenalin starts racing around and clawing at my pores. I'll never forget the week I covered a murder trial in a little mountain town and passed such a sign twice daily. No matter whether it was rainy or foggy or pitch black dark, the words leaped out at me in luminous yellow—the very color, I imagine, of sulphur and brimstone. That week I almost perfected the art of instant repentance.

When Anne McFarland throws in a scriptural scary I sometimes don't read it, tucking it into my pocketbook on the theory that I'll get to it later. One midwinter afternoon after weeks of being stuck indoors at the state capitol, covering the legislature, I got out unexpectedly early and started walking back to the office. More as an excuse to stay out in the sunshine than because I was interested in the merchandise, I strolled, looking in windows.

The air had the cool clean taste of mountain springs, and the midwinter sky was the color of Michaelmas daisies. People who had been hurrying along with their heads bowed against the wintry wind were strolling and sniffing the air, savoring the lagniappe of a springlike day in the knowledge that they might not get another one for weeks and weeks.

Although I had work to do I thought of begonia bulbs and ducked into a seed store. There was a wheelbarrow full of leftover daffodils, and I yearned over them long moments, the thrifty side of me arguing that it was too late to plant them (see, they're sprouting already) and the fool optimist contending that they were gorgeously cheap and, who knows, they might be the eagerest bulbs you ever saw. A clerk saved me from that particular struggle by pointing out the snowdrop bulbs, marked down to a fantastic fifty for fifteen cents.

Well, you can't get fifty anythings for fifteen cents, I decided exultantly, and squandered thirty cents on two little perforated sacks full. They were stamped "Product of Holland," and I opened one to sniff the earthy scent of the tiny bulbs and to hold one between my fingers, marveling at the miracle of a dull, dun-colored little tuber that was going to make me a real show of springtime bloom.

Walking slowly back to the office I even dwelled dreamily on what a lovely bond a handful of snowdrop bulbs constitutes between a woman who digs in the red earth of Georgia and some flaxen-haired Dutch lady working beside a Holland canal. The promise, the potentiality of bulbs awes me. If a warty, misshapen lump like a begonia tuber, for instance, can produce the delicate perfection of a Crimson Ballerina, it does seem that the possibilities in people would be unlimited.

That theme engrossed me happily for several blocks, and then Anne's scrap of scripture fell out of my pocketbook as I reached for something else. As I picked it up I found that for once it wasn't a warning but a benediction:

"Truly the light is sweet, and a pleasant thing it is for the eyes to behold the sun." (Ecclesiastes)

—from *Small Blessings*

Believing

The decisions involved in being a mother are sometimes so frightening you wonder how any woman has the courage to make them. The most courageous woman I ever saw was a big-eyed country girl named Montell Purcell. She took the responsibility of a life-and-death or, as the newspaper called it at the time, death-or-blindness decision on herself.

It was New Year's Eve 1951 when I first heard of the Purcells. A friend whose husband was in the hospital called and told me that while she was waiting out her husband's operation she got to talking to a woman whose five-year-old daughter was in the hospital to have her eyes checked.

"That little girl, that *baby*, has cancer!" cried my friend. "The doctor just told the mother she will have to have her eyes removed or she will die!"

It was what used to be known as a human-interest story and I didn't have much heart for it. It was the holiday season and nobody wants to read—or to write—sad stories. But after a day or two my conscience hurt me and I went looking for the Purcells and their little girl.

They had left the private infirmary where they had received the death-or-blindness diagnosis and gone to the city-county charity hospital, Grady, in the hope of finding better news. I found them in the children's ward there—Frank, the father, a quiet, country-reared man of forty, who had recently been laid off by a small-town textile mill, and his wife, Montell, thirty-three. They sat beside the bed of a frisky, beautiful little girl named Carolyn, who had bright brown eyes and hair to match curling around a piquant face and pulled into a pigtail in the back.

They told me the story.

Carolyn was their only child and although they had to work hard for everything they had, at Christmastime they took special pleasure in buying their little girl everything they dreamed she would like. Before Frank was laid off at the mill Montell had bought and put away Carolyn's Christmas toys and they both felt relieved and happy that the specter of unemployment wouldn't mar Christmas morning at their house. One of the presents Montell was happiest over and the one that cost the most was a new tricycle. Carolyn had seen tricycles and had talked of nothing else in all the weeks leading up to Christmas.

When Christmas morning dawned the child was out of bed before her father could get up and build a fire. She went straight for the Christmas tree and, stumbling a little (her mother thought from excitement), she found the doll. She looked around and at and over the new tricycle—without seeing it.

"She didn't know it was there," her mother said chokily. "The tricycle she wanted so bad."

As the morning passed and Carolyn gradually discovered and played with her toys, Frank and Montell, looking at each other fearfully, began to realize that their little girl, the child with the bright, beautiful eyes, couldn't see.

They had little money and they knew almost nothing about getting around Atlanta, although they had grown up and lived all their adult lives less than fifty miles from the city limits. But they were undaunted in their determination to find the best medical help for Carolyn. I found out later the reason they acted so swiftly was that their first child, a little girl named Mary Marjorie, had died without medical attention of what the father called "a kind of mystery disease" ten years before Carolyn was born. The day after Christmas they took Carolyn to a country doctor who recommended a city specialist and arranged an appointment for them.

It was at the ear-eyes-nose-throat infirmary that they learned for the first time that Carolyn's trouble was not simple nearsightedness

278

which could be corrected by glasses but something which could cost her life. The name the doctor gave it was glioma.

Hoping against hope that the doctor was mistaken, they had come to Grady, the hospital where most Atlanta doctors teach or serve on the staff as consultants. When I found them, Carolyn was being given a series of tests and was being examined by five or six of the city's other leading eye specialists.

They had been in the hospital for two or three days when the results of a clinic held by the entire staff on opthamalogy were made known. A group of reporters had gathered and we stood in the hall with Montell and her parents when an intern brought up the report, a written diagnosis, and read it to them. It said, in effect, that the child did indeed have glioma, that she would have to lose one eye immediately and the other one probably very soon.

There hadn't been much real hope in the Purcells and in Montell's family, the Dinsmores. They were resigned to the operation. Frank, looking stricken, saw no other course.

Surprisingly, when we all turned to Montell, her answer was a low-voiced, "No."

A delay, the young intern explained patiently, might be dangerous.

"No," said Montell again. "We'll wait."

That night she and Frank took Carolyn and, against the doctors' advice, left the hospital. They went to the home of some relatives who ran a truck stop on a four-lane highway twenty miles north of Atlanta. I saw them almost daily and I felt close enough to Montell to ask her how she dared to wait. She was a woman of little education and, of course, no medical skill. How dare she pit her knowledge against the best medical opinion available in the hospitals and medical schools of our town?

It was then she told me about Mary Marjorie.

She and Frank were very young and very poor when Mary Marjorie was born. They lived on a farm in one of the mountain counties, miles from the nearest doctor and with no car. One day the little girl got sick. All day long Montell nursed her, using such home remedies as she knew about, and steadily the child grew worse.

Frank started walking for help and along about dusk he came back home with a borrowed truck. They wrapped Mary Marjorie up and started to the nearest doctor. The child died on the way.

"I know the Lord don't always answer you the way you want Him to," Montell said, "but I believe He answers you. All day long I prayed that He would make my baby well. He didn't answer my prayer that way but I felt He had a purpose and when the answer come I could take it. I'm praying now and I got to wait."

While Montell waited, people all over the world seemed stirred by the story. Soldiers in Korea wrote her, expressing sympathy and encouragement. Convicts in prisons offered their eyes. Some people urged the operation, some warned her against it. The great Helen Keller wrote and told her not to be afraid, blindness was not so bad, a child could give up her eyes and still have a good life. Advice poured in from every corner of the world. Faith healers came and marched and prayed and sang in the yard. Sightseers came just to look at the child and her parents.

And through it all, Montell, a real gentlewoman, held up her head and smiled and thanked people. And waited.

After about a week, Fred Cannon, head of the local Shrine Horse Patrol, called me and said he had been reading the stories about Carolyn and he and his fellow Shriners were deeply concerned. They had no doubt that the child should have the operation but they understood the mother's reluctance and they felt that another diagnosis from a high-placed source would help her decide. Would I ask her if she would take the child to the Mayo Clinic if I would go with her and the Shriners would pay the expense of the trip?

Both Frank and Montell were overwhelmed by the offer. I could see in Montell's white face the hungry hope that this was "the answer."

Gifts for the child came pouring in. "Papa Sunshine," a Jewish immigrant who ran a department store in a poor section of town, outfitted her with new clothes and a warm coat with a hat that had earmuffs for the cold Minnesota weather. There were toys and gifts of money and a big crowd gathered at the airport to see us off on a gray January day.

Carolyn was bouncy and bright-eyed, and Montell, although tired and pale, smiled a lot. And I privately worried that the child might die on the trip.

Wherever the plane stopped—and they were making more stops in 1951—people came out to greet Carolyn and to give her presents or to shout advice to her mother. Not once did Montell plead weariness or fail to smile and express her gratitude. It was night when we landed in Rochester and although the Shriners, wearing their cheery red fezzes, came out to meet us and to take us to the hotel adjoining the big clinic, it did seem a foreign land to all three of us. All that snow and ice, that unbroken, unrelenting whiteness.

The next day we learned that such examinations as Carolyn's take time and it might be several days before they could begin hers. In the meantime, we were to wait. Having a job and children of my own to worry about, I started making arrangements to turn Montell and Carolyn over to the hospital social service people when I saw Montell's courage falter a little. She had been so brave and so strong but she couldn't bear to be left alone now.

The social workers saw it too, and suddenly, miraculously, somebody stamped Carolyn's case "Emergency" and the next morning at daybreak she began her trip through that vast clinic.

All day long the child and her mother went from test to test, from examination to examination. I was waiting for them at dusk in a little room on the ground floor of the clinic. The lights had not been turned on but there was a strange, silvery twilight reflected from the snow outside. I stood at the window looking at the whiteness and the roof line of a little church strung with icicles.

Montell came in quietly. Carolyn, exhausted from the day's ordeal, was asleep in her mother's arms. Montell held in her hand a piece of paper on which somebody had written the verdict.

"Would you read it for me?" she asked.

I took the paper to the window and read. The child did not have cancer, she did not need to lose her eyes. The difficulty she had was caused by a nutritional deficiency. She could go home and be treated in Atlanta.

I looked up and Montell was looking out the window at the little church, with tears streaming down her cheeks.

"Thank you, Lord," she whispered. "I knowed You'd tell me."

Some people believe in miracles. I'm not sure that I do but Montell Purcell does. She said later, "You know all them doctors couldn't have been wrong. The Lord worked a miracle, He did."

If miracles exist, a stubborn, believing mother waited one out for Carolyn. Today Carolyn is a beautiful young married woman with a three-year-old daughter, Stephanie. Frank died in September 1968 and Montell now spends a lot of time with Carolyn and her family and smiles her warm, serene smile when friends remark that Carolyn's eyes are her prettiest feature.

"Did you know," she murmurs with a touch of awe, "she has twenty-twenty vision?"

—from *Mothers Are Always Special*

Praying

The following column received the $2,000 Christopher news-
paper award for the best creative work of "enduring spiritual
significance" in a newspaper.

The lunch counter had that stainless steel and nickel shine indigenous to lunch counters—and in the soft early morning light it looked clean and impersonal but sort of cheerful. We sat there listening to the hiss of the waffle iron, watching the steamy breath of the coffee urn spiraling upward and wondering if Dr. Thornwell Jacobs had thought to include such a place in his Civilization Crypt.

No future civilization can get any idea of what life in the 20th Century was like unless he could see the 20-odd citizens lined up on stools at a gleaming eatery early in the morning.

We looked at these, shoulders hunched over the "two-fresh-eggs-and-buttered-toast" special, faces reflected here and there in coffee urns and stainless steel panels.

There were college students, fugitives from fraternity house cuisine, a somber-looking man with a briefcase (could it be his wife was a late-sleeper?), two young nurses, a little rumpled and hollow-eyed after a night on duty at the nearby hospital, a family with a little girl, and a sullen teenager impartially distributing lipstick between her coffee cup and cigarette.

The lunchroom was quiet except for the occasional sharp crack of an eggshell in the counterman's expert hand, the sputter of frying bacon, and the bored voice of a customer, ordering more coffee.

The counterman turned a radio on a shelf up a little and war news clattered out. New raids on Communist air bases in Manchuria, possibility of Reds massing to send "full air power into Korea." Abruptly he switched it off and stood absently wiping the already spotless counter.

We thought of his customers, 20-odd people, each engrossed in his own thoughts, encased in his own shell—inconspicuous, anonymous, brought together by nothing more binding than the tribal custom of eating in the morning. They did not even have real ravening hunger in common...just eating because people do.

And then at the end of the counter the little girl said in a carrying voice. "Mother, don't we ask the blessing here?"

The counterman stopped wiping and grinned at her suddenly.

"Sure we do, sister," he said. "You say it."

She bowed her smooth little head. The young counterman turned and glared briefly at his customers and bowed his head, too. Up and down the counter heads went down, the nurses, the students, the man with the briefcase, and then, slowly, the teenager.

The breathless little voice was loud in the room:

"God is great, God is good. Let us thank Him for our food. By His hand we are fed, He gives us our daily bread. Amen."

Heads went up along the counter. Eating was resumed but somehow the atmosphere had subtly changed. The man with the briefcase smiled and remarked to the nurses that he had a new baby in their hospital.

Conversation became general. The counterman smiled at the students and said, "Well, I won't be seeing you after this week. I reckon I'm going to Korea." They paused, paying their check, to talk with him about it.

Somehow a tenuous bond of friendliness and mutual confidence had grown up in the room and the little girl, oblivious to what she had done, lathered her waffle with syrup and ate it happily.

—from the *Atlanta Journal* and the *Atlanta Constitution*, Sunday, April 8, 1951

Permissions